AF531194

Renovating for Living

RENOVATING FOR LIVING

LOFT

Idea and concept: Paco Asensio

Editorial coordinator: Catherine Collin

Editor and original texts: Llorenç Bonet

English translation: Michael A. Brunelle

Copy editing: Addenda
www.addenda.es

Art direction: Mireia Casanovas Soley

Layout: Jonatan Roura

Via Laietana 32, 4° Of. 92
08003 Barcelona, Spain
Tel.: +34 932 688 088
Fax: +34 932 687 073
loft@loftpublications.com
www.loftpublications.com

ISBN 10: 84-95832-52-6
ISBN 13: 978-84-95832-52-8

Printed and bound in China

Introduction

Sometimes tackling the renovation of a building is more complicated than building a new one, not only because of the historic value of the part that must be preserved, but also because of the state of the structure itself since we rarely know what condition it is in before beginning the project. Furthermore, the act of working on an existing building is a challenge for any architect since it means developing adaptive strategies that are very different from those that would be developed for a new construction.

The reasons for renovating a house instead of building one from scratch are many, although most frequently it is because there are laws that prohibit its demolition or because it is cheaper to make use of the structure. In both cases the design must respect these premises, while at the same time fulfill the requirements of their future inhabitants and their lifestyles.

Since World War II the European tendency to respect buildings from the past has led to a certain stylistic mannerism, and many projects have resulted in either a misunderstood quaintness or in the so-called

restorations of buildings where only the façades are preserved and in reality new constructions are built. In contrast to these techniques, an enlightened approach has appeared that treats the renovation as if it were adapting an old factory to today's requirements, leaving the dialogue with the past as a secondary concern. Despite the apparent aggressiveness of this approach, a striking use of modern materials is often more respectful than interventions that try to copy forms and techniques that are no longer in use out of supposed respect for the past.

The sensitivity of the architect carrying out the renovation is of utmost importance, since he must combine the client's wishes with the realities of the structure; and the strategies that he is able to develop and that the budget allows will dictate the final form of the building.

RENOVATING FOR LIVING

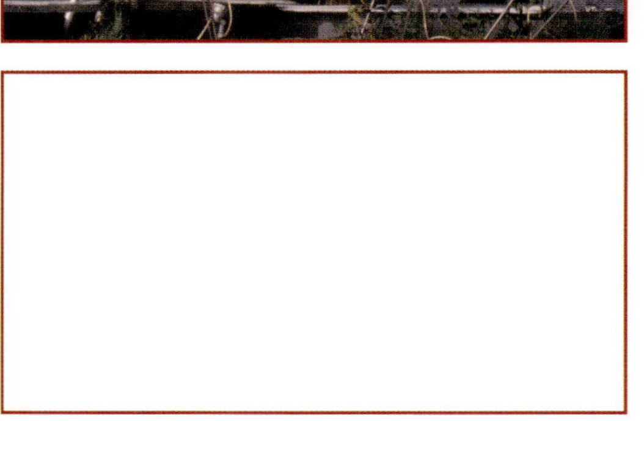

House in Malvern

Architect: Greg Gong

Photographs © John Gollings

Location: Melbourne, Australia

HOMES ARE REMODELED AT LEAST ONCE EVERY GENERATION; THEY MUST INEVITABLY BE ADAPTED TO TECHNOLOGICAL ADVANCES AND TO THE EVOLUTION OF THE LIFESTYLES OF THEIR INHABITANTS.

House in Malvern

This house located on the outskirts of Melbourne was built in 1930 and renovated in 1960 with the construction of a new wing. The latest adaptation brought the entire house up to date and totally rearranged the interior. The renovation was centered on the rear area of the house, where most activities are carried out and which has a garden that enjoys full sun. On the other hand, the façade still dates to 1930, which causes some surprise upon entering the house, whose interior is modern and functional. The space that contains the studio, previously the kitchen, is the first element that appears and it acts as a transition between the old part and the new. In addition to changing its use, skylights were installed to make use of the natural light. The kitchen is now located in the new addition; a large room combines the cooking, living, and dining spaces, and a large opening facing the garden makes this room the heart of the house. Melbourne's pleasant climate allows the exterior space to be used nearly year round, so the dining room's large sliding door is almost always open. The third bedroom is also in this addition; its translucent window admits light and at the same time allows privacy, and its orientation towards the garden catches the first rays of the morning sun.

Remodeled roof plan and ground floor plan

Pre-exist roof plan and ground floor plan

Elevation

Section

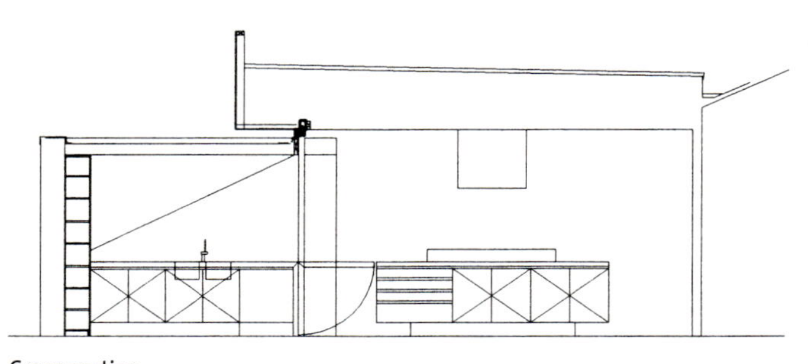

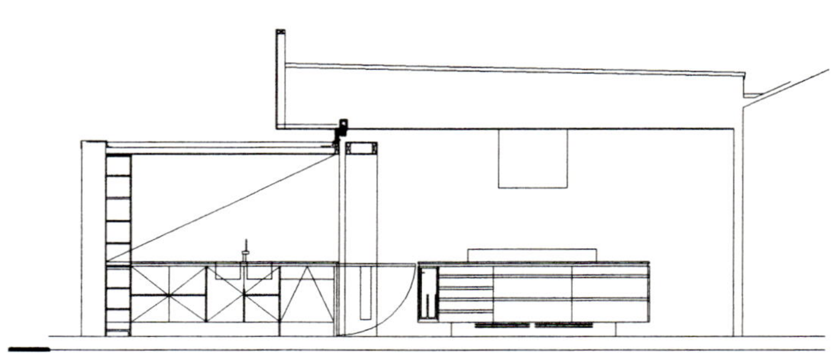

Croos section

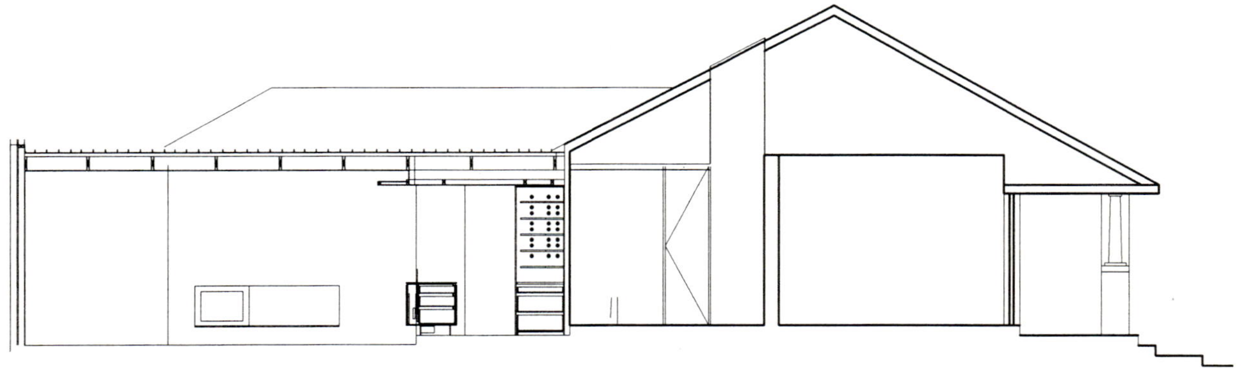

Longitudinal section

The use of translucent glass allows natural light to flow to the most private areas of the house.

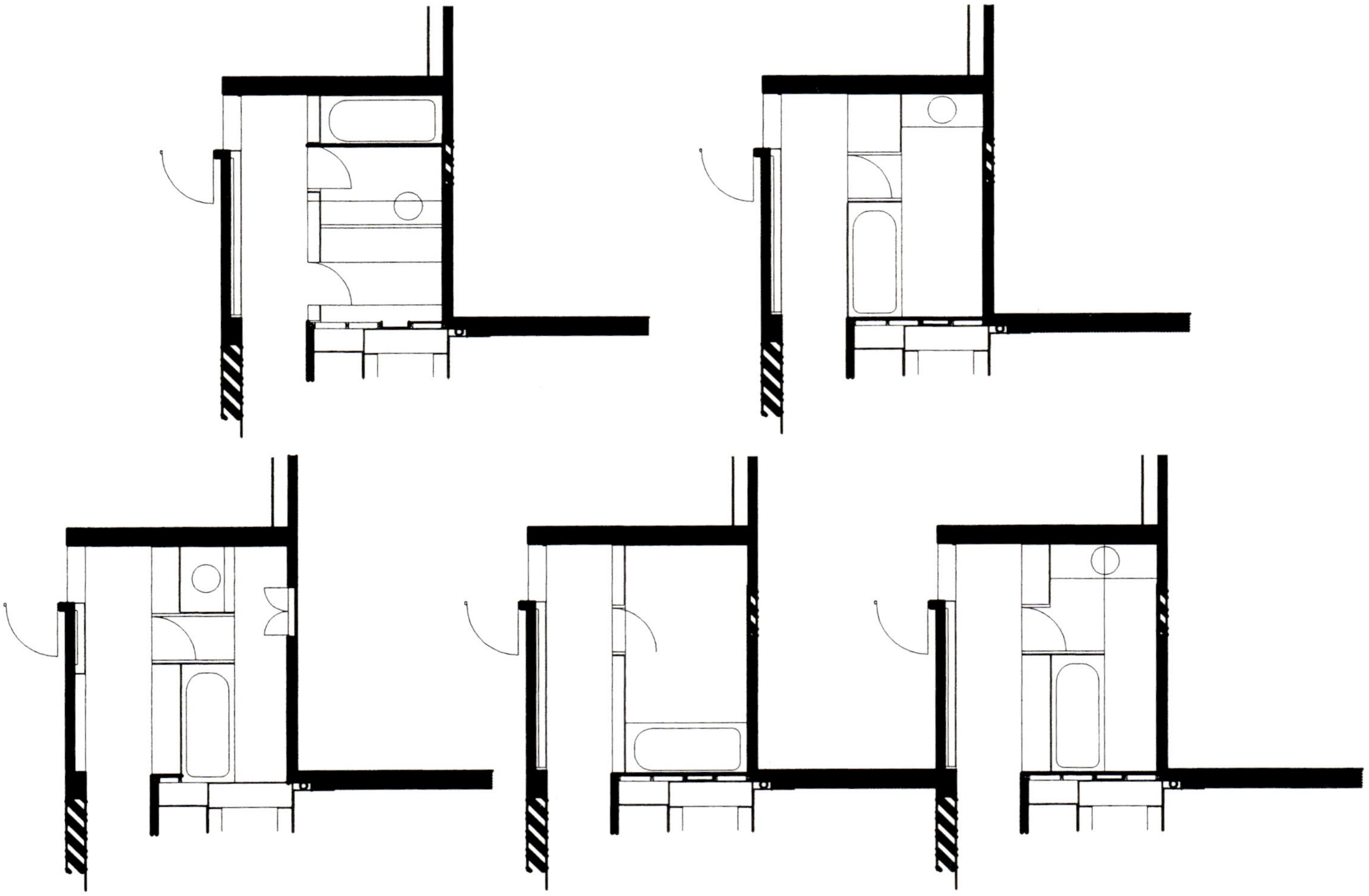

Hipothetical bathroom plans

0 1 2

Loft in Jersey City

Architects: Abelow Connors Sherman

Photographs © Michael Moran

Location: Jersey City, New Jersey, USA

Public and private spaces are mixed in this three-story heterogeneous loft, notable for its spaciousness.

Loft in Jersey City

The client on this project was a musician and producer who wanted to enjoy all the advantages of a conventional home, office, and a recording studio. These requirements were very creatively developed in a space that had been used as a warehouse and a stable for horses, and that still preserved its brick walls, the framework of wooden posts and beams, and the slanted ceiling. The spacious industrial character of the new loft allowed connections between the three levels where the different rooms were inserted. The ground floor was reserved for the recording studio to take advantage of the acoustic qualities of the open space. This level also contains a living room, the kitchen, the dining room, a library, and a room for the computers. The bedrooms, the control room, and the editing room are located on the two others floors, without ever interfering with the relation between the private and public spaces. The use of different materials is highlighted and gives the entire setting a heterogeneous feeling.

The project designers chose to work with very diverse materials, among which steel and wood predominate.

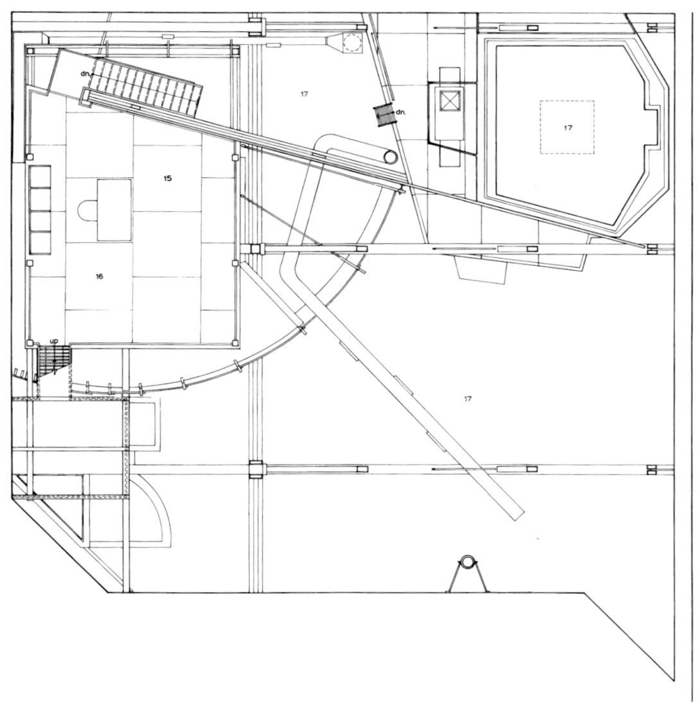

Ground floor

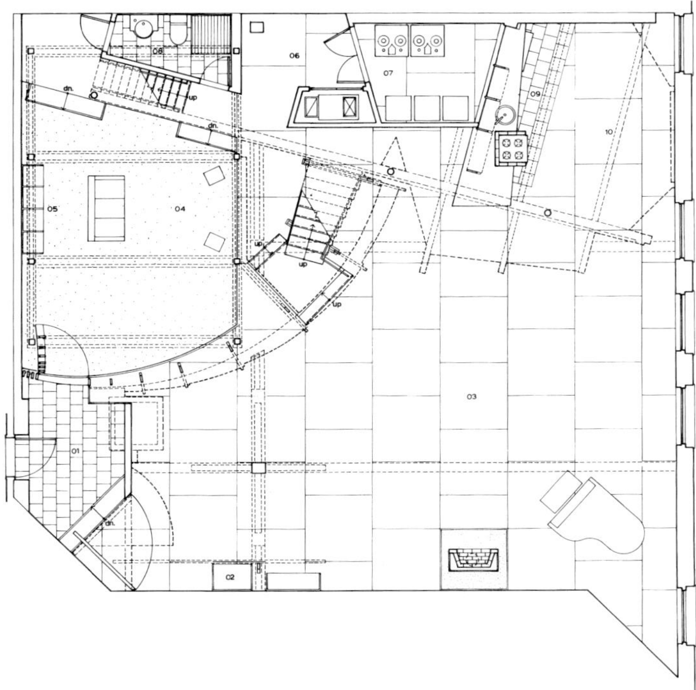

First floor

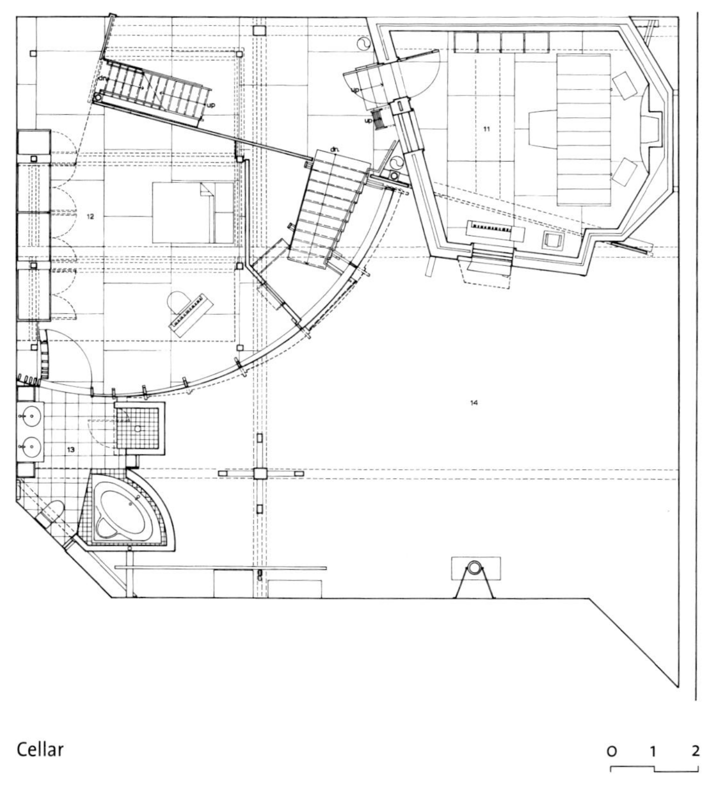

Cellar

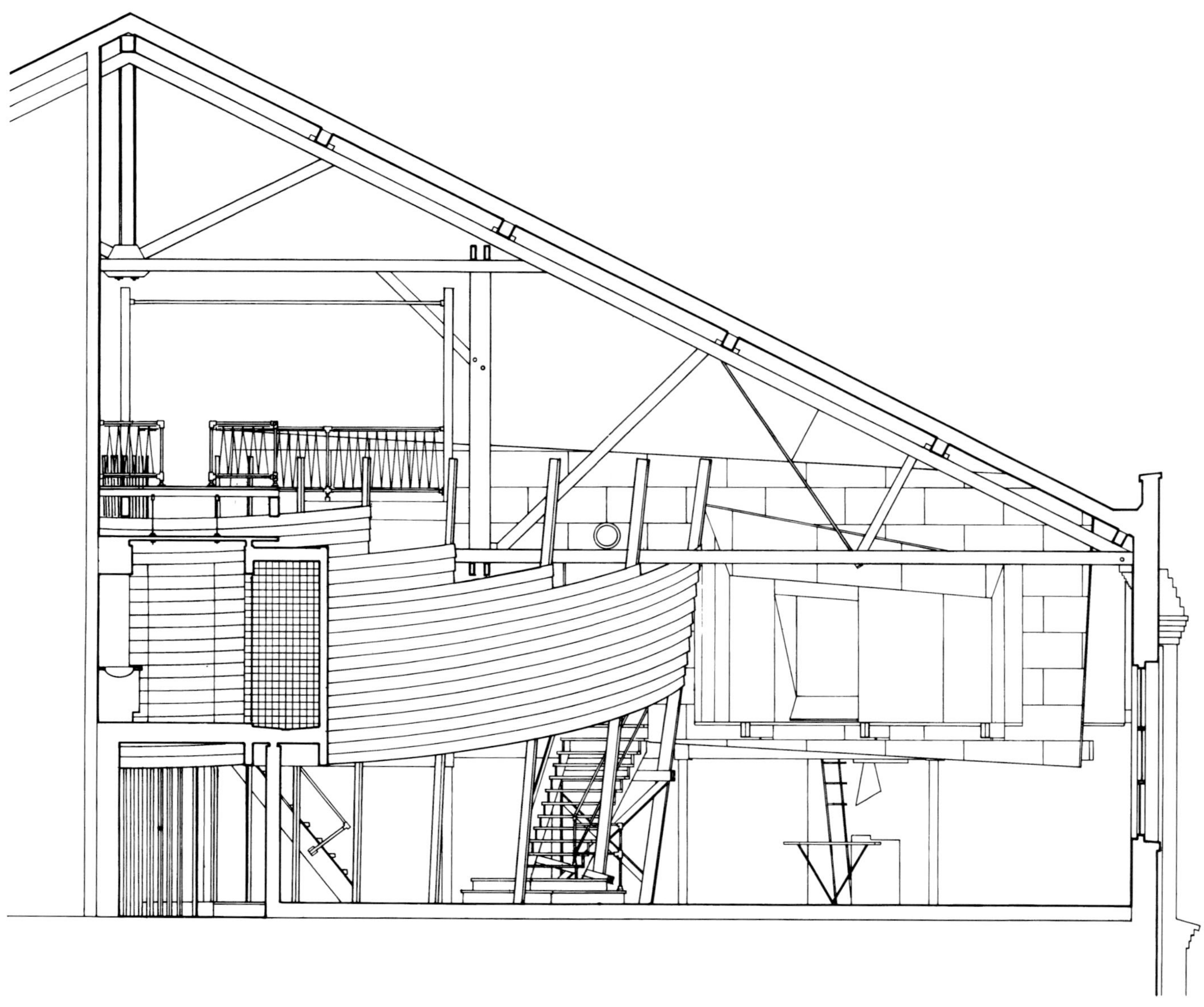

Section

The light that flows through the skylight illuminates the framework of the internal structure, putting the different elements in striking relief.

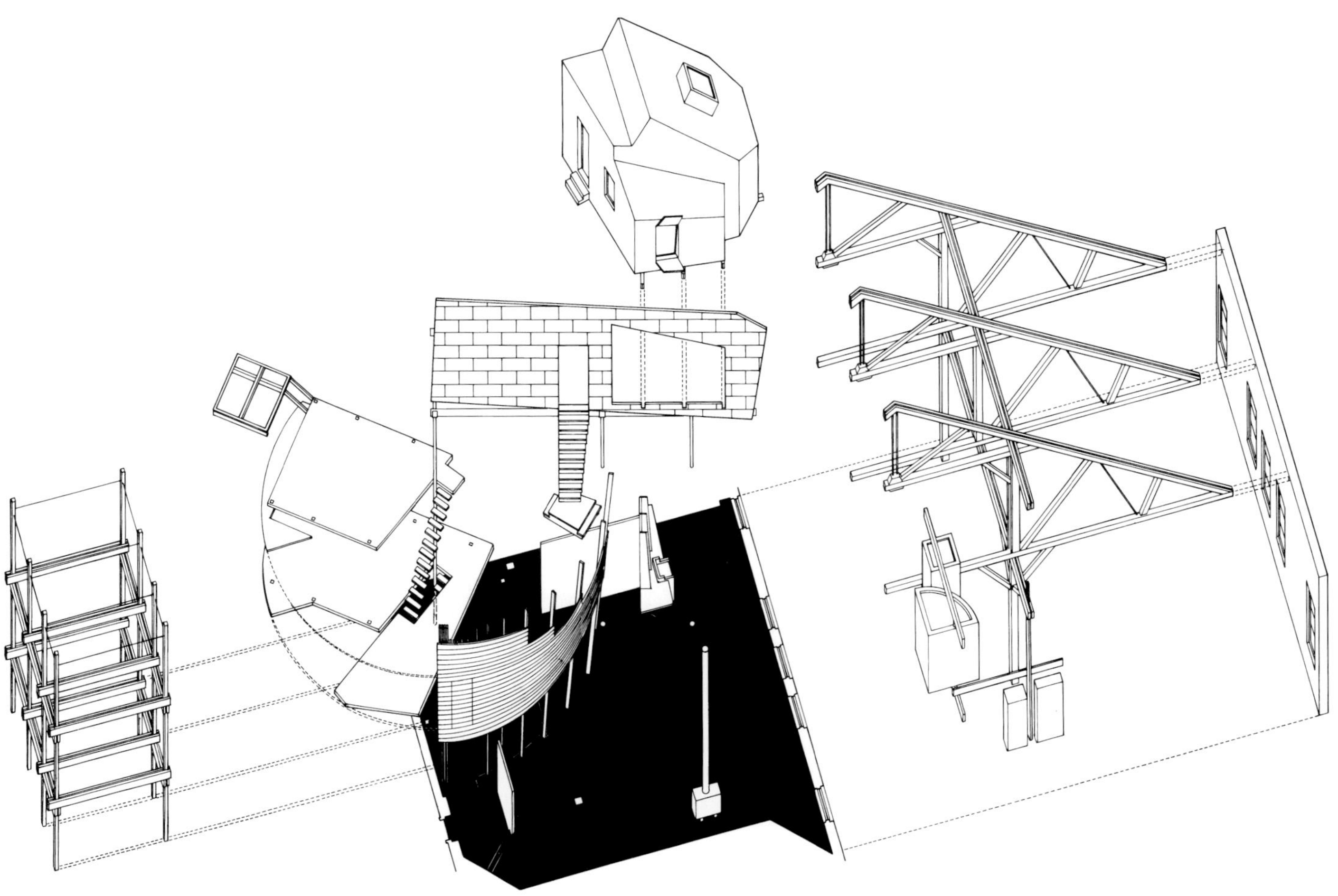

Axonometry

ISN House

Architect: Ogris:Wanek Architects

Photographs © Ferdinand Neumüller

Location: Klagenfurt, Austria

BOLD FORMS MUST BE USED WHEN FACED WITH CERTAIN CHALLENGES, LIKE IN THIS CASE WHERE THE RENOVATION IS AS STRIKING AS IT IS RESPECTFUL WITH THE ORIGINAL BUILDING.

ISN House

This typically Nordic mid-century house is found within a residential area full of monotonous buildings, in what is now a central neighborhood due to the growth experienced by the city in the past fifty years. When faced with updating the home for its new owners, the architects defended the concept of maintaining, up to a point, the traditional image that is seen from the street, while at the same time designing a more evident renovation in the back, visible only to the family and their neighbors. A minimal enlargement of the entry door alerts the visitor to what is found inside; the same thing is true of the enlargement of the first floor, which can only be seen from the street if one is paying close attention. This allows the traditional outline of the building to be kept while giving it a contemporary and mysterious feeling. This willingness to not violate the structure paired with the striking forms and colors in the back turn this project into an example of how residential neighborhoods can be given a little character without having to make drastic changes. The materials used are easy to find and the construction techniques are traditional in this country, reducing possible technical and budgetary problems.

A novel form, created using traditional techniques and materials, stands out from the rest of the surrounding buildings.

Model

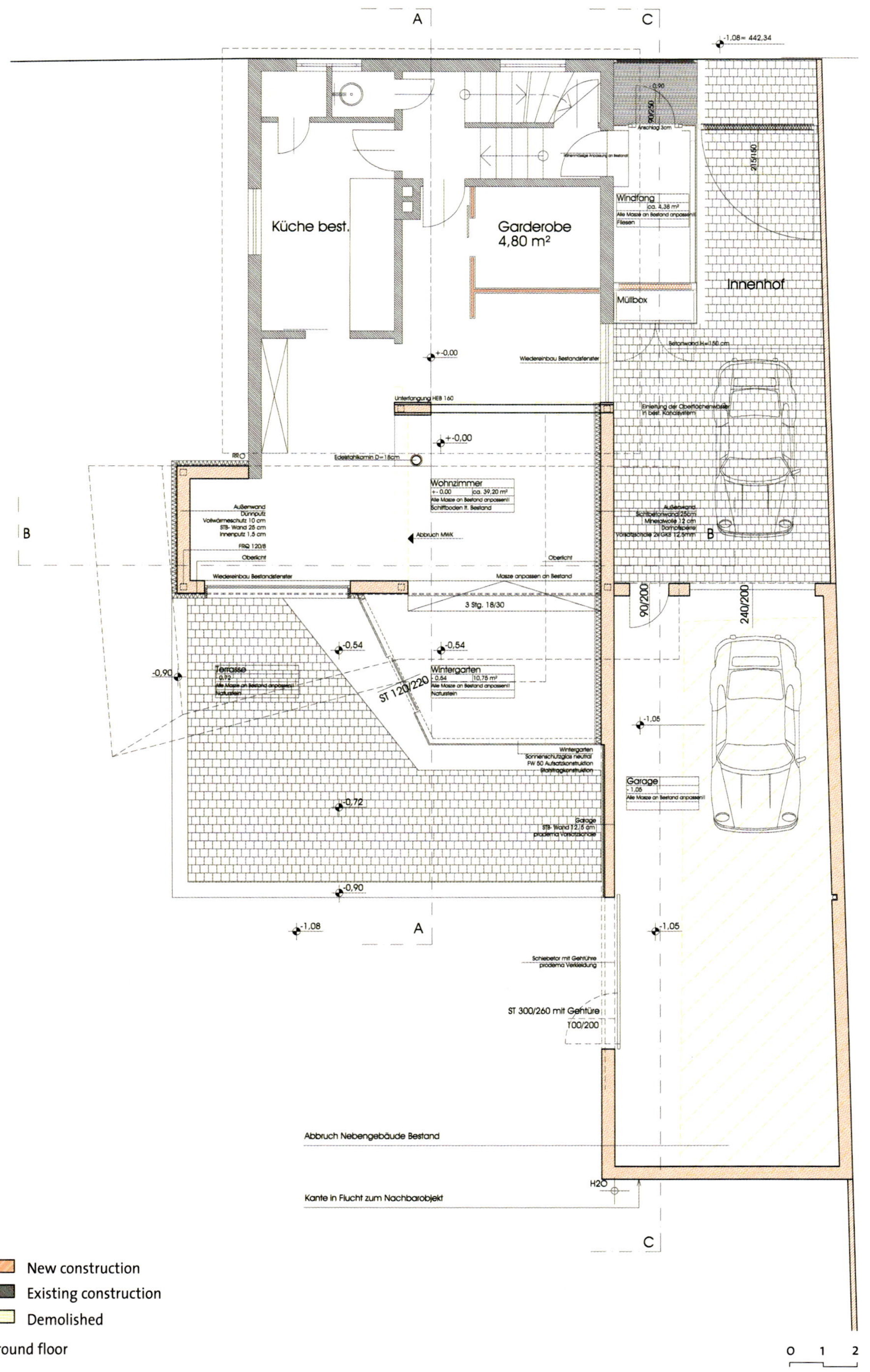

Ground floor

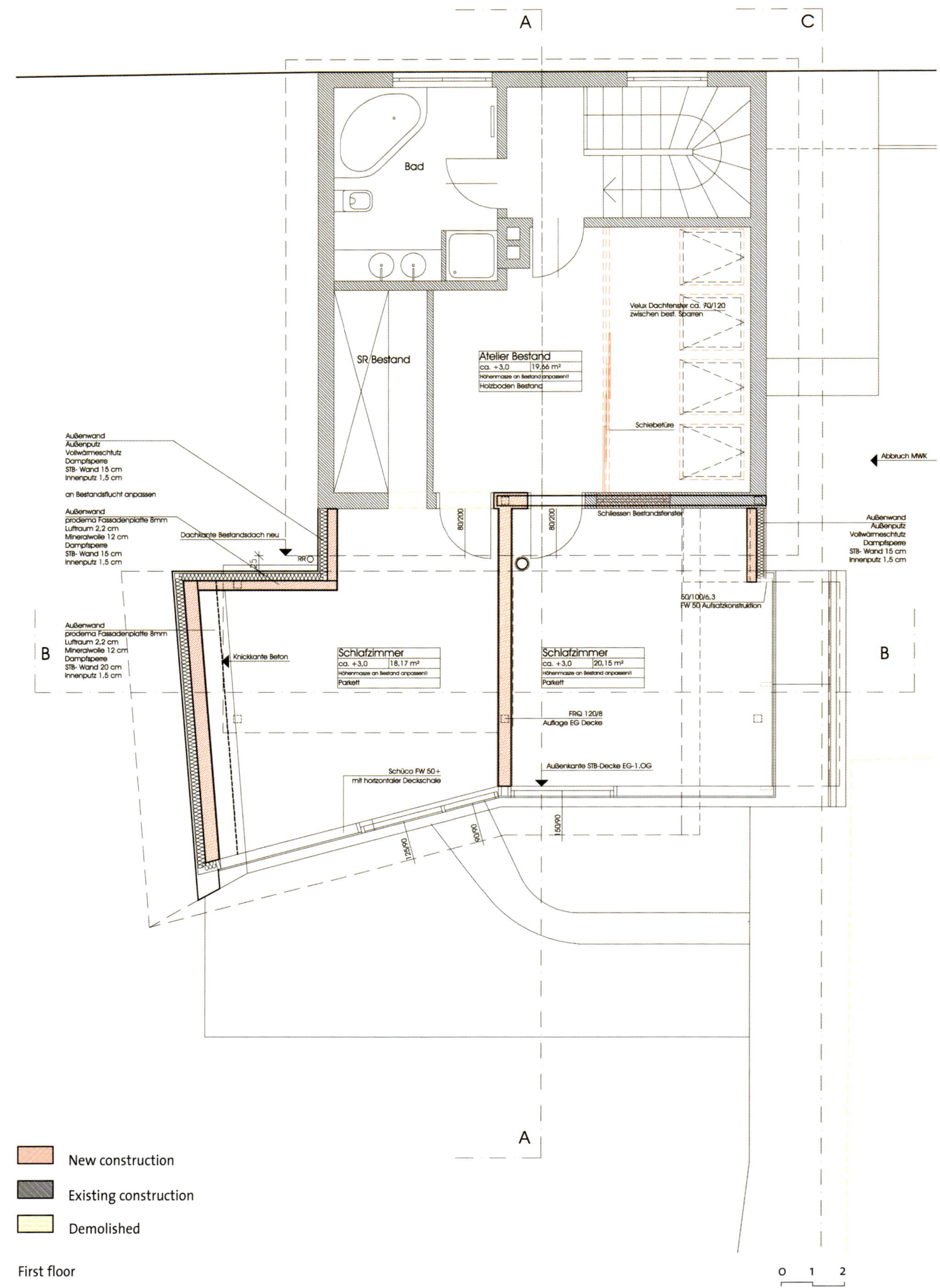
A
C
Bad
SR Bestand
Atelier Bestand
ca. +3,0
19,66 m²
Höhenmasze an Bestand anpassen!!
Holzboden Bestand
Velux Dachfenster ca. 70/120
zwischen best. Sparren
Schiebetüre
Abbruch MWK
Außenwand
Außenputz
Vollwärmeschtutz
Dampfsperre
STB- Wand 15 cm
Innenputz 1,5 cm
an Bestandsflucht anpassen
Außenwand
prodema Fassadenplatte 8mm
Luftraum 2,2 cm
Mineralwolle 12 cm
Dampfsperre
STB- Wand 15 cm
Innenputz 1,5 cm
Dachkante Bestandsdach neu
RR
80/200
80/200
Schliessen Bestandsfenster
Außenwand
Außenputz
Vollwärmeschtutz
Dampfsperre
STB- Wand 15 cm
Innenputz 1,5 cm
50/100/6,3
FW 50 Aufsatzkonstruktion
B
Außenwand
prodema Fassadenplatte 8mm
Luftraum 2,2 cm
Mineralwolle 12 cm
Dampfsperre
STB- Wand 20 cm
Innenputz 1,5 cm
Knickkante Beton
Schlafzimmer
ca. +3,0
18,17 m²
Höhenmasze an Bestand anpassen!!
Parkett
Schlafzimmer
ca. +3,0
20,15 m²
Höhenmasze an Bestand anpassen!!
Parkett
B
FRQ 120/8
Auflage EG Decke
Außenkante STB-Decke EG-1.OG
Schüco FW 50+
mit horizontaler Deckschale
125/90
90/90
150/90
A
New construction
Existing construction
Demolished
0 1 2

First floor

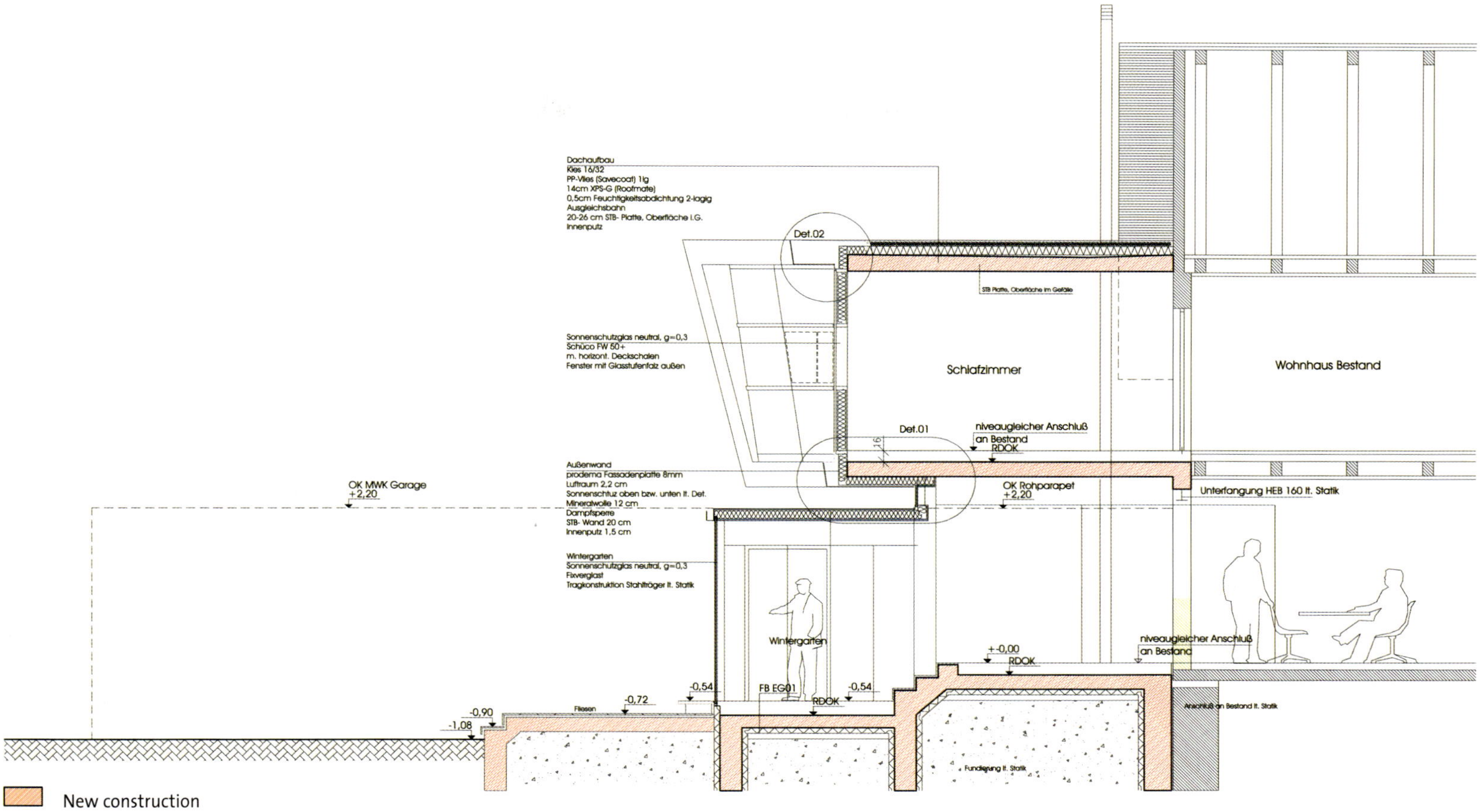

New construction

Existing construction

Demolished

Section

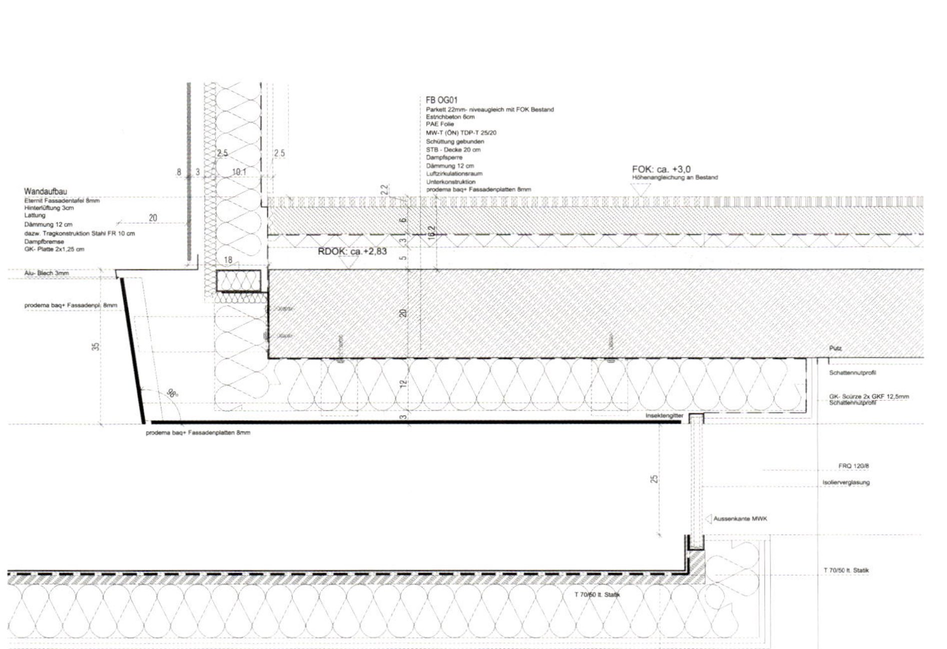

Roof construction detail

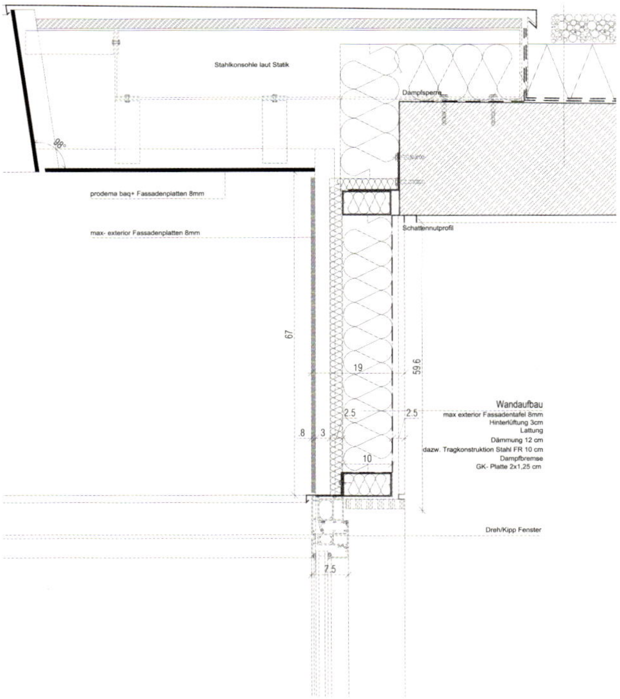

Wall construction detail

Because of its orientation, the second floor bends into an angled form striving for more light.

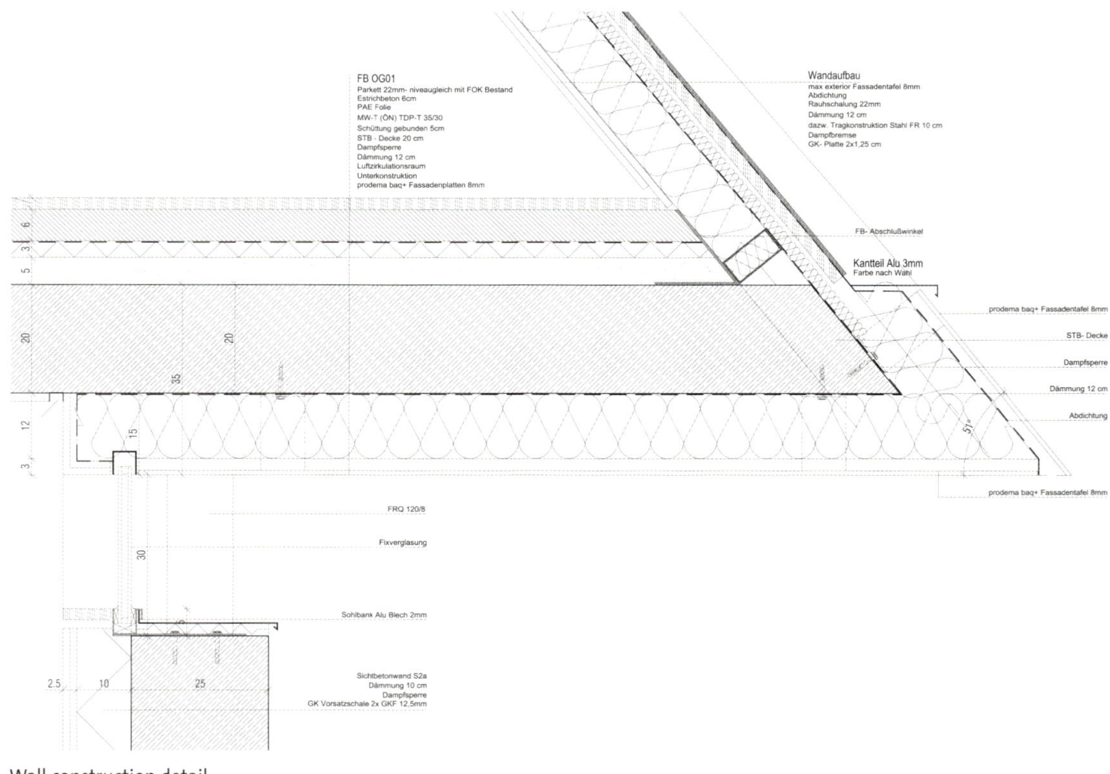

Wall construction detail

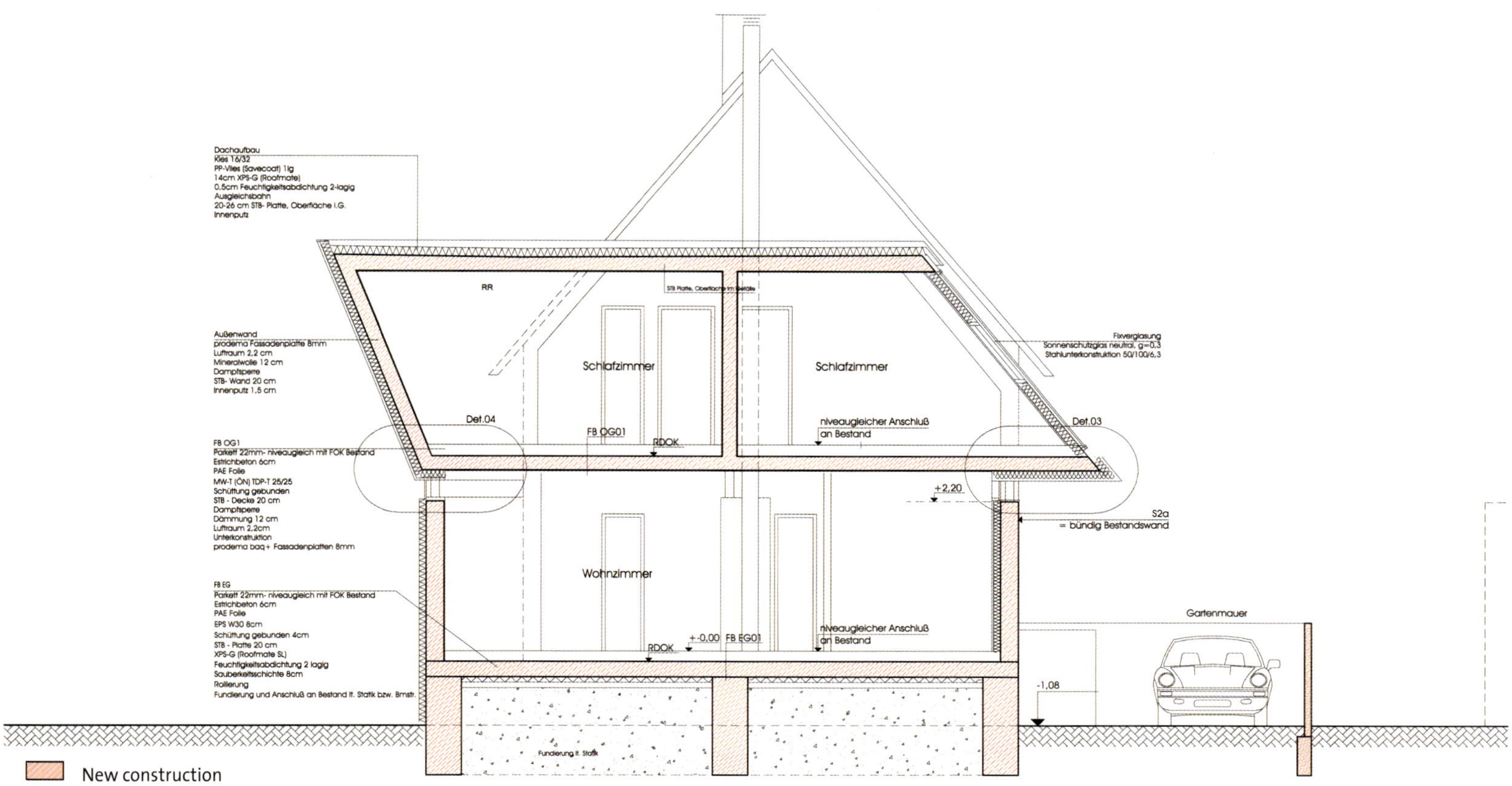

Dachaufbau
Kies 16/32
PP-Vlies (Savecoat) 1lg
14cm XPS-G (Roofmate)
0.5cm Feuchtigkeitsabdichtung 2-lagig
Ausgleichsbahn
20-26 cm STB- Platte, Oberfläche i.G.
Innenputz

RR

STB Platte, Oberfläche im Gefälle

Außenwand
prodema Fassadenplatte 8mm
Luftraum 2,2 cm
Mineralwolle 12 cm
Dampfsperre
STB- Wand 20 cm
Innenputz 1,5 cm

Schlafzimmer

Schlafzimmer

Fixverglasung
Sonnenschutzglas neutral, g=0,3
Stahlunterkonstruktion 50/100/6,3

Det.04

FB OG01

RDOK

niveaugleicher Anschluß
an Bestand

Det.03

FB OG1
Parkett 22mm- niveaugleich mit FOK Bestand
Estrichbeton 6cm
PAE Folie
MW-T (ÖN) TDP-T 25/25
Schüttung gebunden
STB - Decke 20 cm
Dampfsperre
Dämmung 12 cm
Luftraum 2,2cm
Unterkonstruktion
prodema baq+ Fassadenplatten 8mm

+2,20

S2a
= bündig Bestandswand

Wohnzimmer

FB EG
Parkett 22mm- niveaugleich mit FOK Bestand
Estrichbeton 6cm
PAE Folie
EPS W30 8cm
Schüttung gebunden 4cm
STB - Platte 20 cm
XPS-G (Roofmate SL)
Feuchtigkeitsabdichtung 2 lagig
Sauberkeitsschichte 8cm
Rollierung
Fundierung und Anschluß an Bestand lt. Statik bzw. Bmstr.

RDOK +-0,00 FB EG01

niveaugleicher Anschluß
an Bestand

Gartenmauer

-1,08

Fundierung lt. Statik

New construction

Existing construction

Section

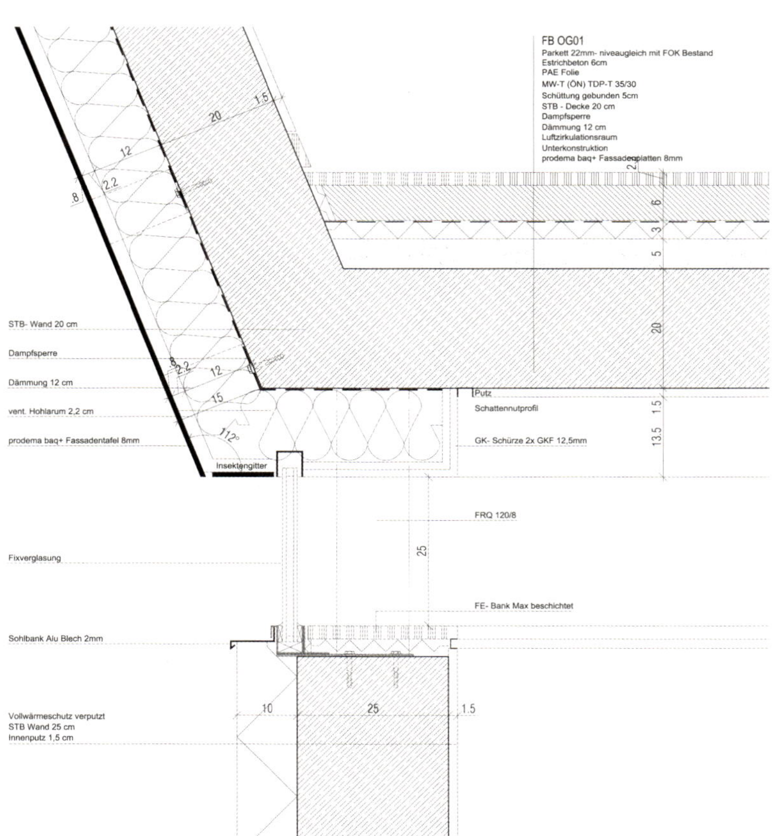

Wall construction detail

Elevation

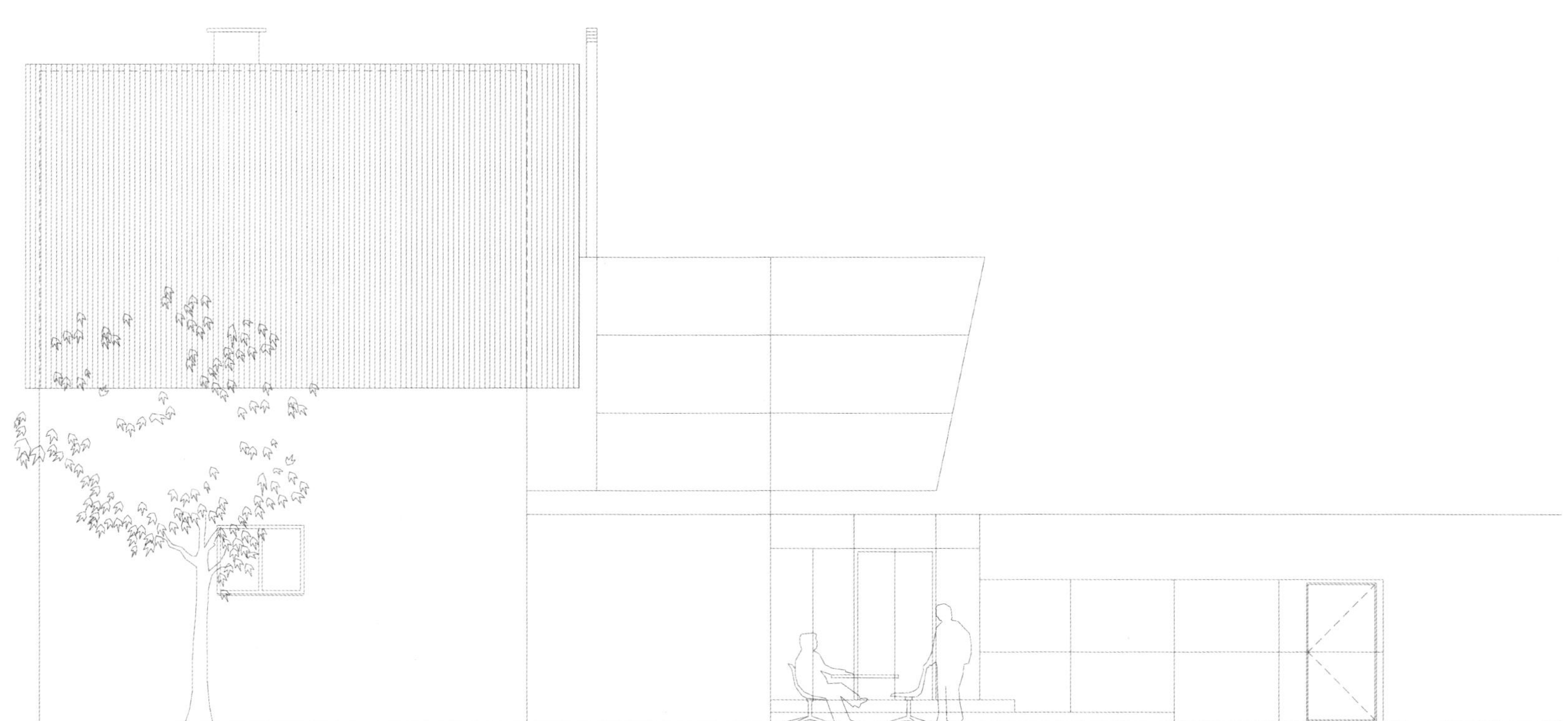

Elevation

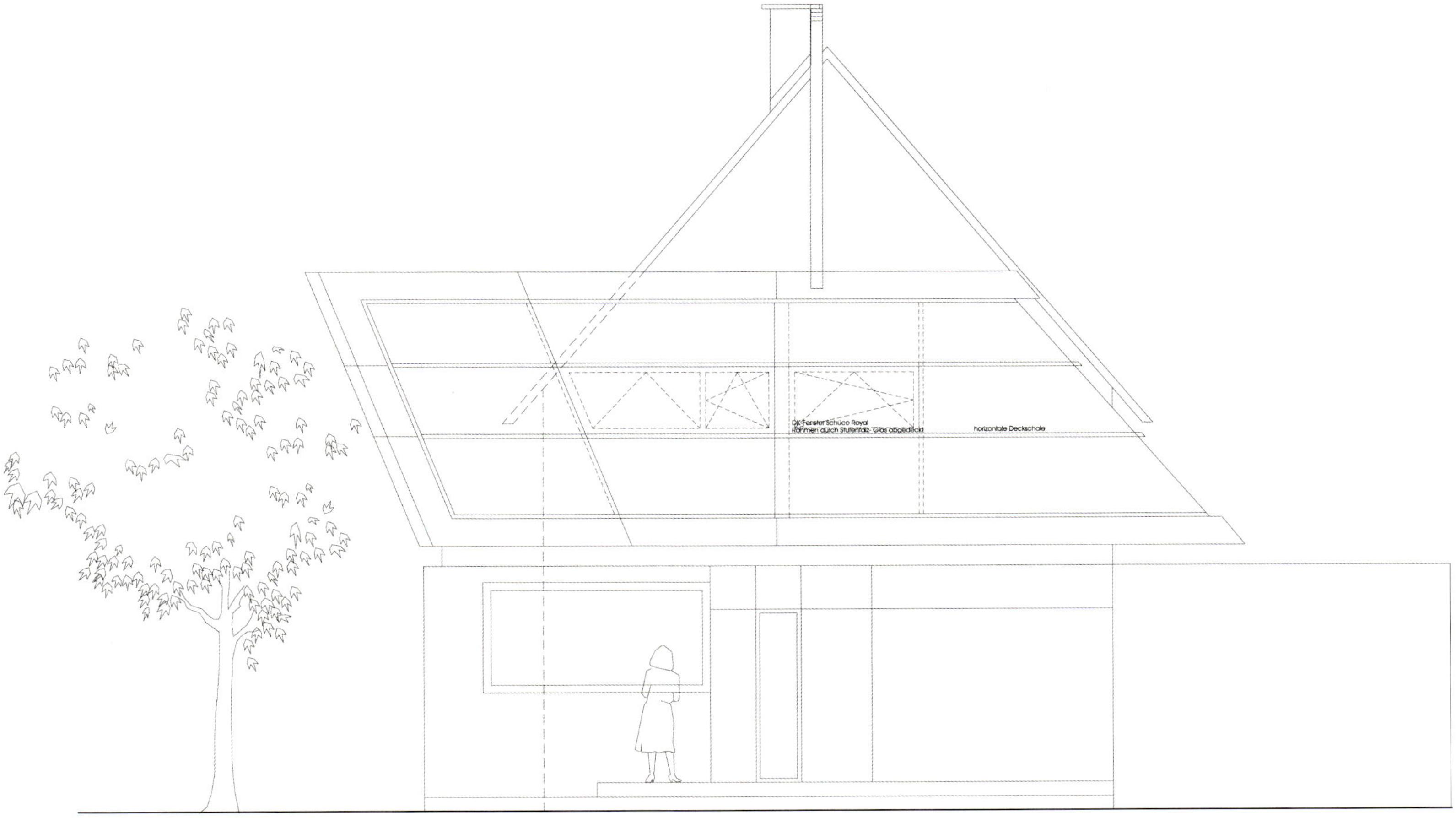

Elevation

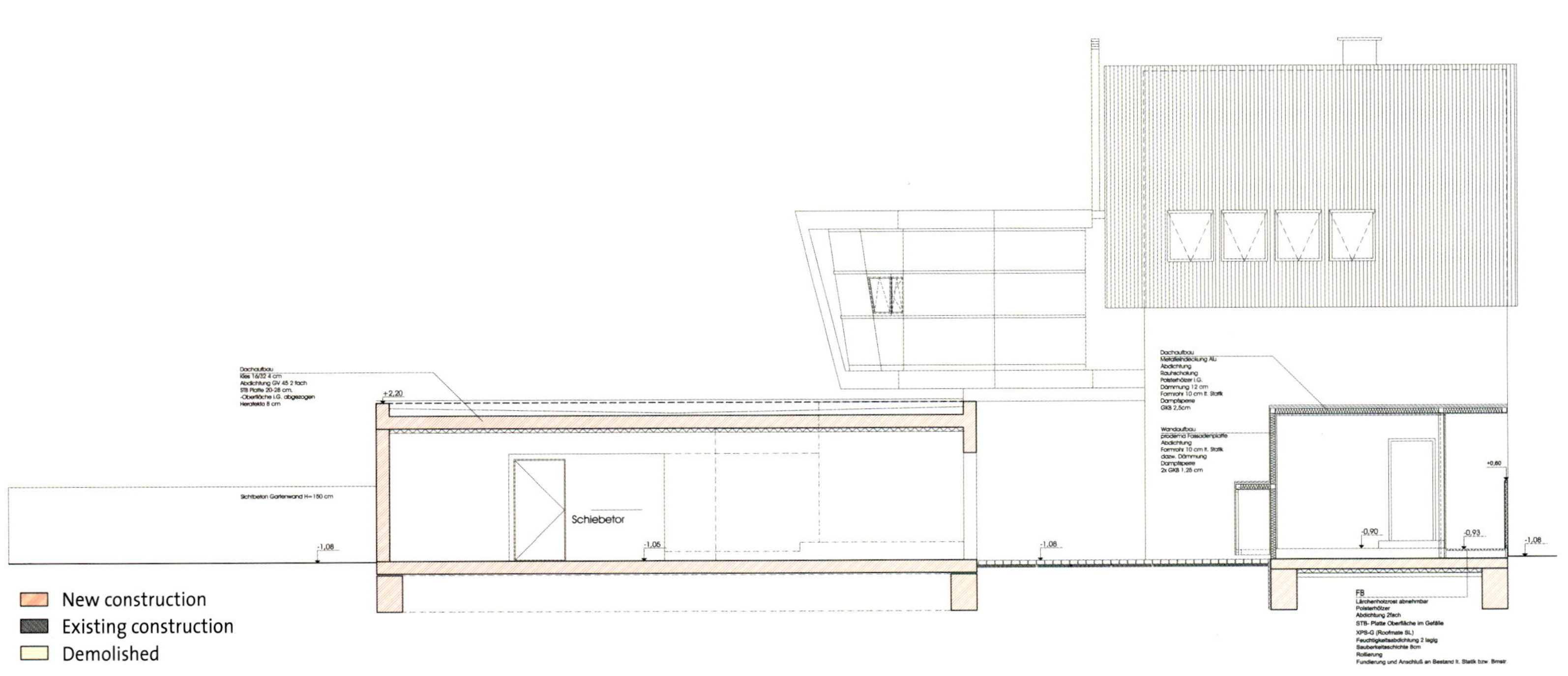

Longitudinal section

Apartment in Sant Andreu

Architect: Agustí Costa

Photographs © David Cardelús

Location: Barcelona, Spain

The renovation of this apartment, whose budget amounted to 20,500 dollars, was approached as an exercise in restraint and in not doing more than what was strictly necessary, where quality was achieved through economic solutions.

Apartment in Sant Andreu

Lighting was one of the problems that had to be resolved; the only rooms with natural light were the living room and the studio, located at each end of a long hallway, and the rest of the rooms of the house –two bedrooms, the bathroom, and the kitchen –are between the two and do not have any windows. Various openings were made in the walls to allow light to flow in and create more of a sense of space and communication. Gutting the rooms was not in the budget nor was it advisable in such an old building where the walls supported part of the structure's weight. These openings fulfilled different functions: for passing plates between the kitchen and the dining room, and as an interior window between one of the bedrooms and the studio, giving both rooms different perspectives. There is also a small opening between one of the bedrooms and the bathroom so that natural light reaches even the remotest areas of the house. The lighting of the long hallway was resolved with a line of fluorescent lights along its length. This element acts to unify the space along with the melamine surface that runs from one end to the other of the house and functions as a bookshelf in the studio, a counter in the entrance, and an auxiliary table in the kitchen. The doors in the hallway are metal screen instead of traditional glass, to conduct the flow of light as well as control ventilation to avoid bothersome drafts.

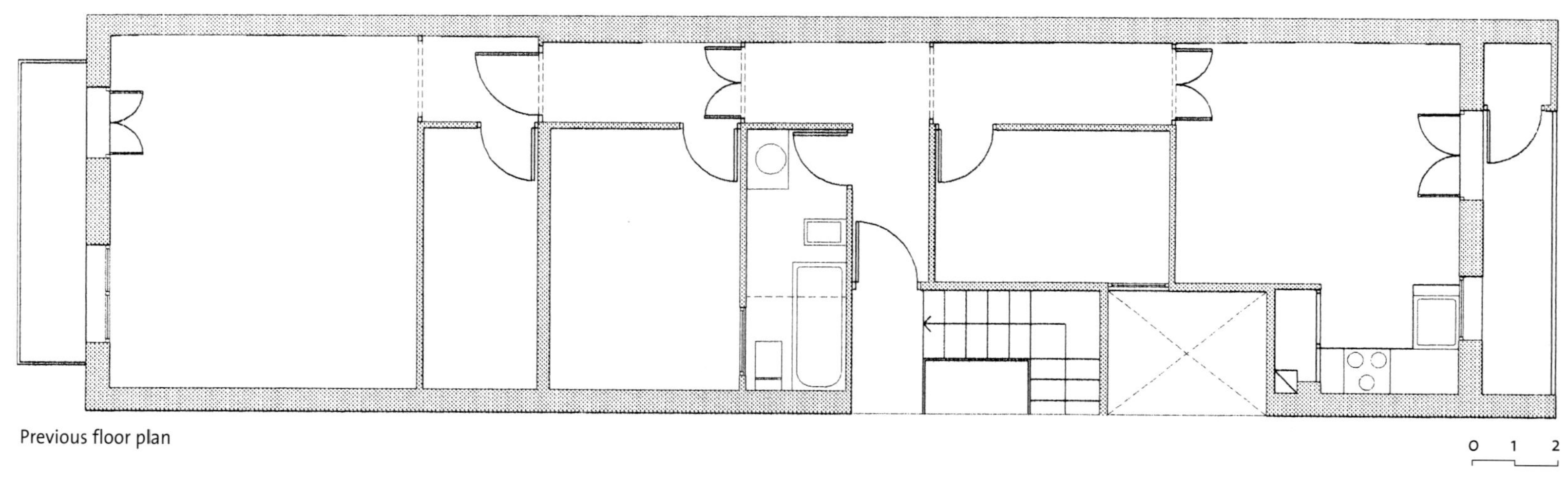

Previous floor plan

0 1 2

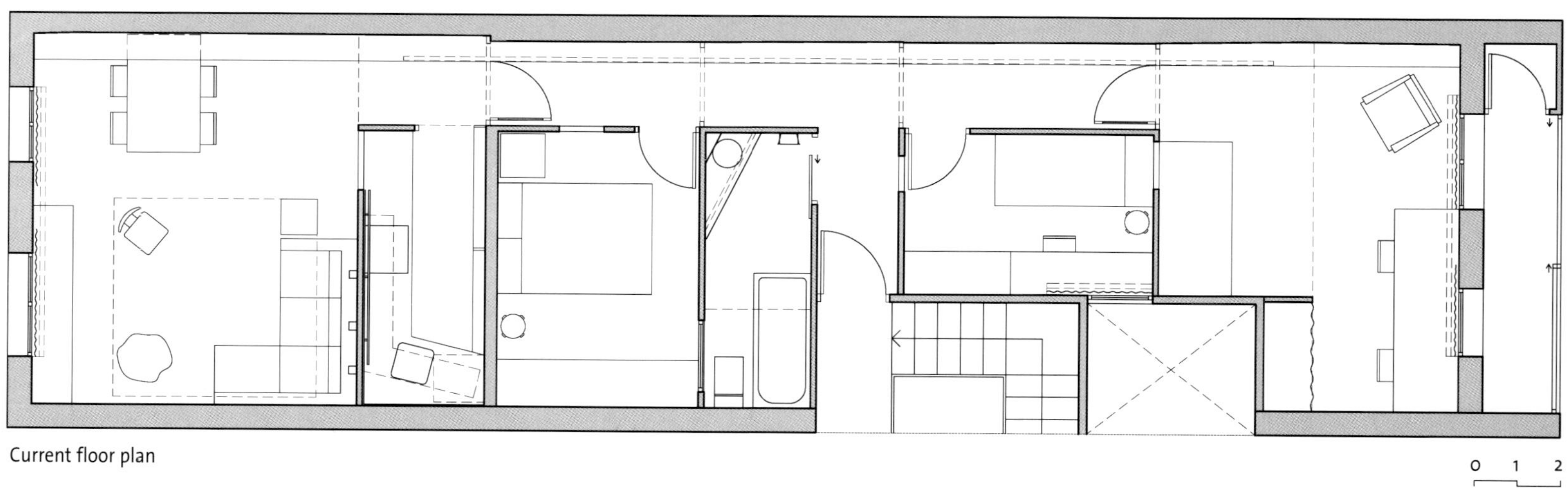

Current floor plan

0 1 2

The small windows created in the interior wall light into the bedroom and allow different views between the rooms.

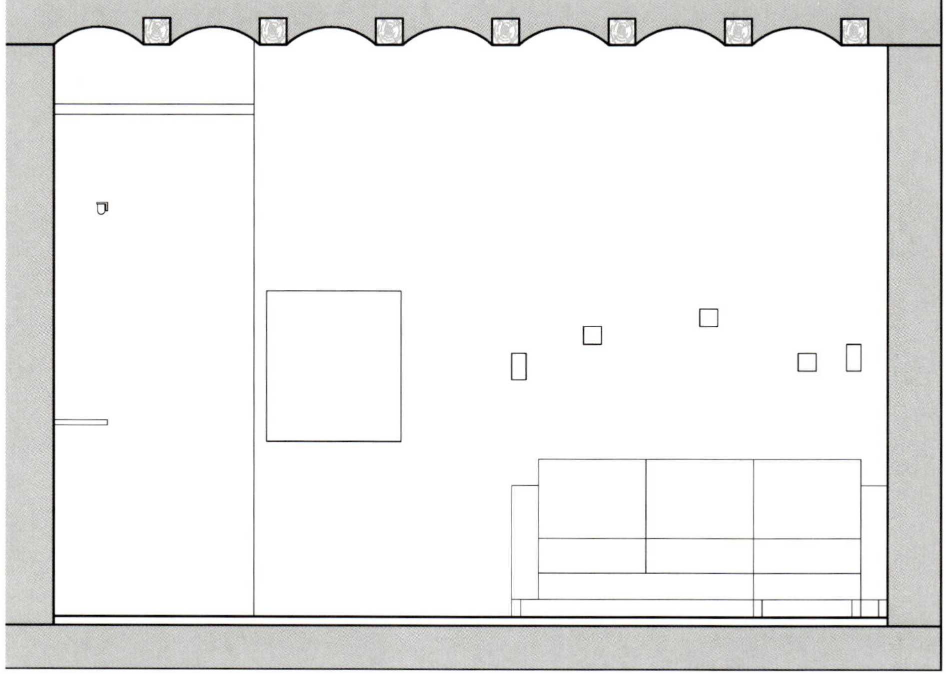

Section of living room

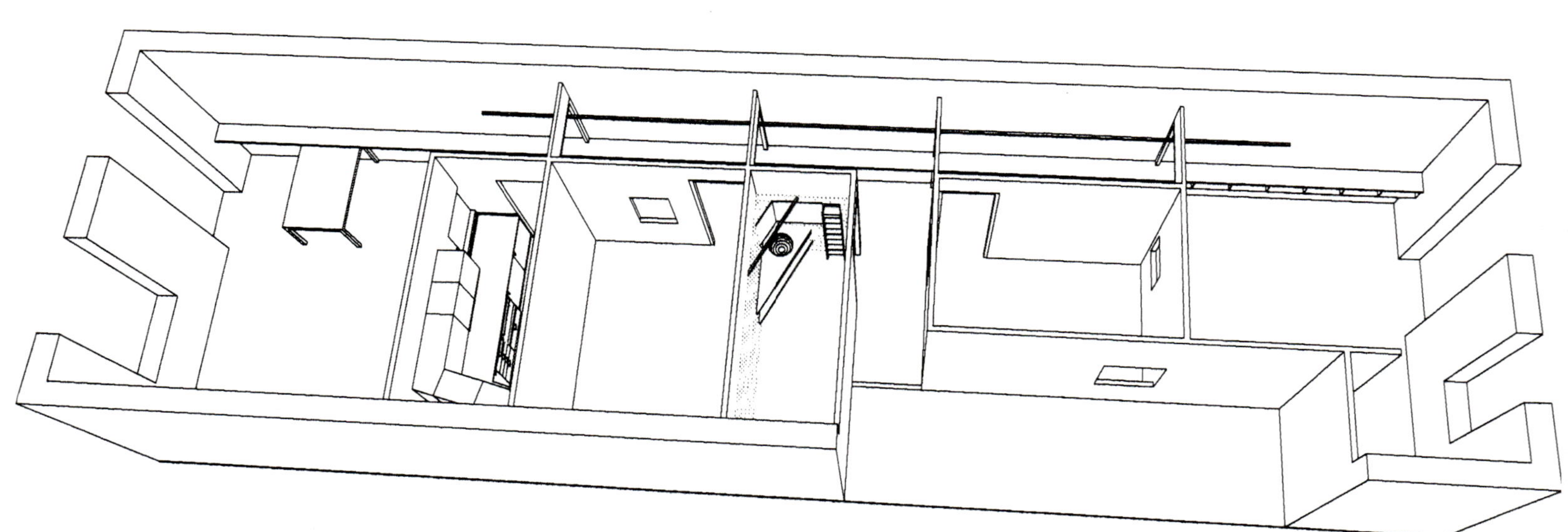

Axonometric view

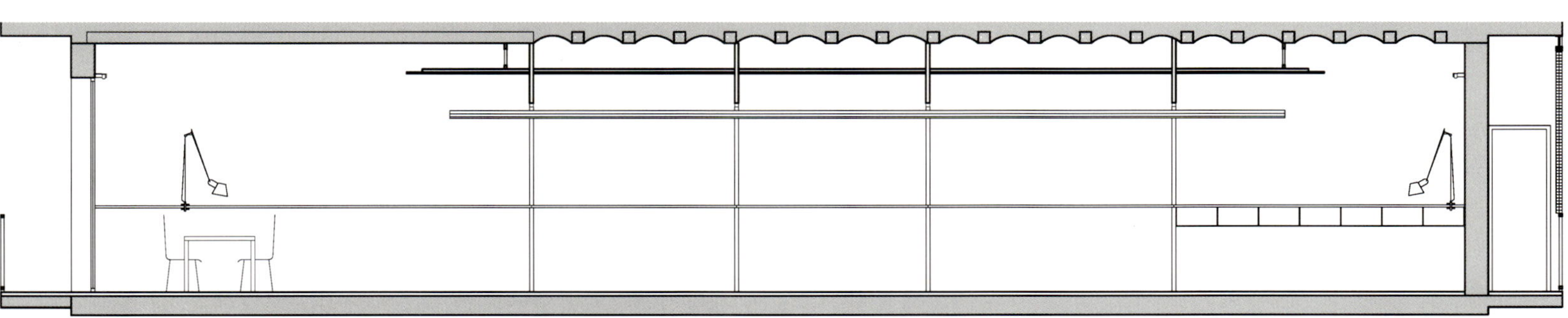

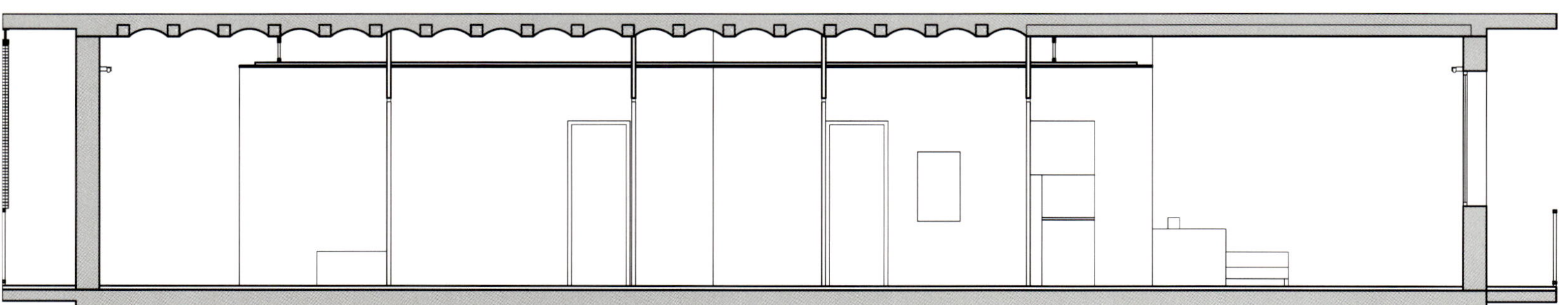

Longitudinal sections

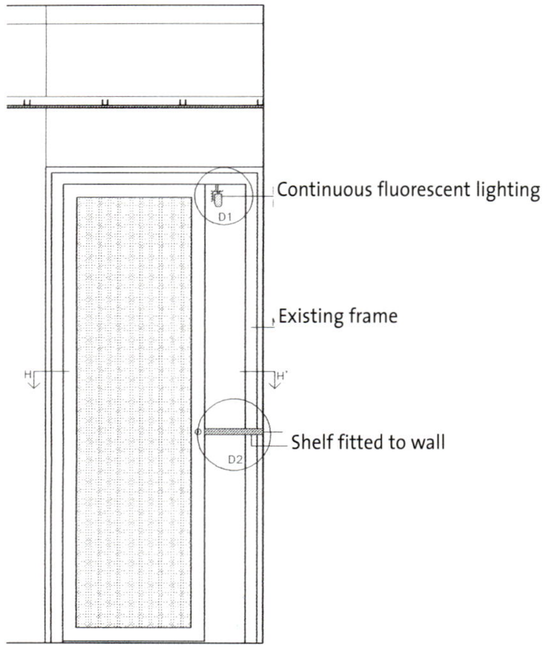

Section

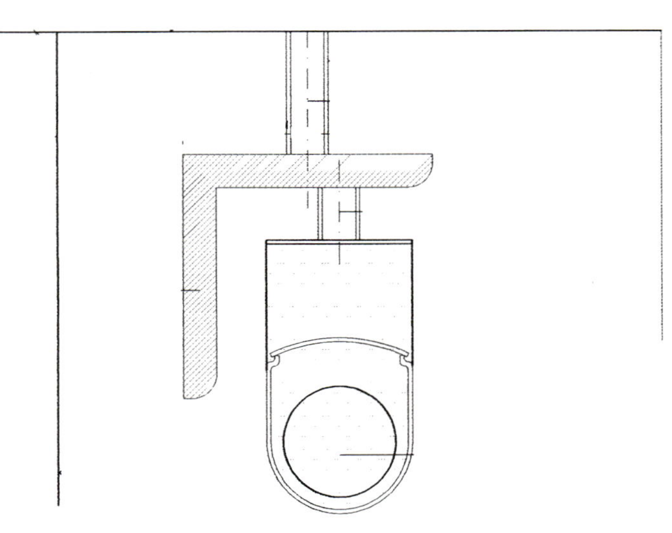
Fluorescent construction detail

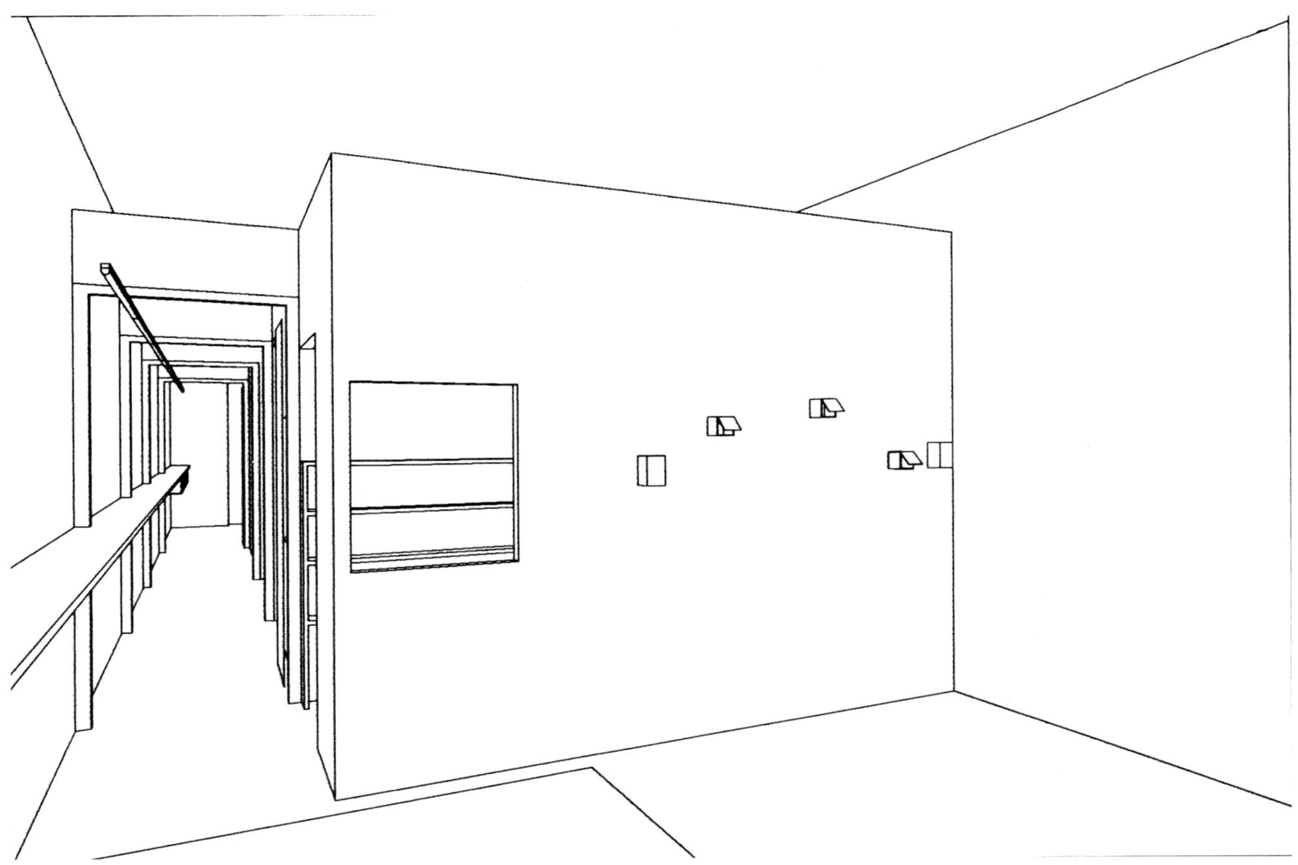

Perspective from living room

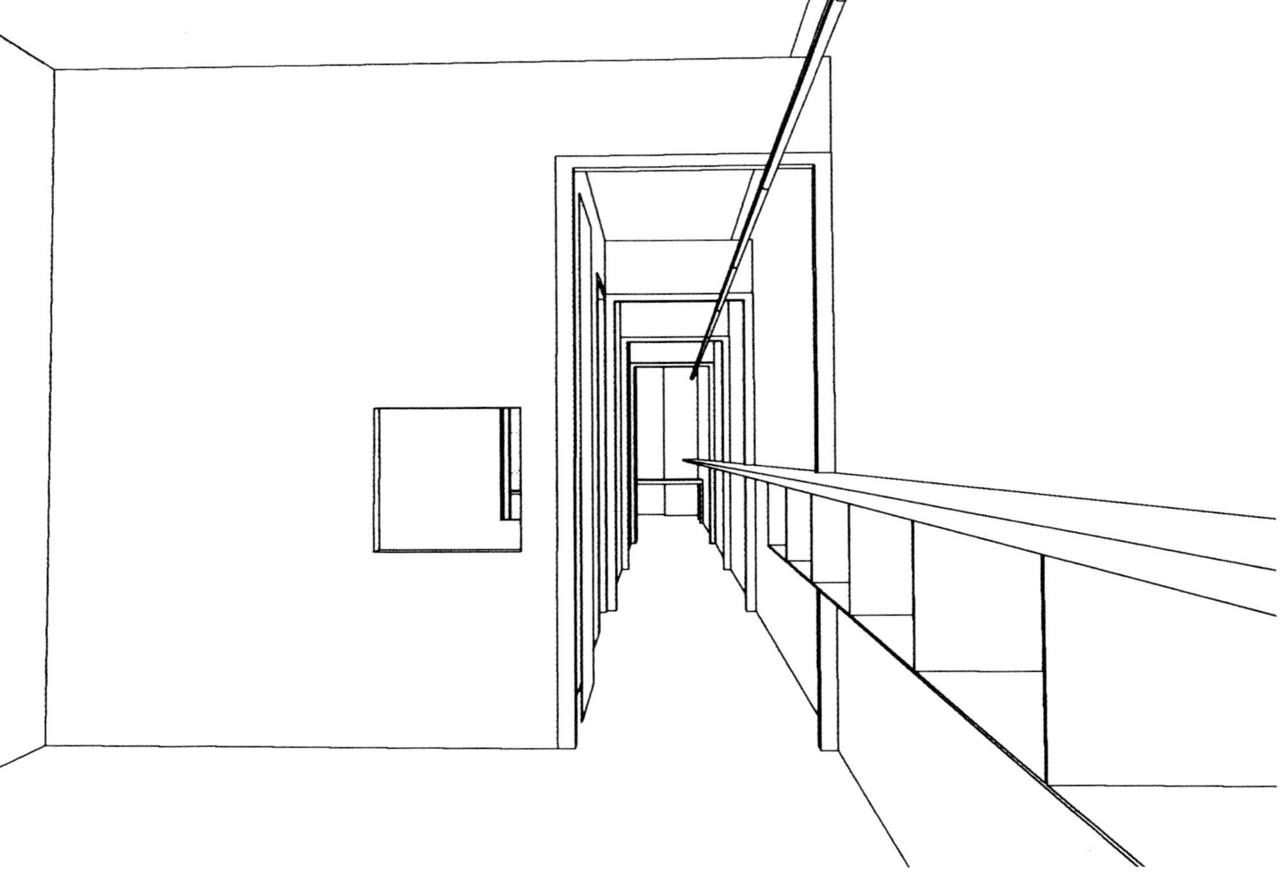

Perspective from studio

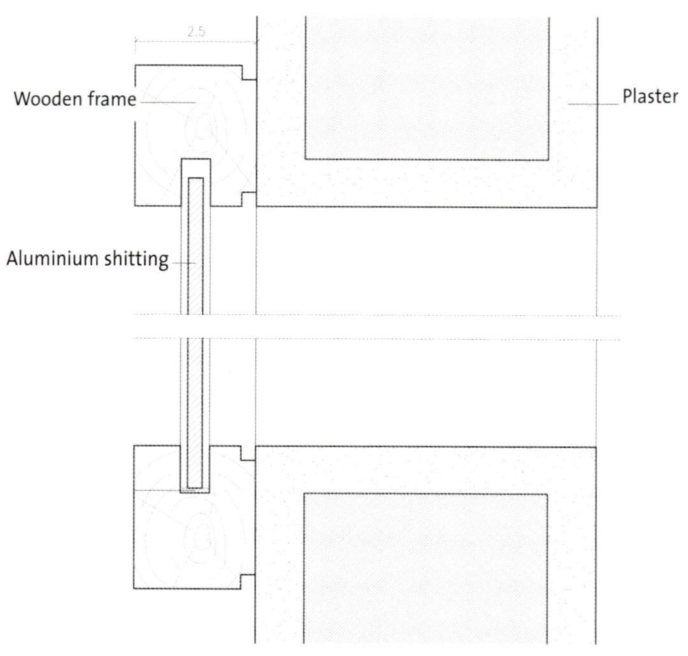

Detail of interior structure

Elevation

Section

Bento Box Apartment

Architects: Procter & Rihl

Photographs © Nathan willock

Location: London, United Kingdom

Constructed in the mid-1960's, the building where this project was carried out has several levels where simple apartments sit above office spaces.

Bento Box Apartment

This apartment consists of a studio with a stairway that connects to the bedroom and a terrace. The spaces were poorly designed, with an uncomfortable stairway and a terrace that is too big compared to the dimensions of the apartment. The interior space was extended upward and outward to create views of London to the east and the west. The apartment was reversed, putting the kitchen and living room on the upper level while the bedroom, entryway, bathroom, and studio were placed on the lower level. The apartment was thus remodeled completely including parts of the façade (windows and sliding doors) and thermal insulation in the ceiling. In general, the space was modified to give the impression that it was enlarged, thanks to the strategic placement of mirrors. The details also contribute to an increased feeling of space. A window without a frame and light flowing from the ceiling create the feeling that the walls are extended, floating toward the outside. The space is defined through the subtle use of different materials without needing to separate the environments. This way more contrasts are created between the materials inside the apartment. In the same way, the materials are able to unite the spaces. For example, the marble in the entryway extends to the bathroom.

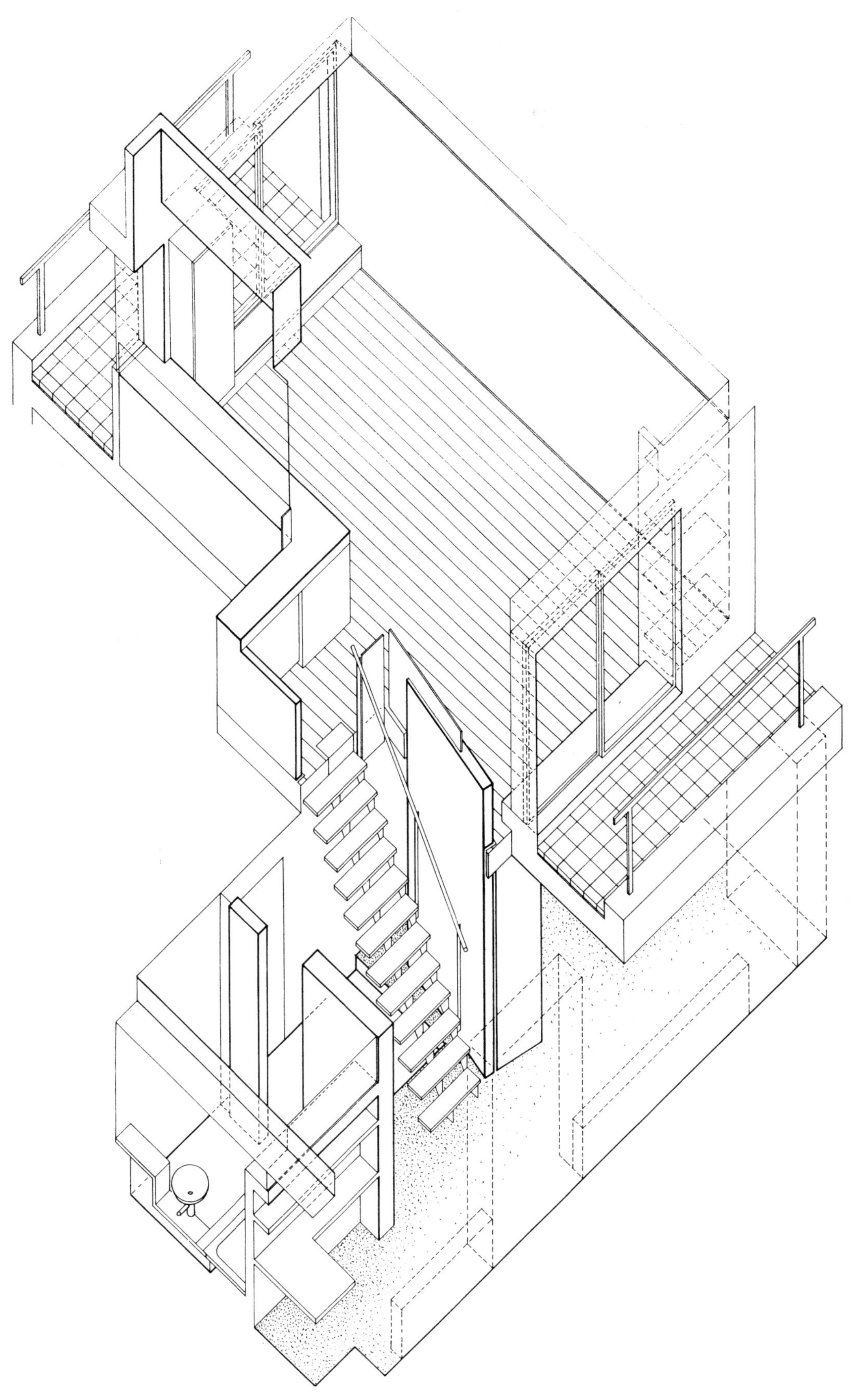

Axonometry

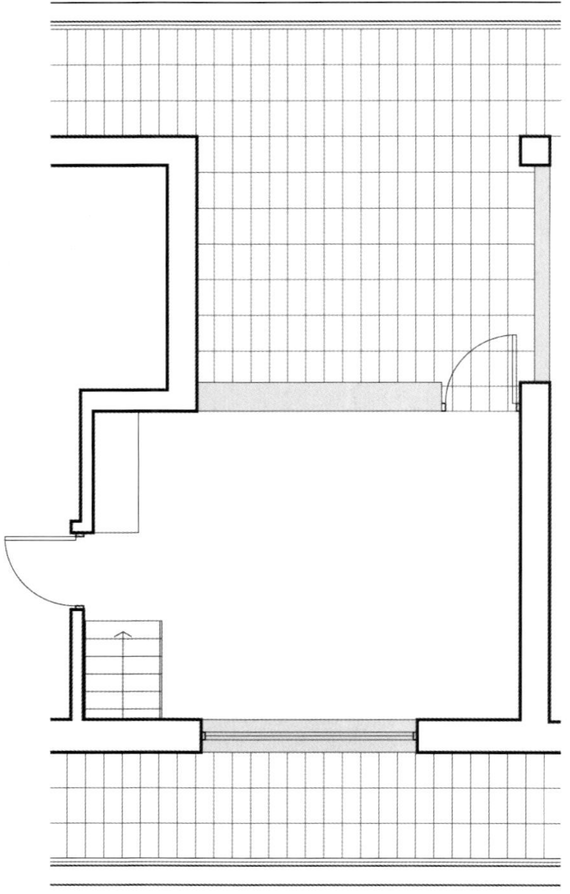

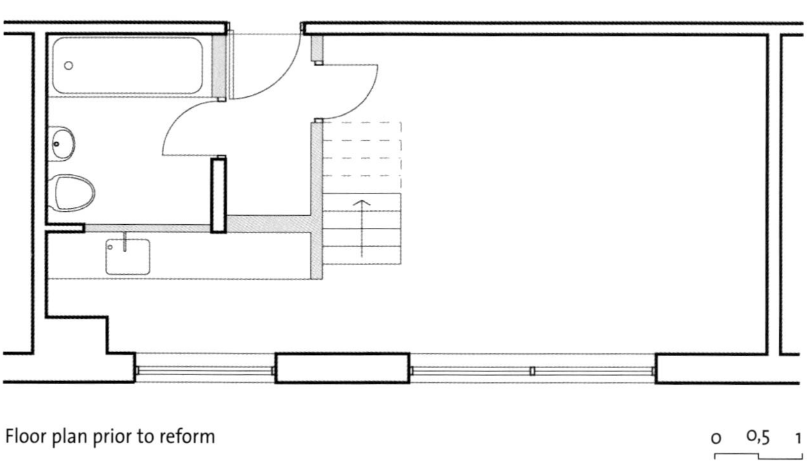

Floor plan prior to reform

0 0,5 1

The custom-made tables were designed to be graceful elements within the space.

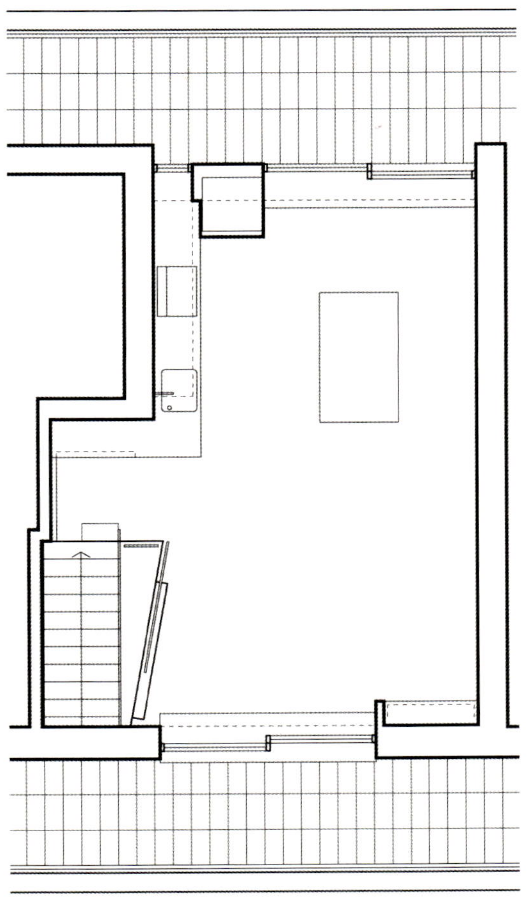

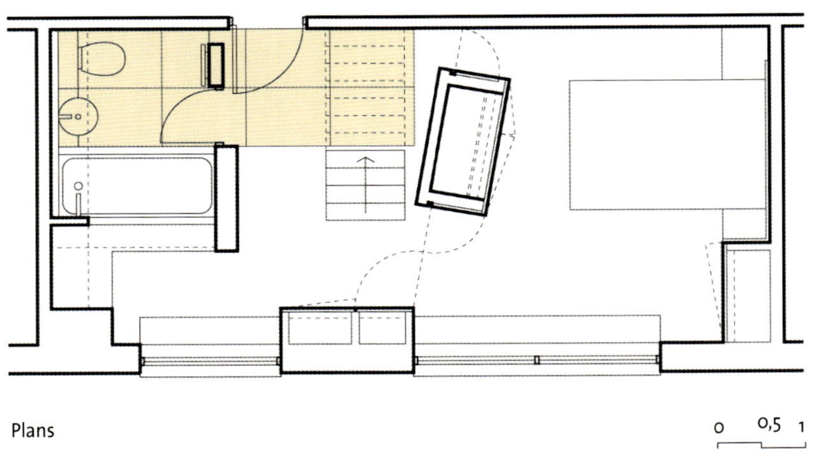

Plans

0 0,5 1

House in Tiana

Architect: Alfons Soldevila

Photographs © Jordi Miralles

Location: Tiana, Spain

The gentle pergola at the entrance is an element that does not alter the building, yet it provides it with a new terrace and a shaded space, as well as a new access.

House in Tiana

A radical change in the layout was required to transform this old farmhouse into a home and adapt it to modern requirements. The old house had storage on the ground level, leaving only the two upper levels for living space. In addition, the upper levels were a bit dark because of the layout of the rooms and the narrow windows typical of old buildings. The renovation adapted the new design to the existing structure; the long façades were all conserved while the short ones, oriented towards the sea and mountains received large windows, a relatively simple task since the brick walls were not load bearing. The windows were installed with channels that could easily be attached directly to the brick and put into use quickly. The new interior layout foresaw larger rooms all facing the outside, and a very large and light-filled stairway. The most innovative element of this design was the very large new terrace on the level of the second floor. Its thin steel framework looks so light that it does not detract from the original structure. This structure, besides adding square feet as a terrace, acts as a porch for the lower level, and is reminiscent of the fine trellises for ivy and climbing plants on rural houses.

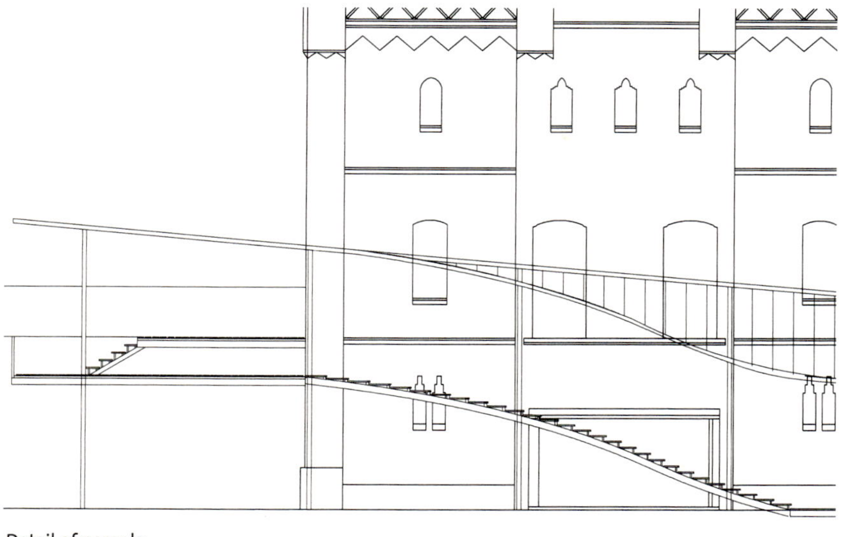

Detail of pergola

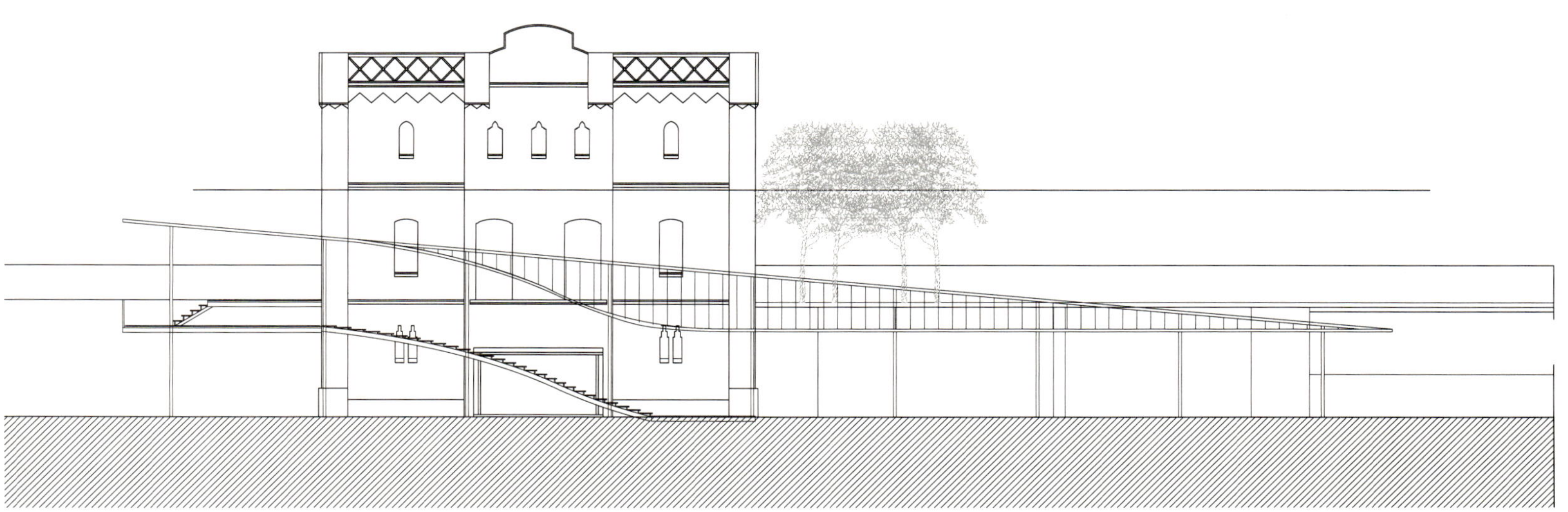

Elevations

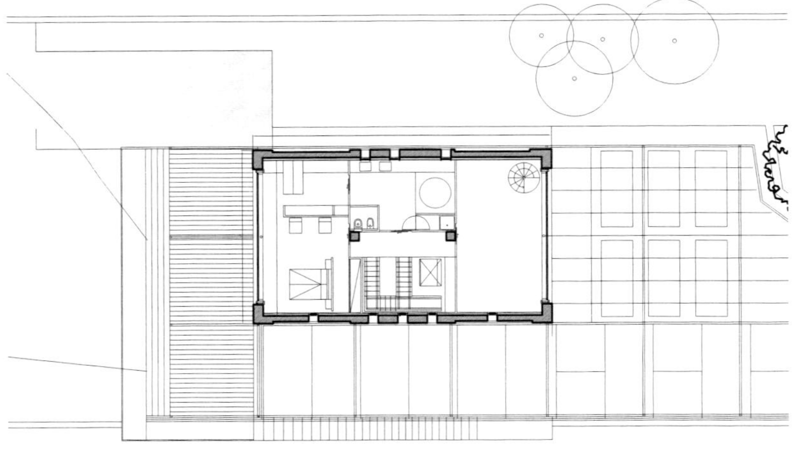

Second floor

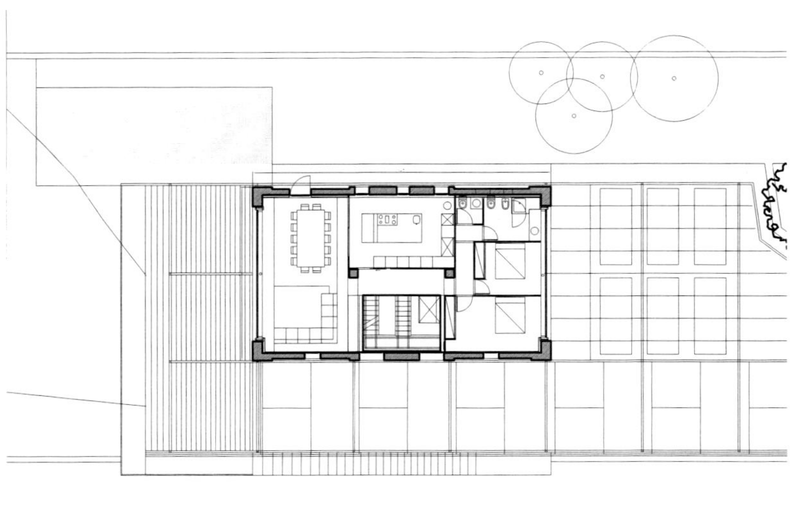

First floor

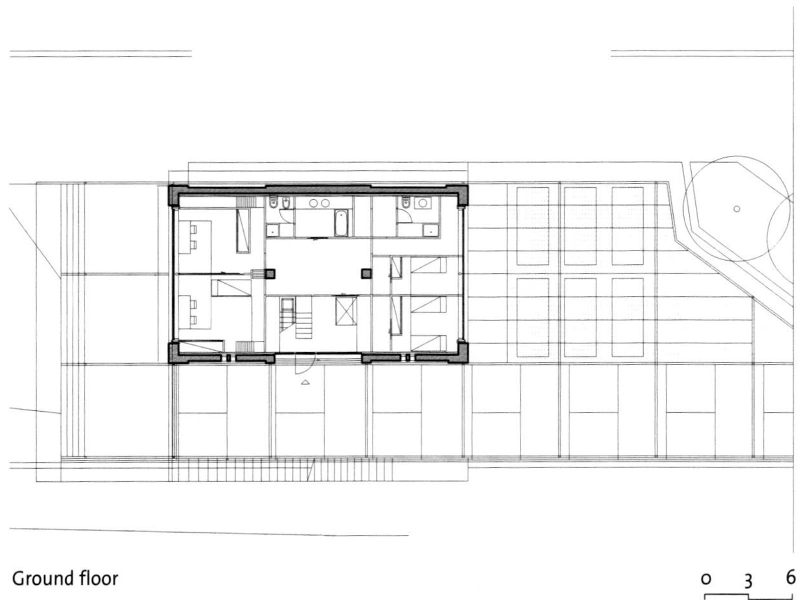

Ground floor

The lightness of the stairway allows natural light to flow to the ground floor and acts as a communicating space between the different levels.

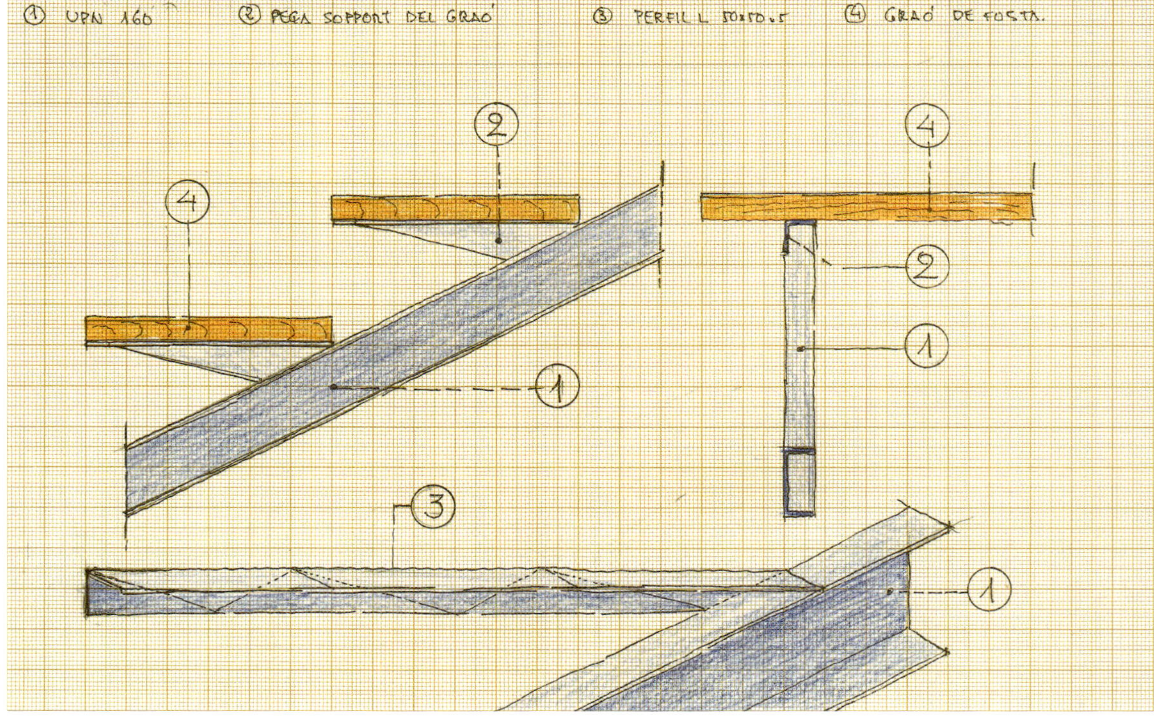

Stairway construction detail

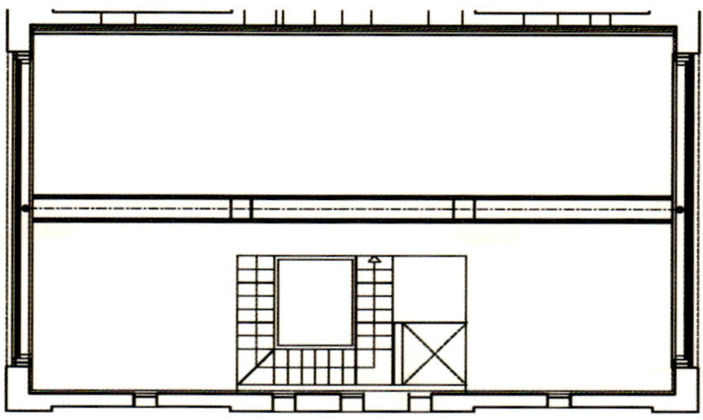

Third floor

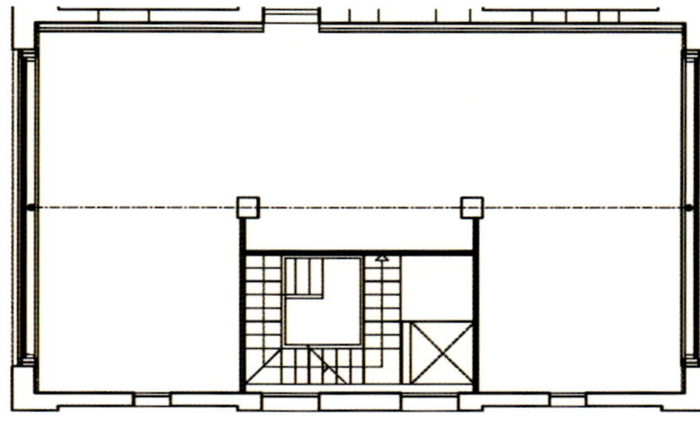

Second floor

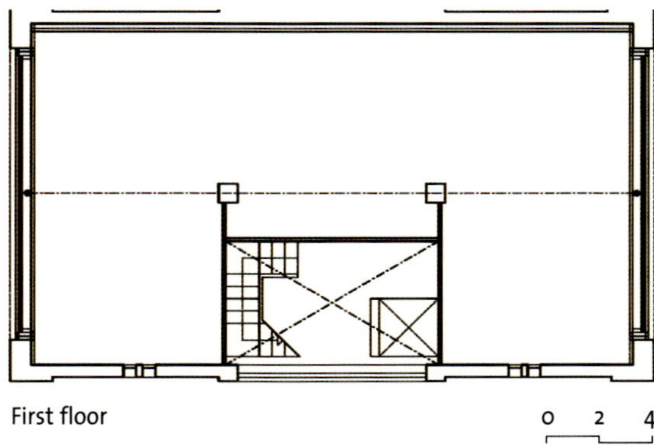

First floor

0 2 4

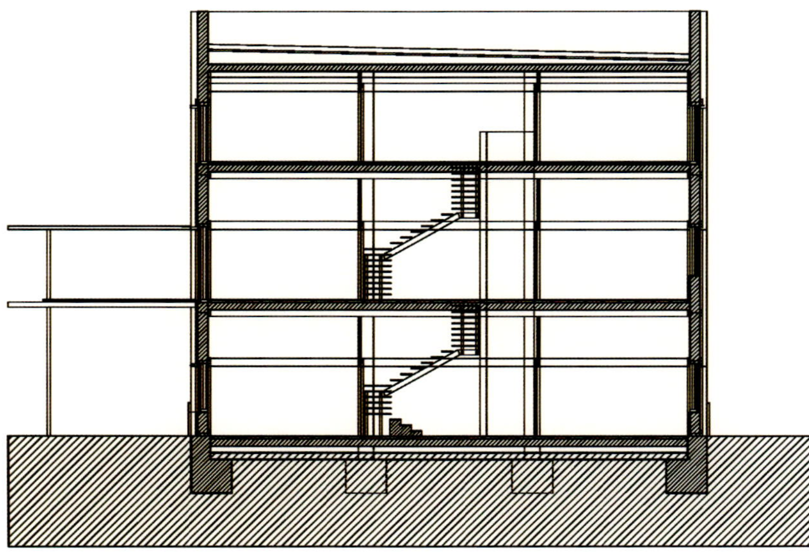

Section

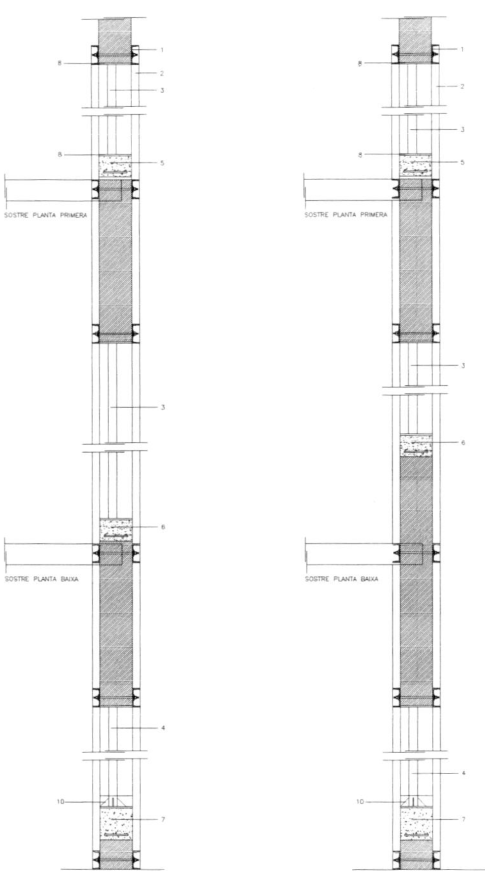

Wall construction detail

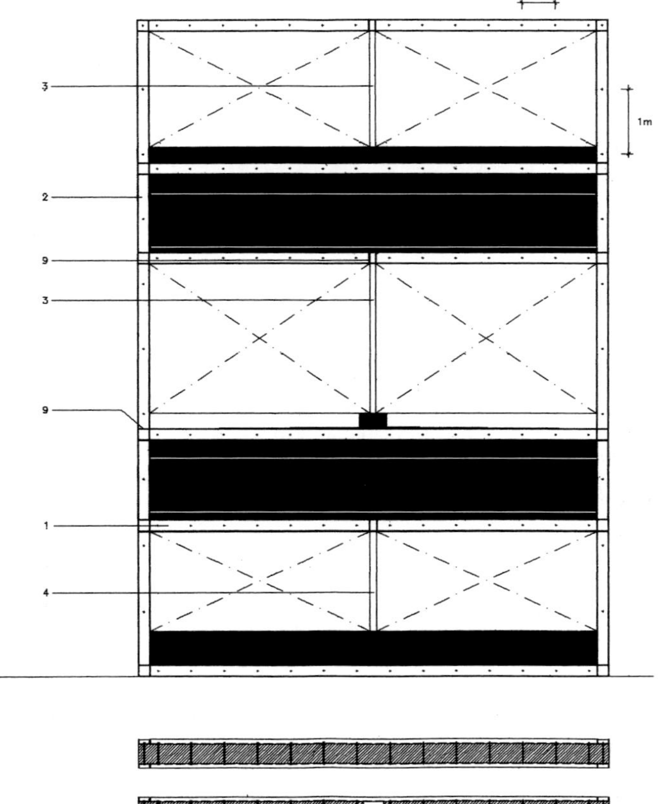

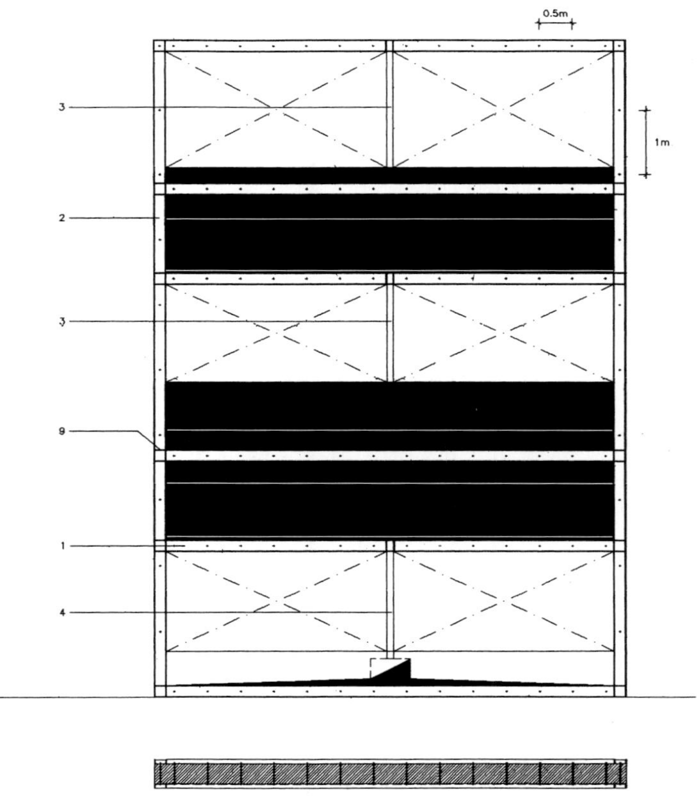

Glass wall construction detail

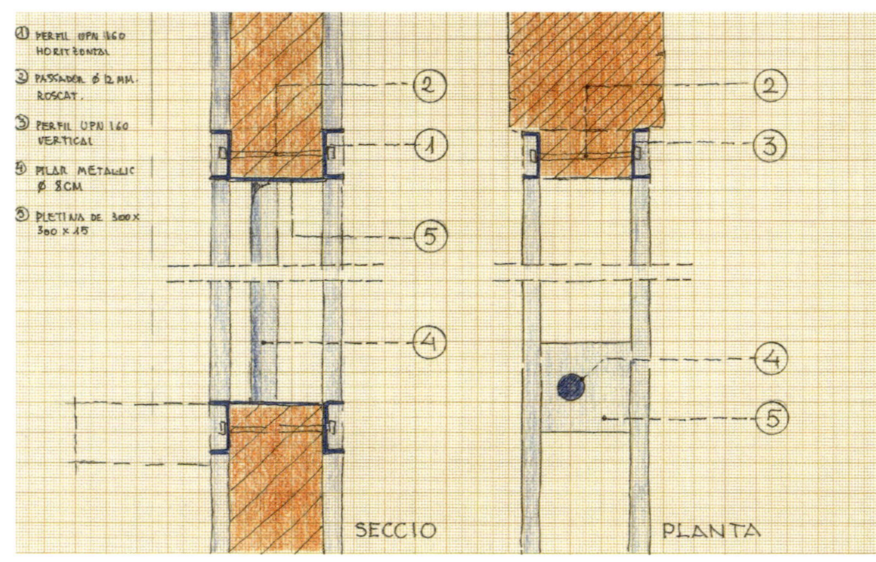

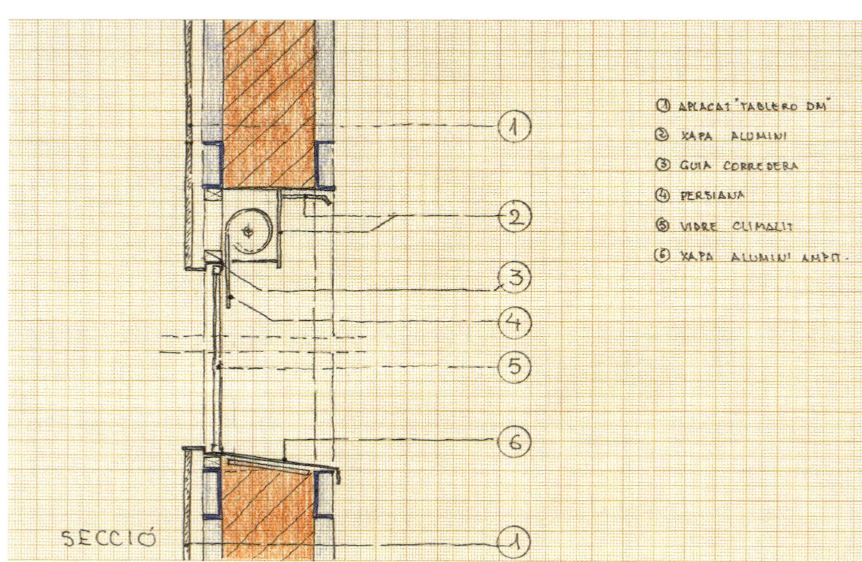

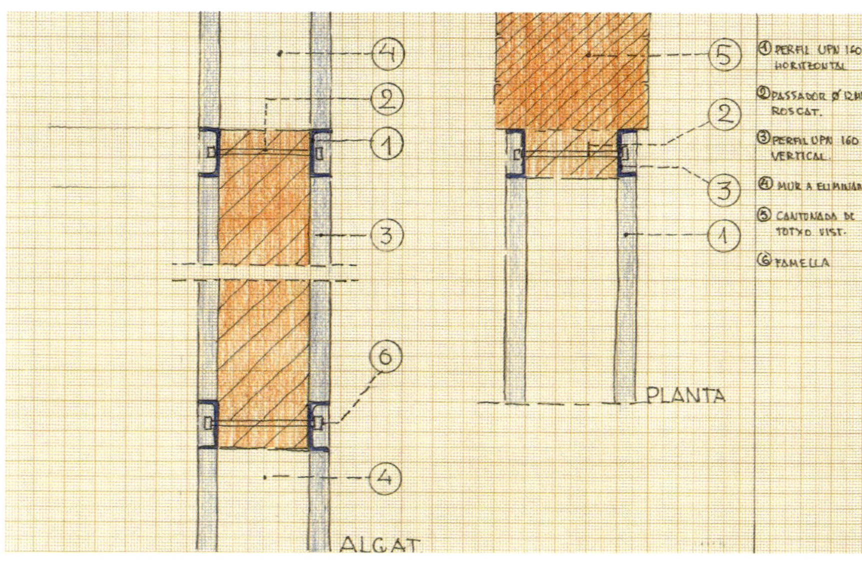

Glass wall construction details

House in Piazza Novona

Architect: Roberto Silvestri

Photographs © Ernesta Caviola

Location: Rome, Italy

This house stands as an example of an open plan whose uniqueness lies in the fact that not all functions are grouped in a single space, which often occurs when renovating urban spaces. Here a public area and a private area coexist in an intelligent layout.

House in Piazza Novona

The design for the renovation of this house done for a film director had to combine the requirements of a home with the public activities of the owner. The solution was a space that maintains the footprint of the structure of a traditional home, but with rooms connected by multiple openings that do not turn it into a single open space. The entrance has three large travertine steps supported by a light steel structure, which announces the mixing of materials in the entire apartment that strives to create an austere, warm, and very human interior. The dark parquet contrasts with the white walls, and the steel walls, rarely used in interiors, add a touch of sobriety and warmth. The sliding doors that separate this space from the rest of the house go perfectly well with the steel, since they are acid etched glass that add a translucent texture that is at the same time similar to that of the walls. The wide hallway leads to a small terrace located next to a small and functional kitchen that is nothing more than a widened hallway, perfect for this type of dwelling. The bedroom is simple and of small size following the owner's express wishes; the bathroom, however, has a somewhat fancier decoration, especially the flooring.

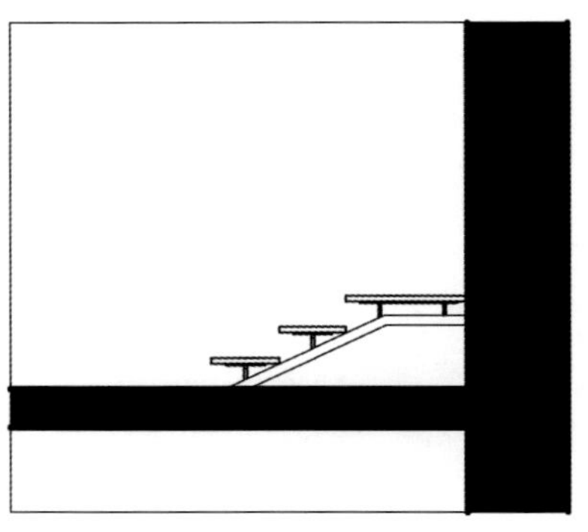

Stairway construction detail

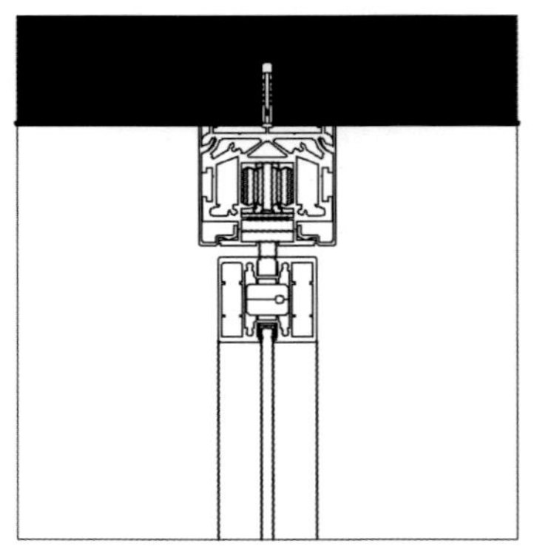

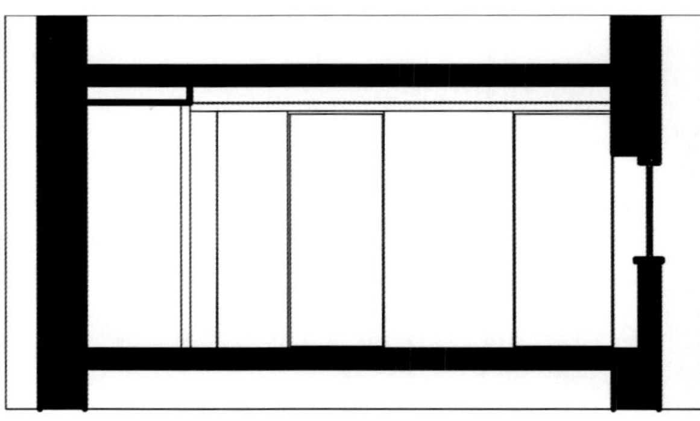

Section A-A'

Detail of sliding door

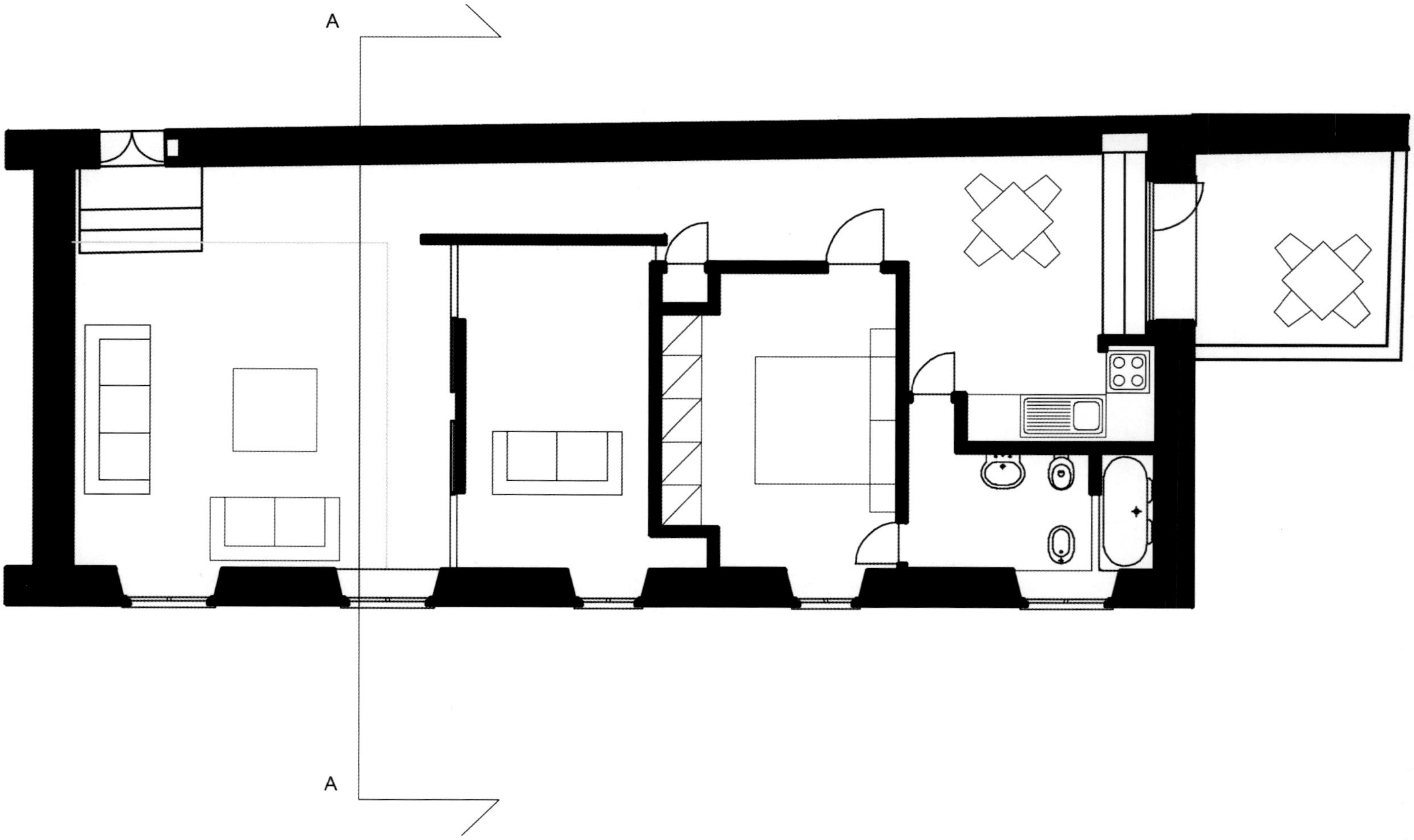

A

A

Plan

0 1 2

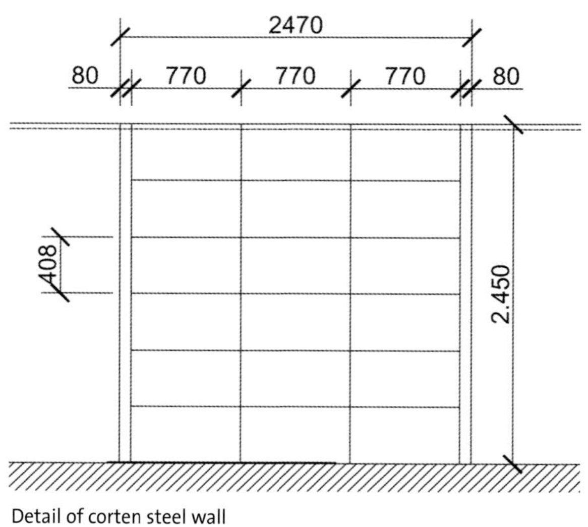

Detail of corten steel wall

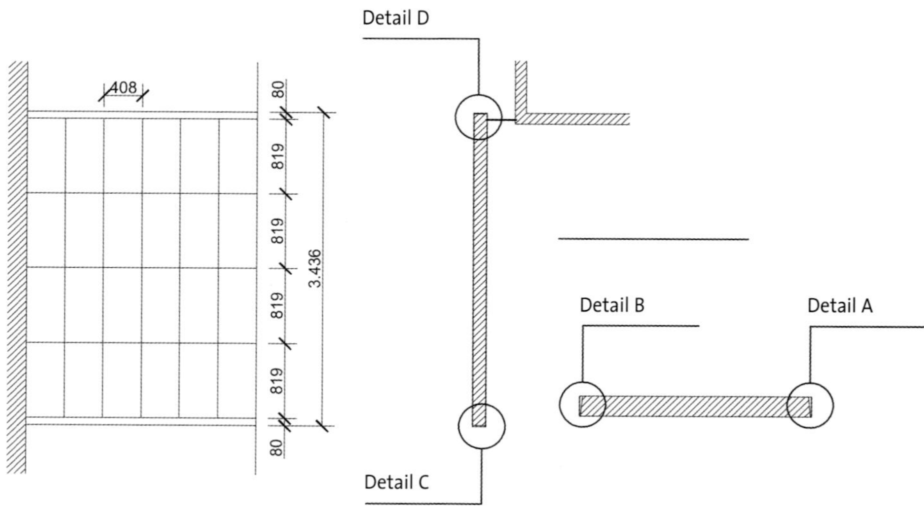

Sketch of new walls

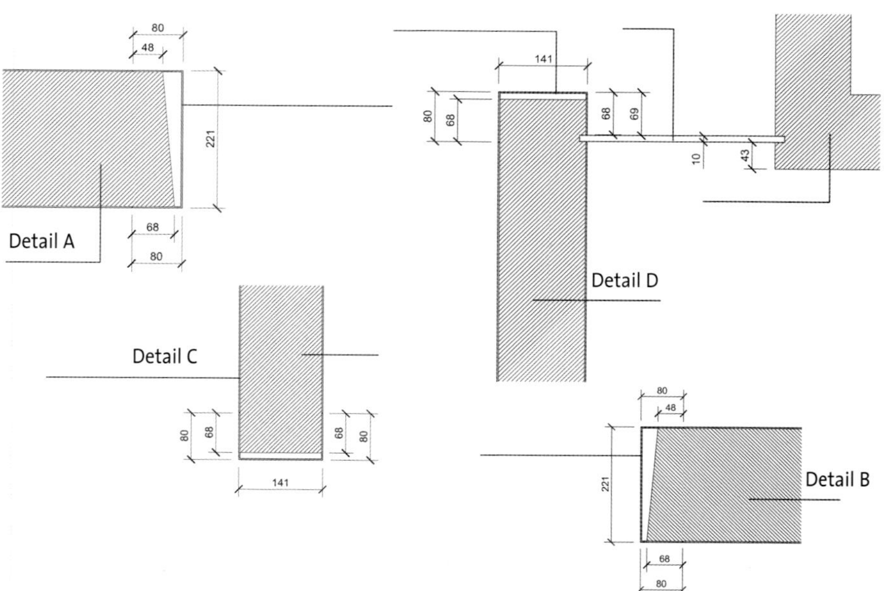

Construction details

Soup Kitchen

Architect: Christof Swartz/Swartz Design

Photographs © Swartz Design

Location: Hamburg, Germany

CONVERTING HISTORIC BUILDINGS TO HOMES IS A PRACTICAL SOLUTION FOR MAKING USE OF STRUCTURES THAT WOULD OTHERWISE REMAIN ABANDONED.

Soup Kitchen

The Soup Kitchen building was built during the 1830's and was planned to be a center for housing poor people, a type of institution that was very popular during the first industrial revolution. It fulfilled this function until 1920, when it was abandoned, and it came back into use after World War II, occupied by small industrial shops until 1995. Now at the beginning of the 21st century it has become a residence, although the remodeling has a rather disordered look. Today, after the remodel, the building contains seven lofts; three of them hold offices, while the rest combine apartments with studios. In all of them there was an attempt to maintain the characteristic elements of the old building, while adapting the spaces to the needs of a modern and comfortable home, with new utility installations, parquet flooring, and an occasional wall to separate spaces. The large fireplace that was used for cooking as well as for heating the various rooms was one of the most interesting elements to be preserved given its symbolic form, despite the fact that it meant losing the great amount of floor space that it occupied. This and other elements that before fulfilled a specific function, like the very thick brick walls, are now ornaments that give the building the additional values of quality and history.

The comforts offered by the new apartments do not clash with the preexisting structure, like this modern kitchen that is no less functional despite having been located in a dead space between two floors.

Elevation

Section

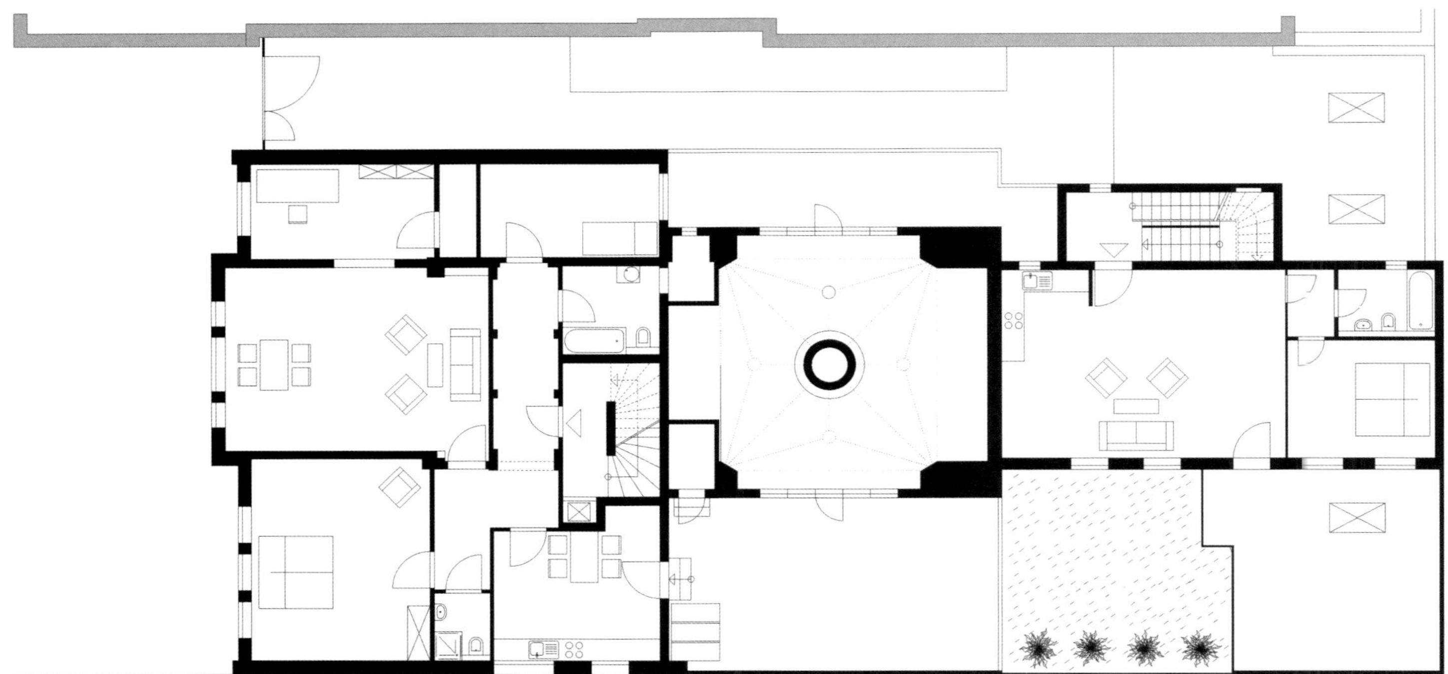
First floor

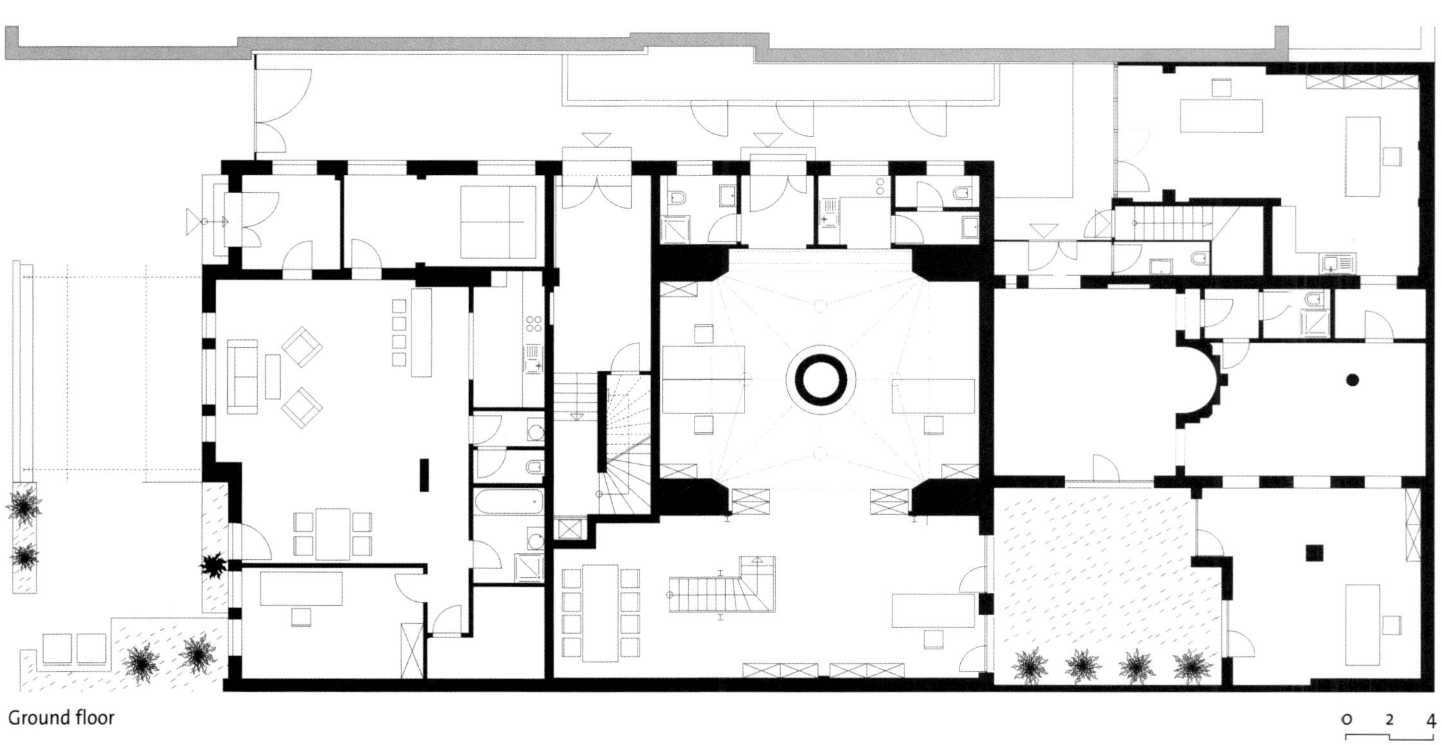
Ground floor

0 2 4

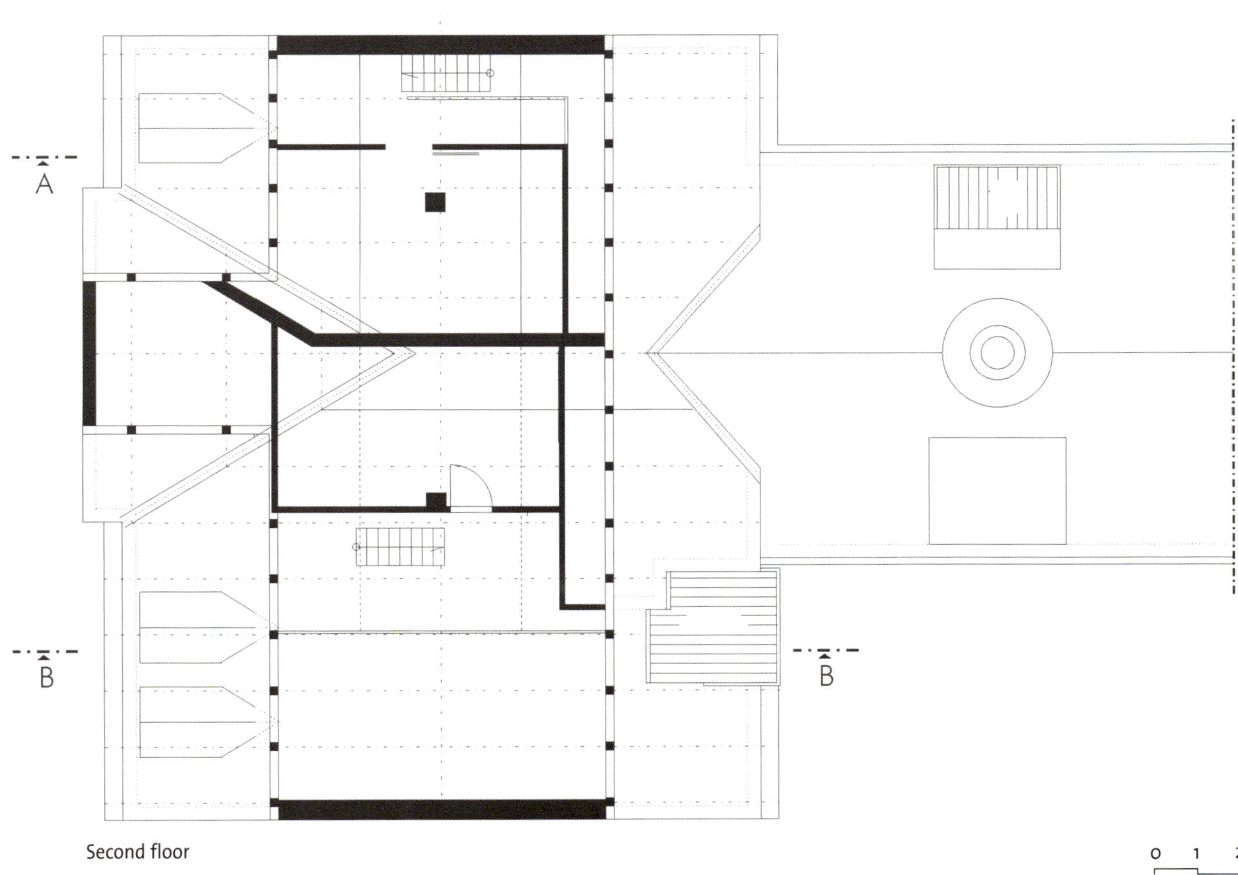

Second floor

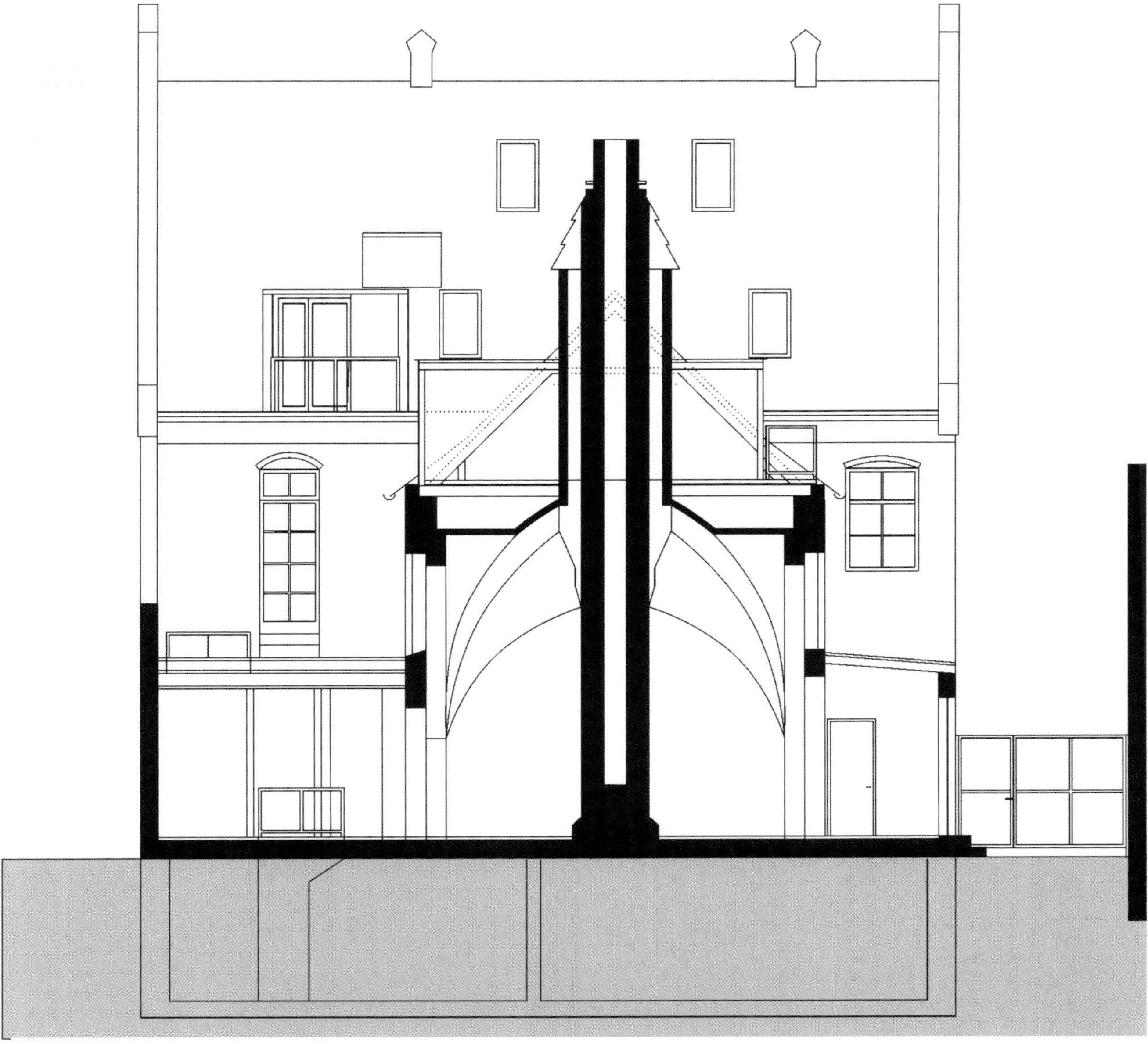

Section

Welcome Center

Architects: Carmen Quintana & Carmelo García

Photographs: © Quintana & García Arquitectos

Location: Las Palmas de Gran Canaria, Spain

Remodeling this house was a matter of removing the past additions to leave a clean space that respected the original 16th century structure that would work well in its new use.

Welcome Center

Located in the old neighborhood of Vegueta in the center of the city of Las Palmas, the old use of the residential building being remodeled was to be changed to administrative uses. Despite this, it was decided to fully respect the original 16th century structure given the advantages this supposed. The distribution around the patios allowed good ventilation and natural light in all the spaces, and it also had a good traffic pattern both horizontally and vertically, as well as a number of good views and spatial transitions. A study was done first, detailing the state of the building, which detected some problems with dampness and seepage that had to be repaired. But the architectural richness that was uncovered after the removal of the different elements added in recent eras included an impressive 20 foot wide arcade and wood porches in one of the patios, ornaments hidden by posterior additions that now add value to the building. Despite the remodeling, there was no plan to inhabit the building. The project has become an example of economy and quality, and demonstrates that remodeling for modern use is possible.

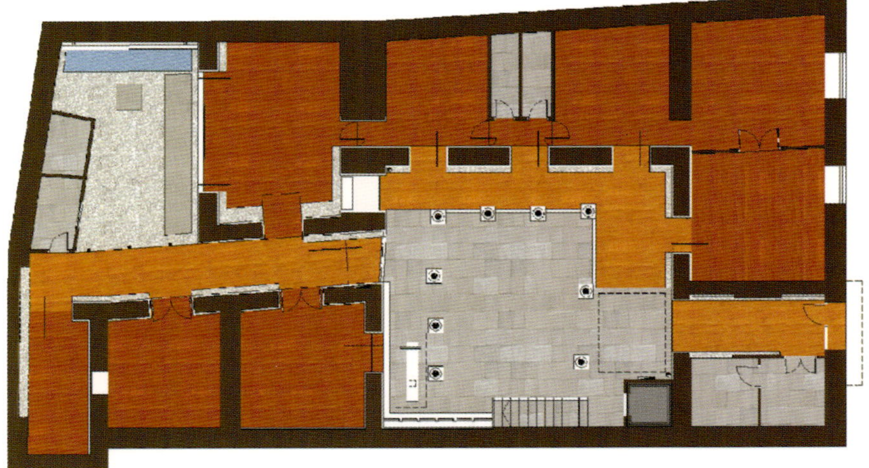
Ground floor

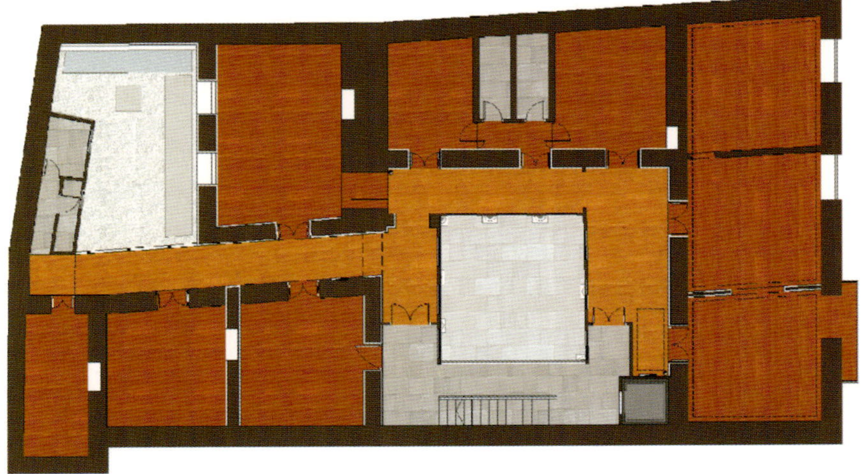
First floor

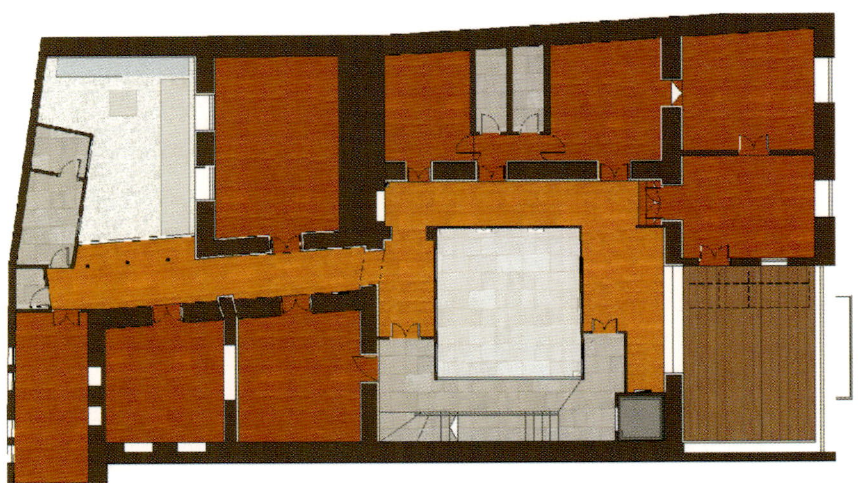
Second floor

0 2 4

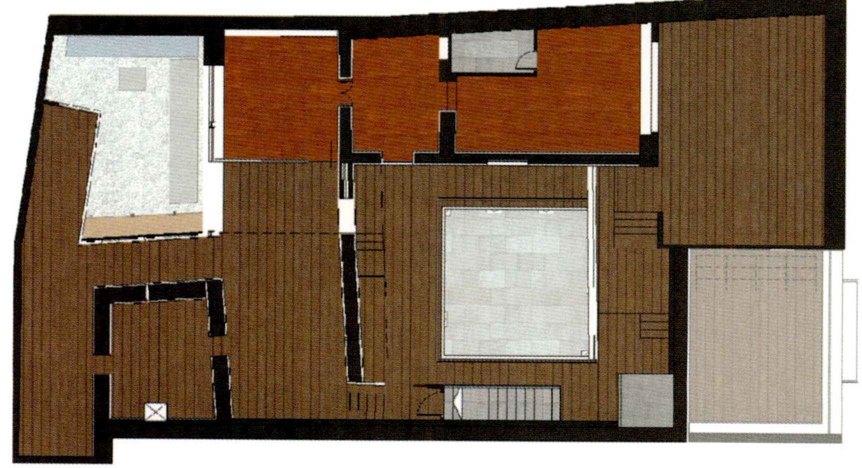

Attic

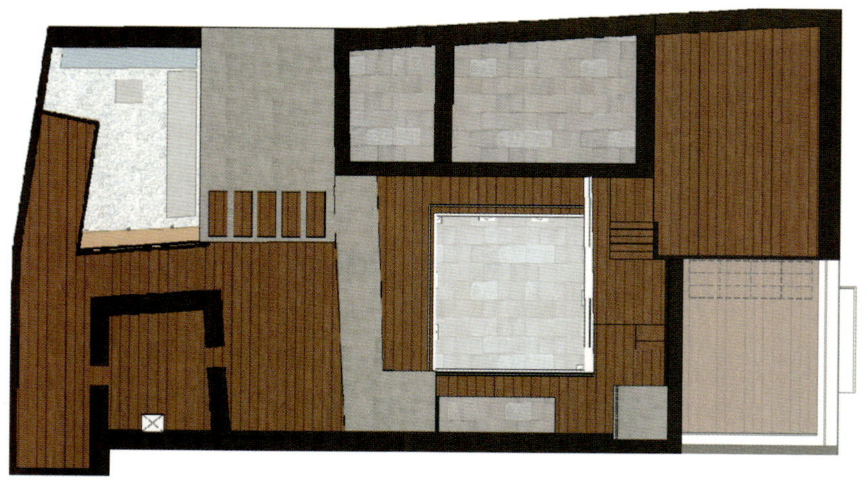

Roofs

0 2 4

Longitudinal section

Sevenig-Goergen

Architects: Bruck & Werckerle Architects

Photographs © Lukas Roth, Ruedi Walti

Location: Luxemburg, Luxemburg

The addition of new rooms was carried out by creating a rectangular structure that, instead of trying to blend in with the old building, uses its form and color to act as a transitional element between the garden and the building.

Sevenig-Goergen

Enlarging this duplex required adding a kitchen and a bedroom to the ground floor, and a bathroom on the top floor. This was accomplished by building a two-level annex that the project designers decided to paint in a bright color that would make it stand out from the surrounding landscape rather than trying to hide it. This new paneled wood structure, with its straight lines and large windows, was built on a concrete pad. The challenge of this commission was placing a bathroom in a space without windows that is also the passageway to the bedrooms. The lack of light was remedied by installing translucent glass walls to let in light from the adjacent rooms. The original house was completely left alone, but some of its elements were manipulated with the intention of emphasizing their characteristics. Thus, the stairway box was painted a bright saffron yellow color that contrasts with the rest of the white painted spaces.

Given the small size of the addition, it was decided to use a light and easy to handle material like wood, a reason that the project took very little time to complete.

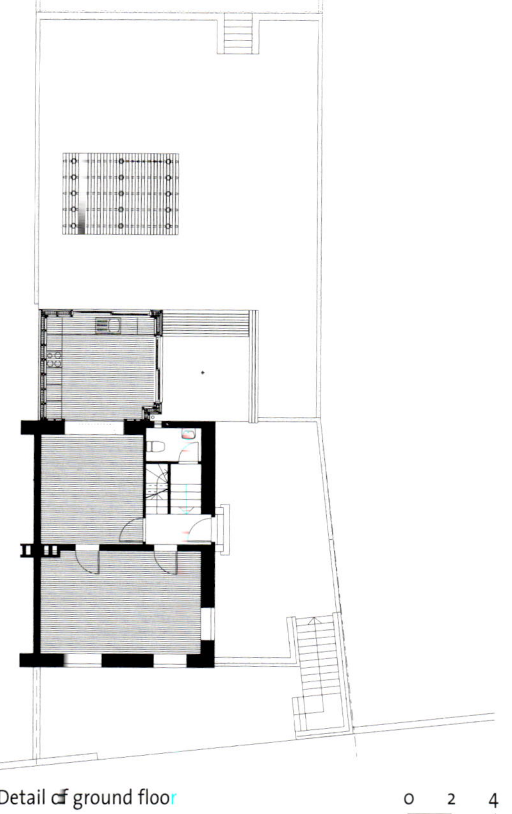

Detail of ground floor

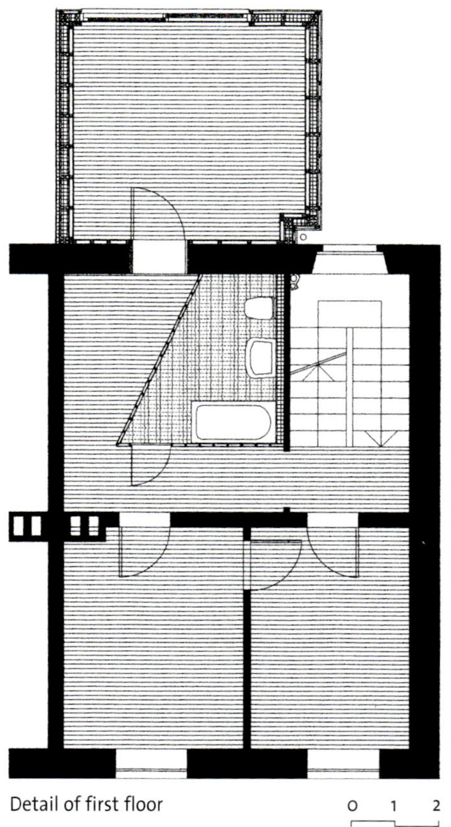

Detail of first floor

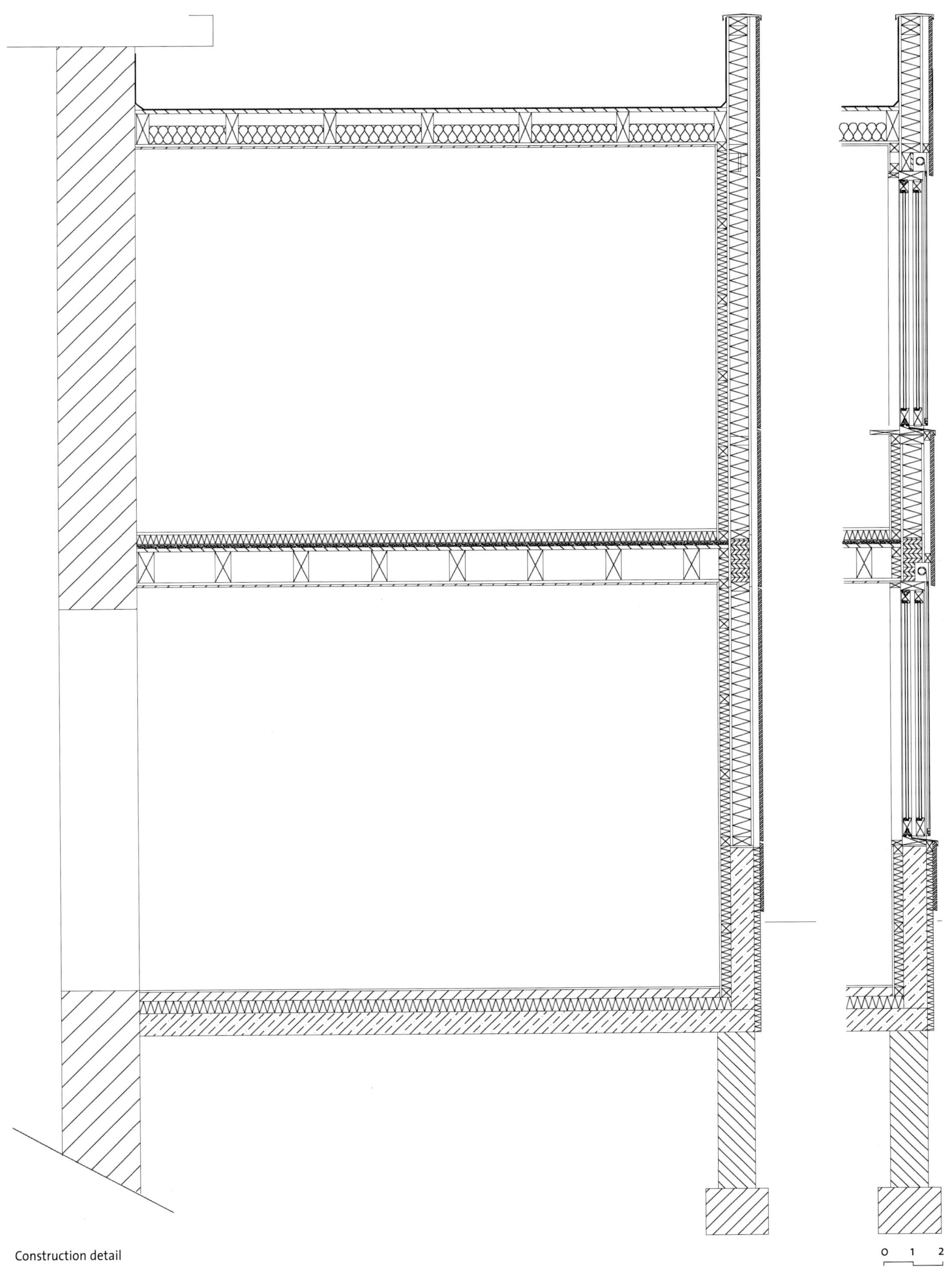

Construction detail

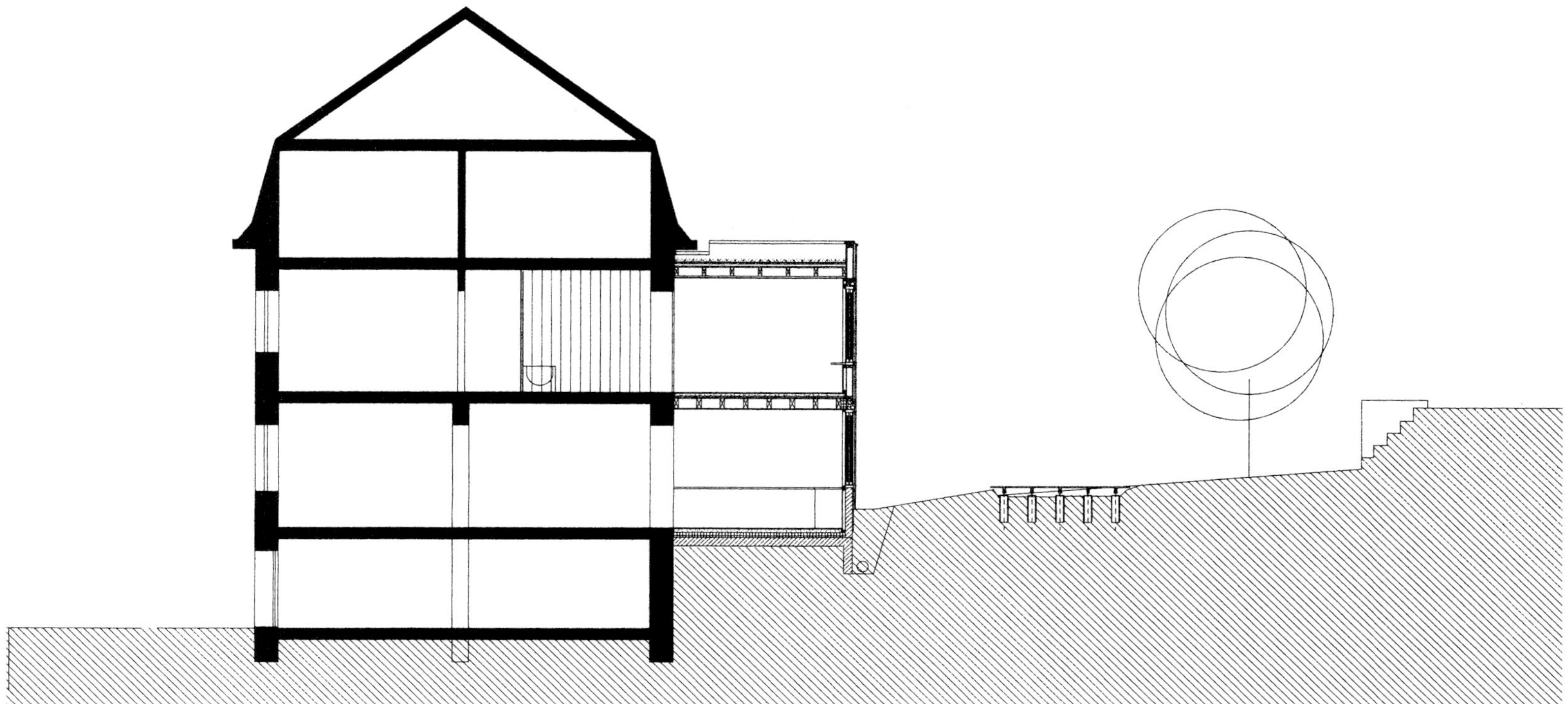
Section

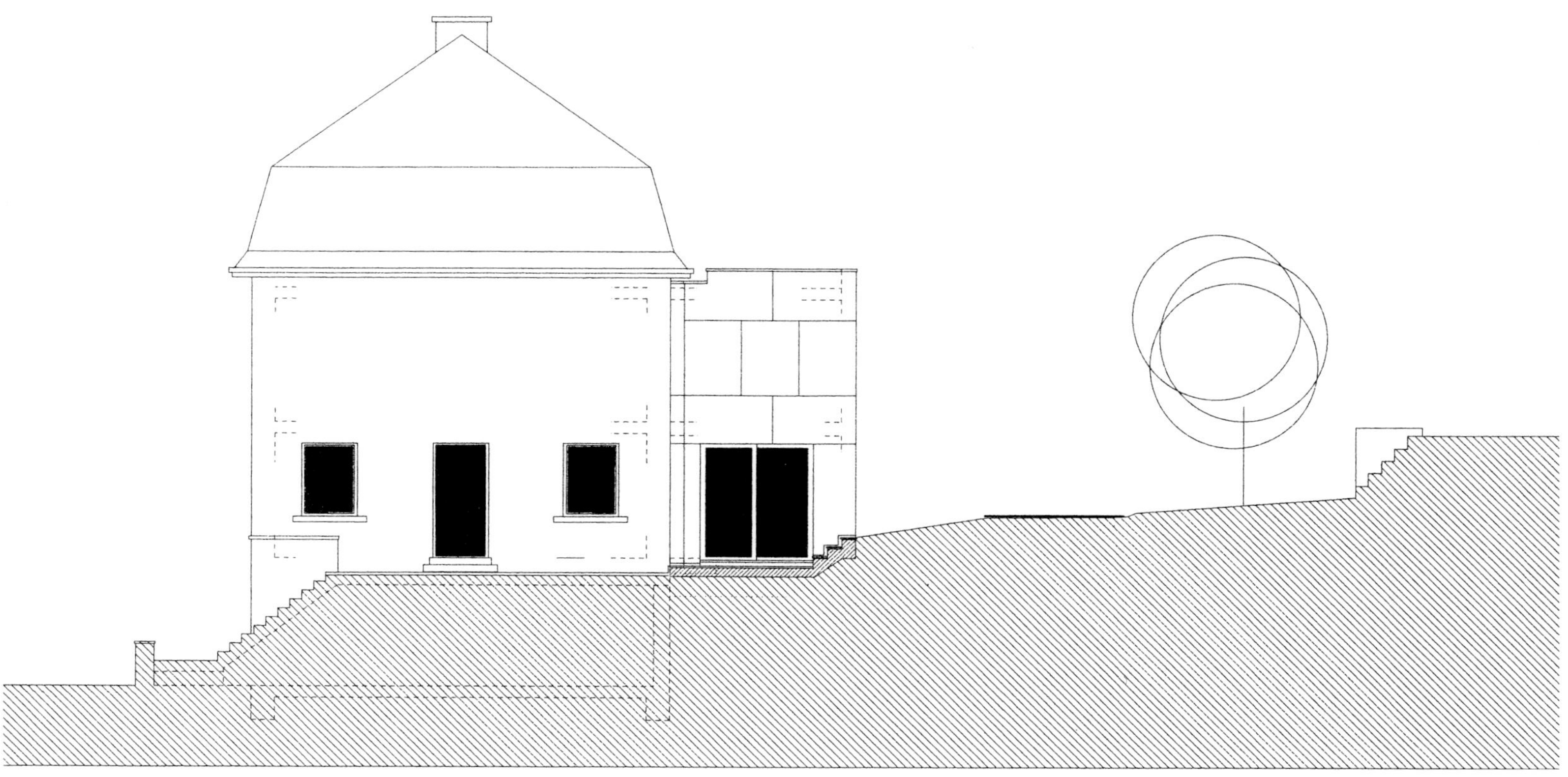
Elevation

First floor of enlargement

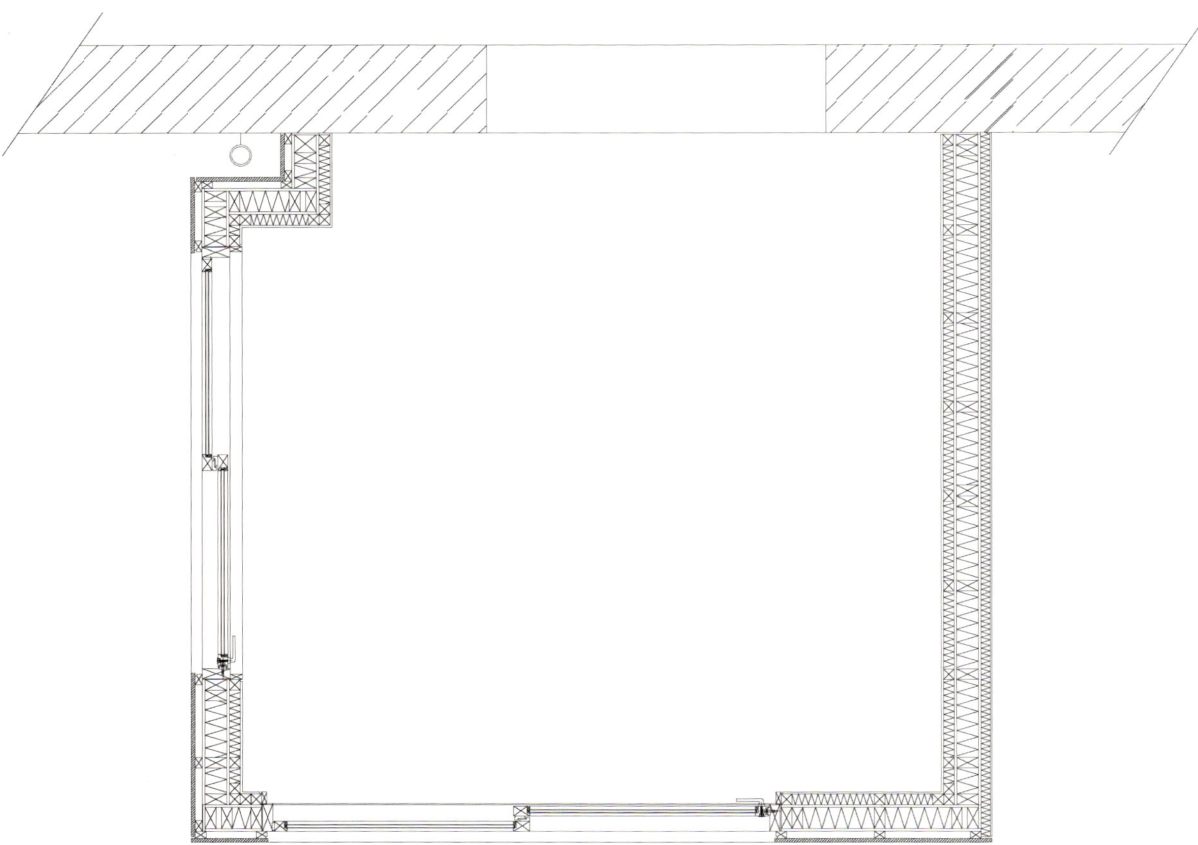

Ground floor of enlargement

Tall Acres

Architects: Studio for Architecture

Photographs © Studio for Architecture

Location: Rochester, NY, United States

The addition to this house was based on juxtaposing the gable-roofed building against the new rectangular one, establishing a dialogue of balance and opposition between the two.

Tall Acres

The design for remodeling and enlarging this typical American home took the form of an addition with a very different shape from the rest of the house. The flat roof and the pierced concrete contrast with the gable roof of the original building and its vinyl clapboard siding that was typical of prefabricated homes in the 1970's. The monolithic presence of the addition dominates the house, despite its smaller size, because the regularity of its shapes and the dark colored concrete give it a stronger appearance. This juxtaposition is less evident in the interior, since the transition between the spaces is smoother. The new building is an enlargement of the old dining room, and it now fulfills the functions of kitchen, living room, and dining room. In addition, the enlargement can be read as a new kind of relationship between the house and the garden; it has gone from being an area relegated to the rear of the setting to being the protagonist thanks to the large windows of the new building. On another level, a new communication between spaces is created by a small interior window that lets the new dining room visually communicate with the old attic, which now contains a studio.

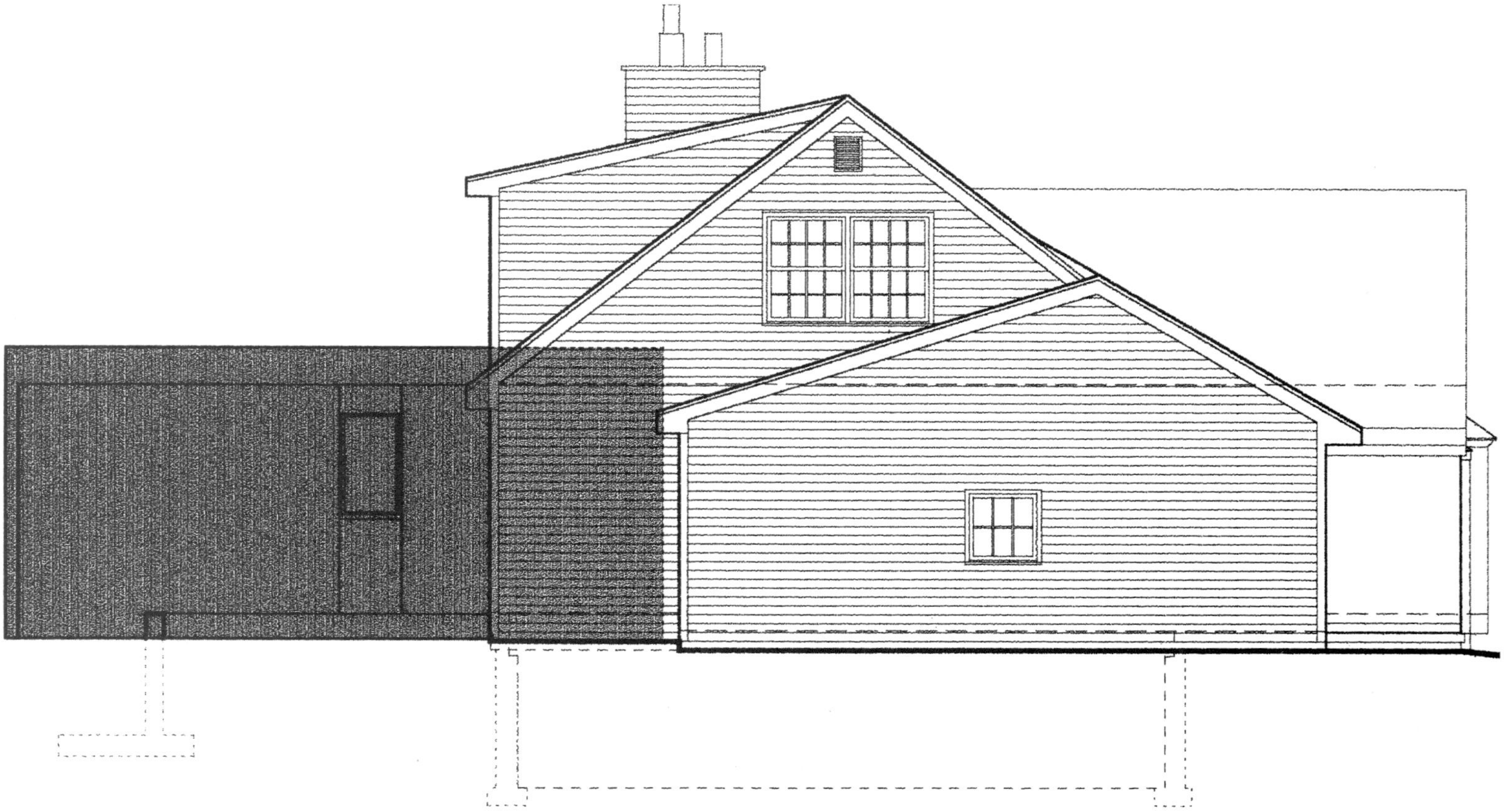

Elevations

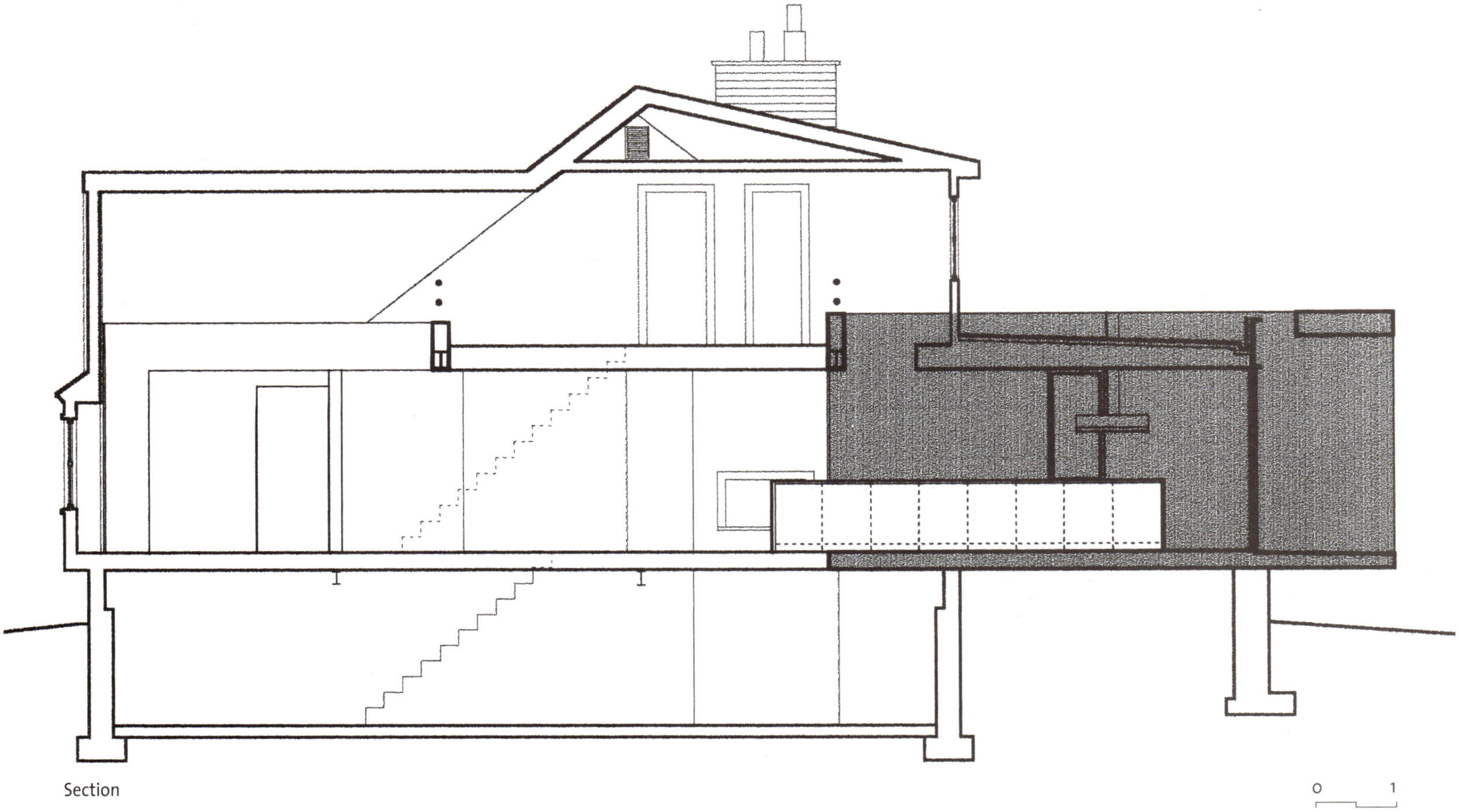

Section

0 1

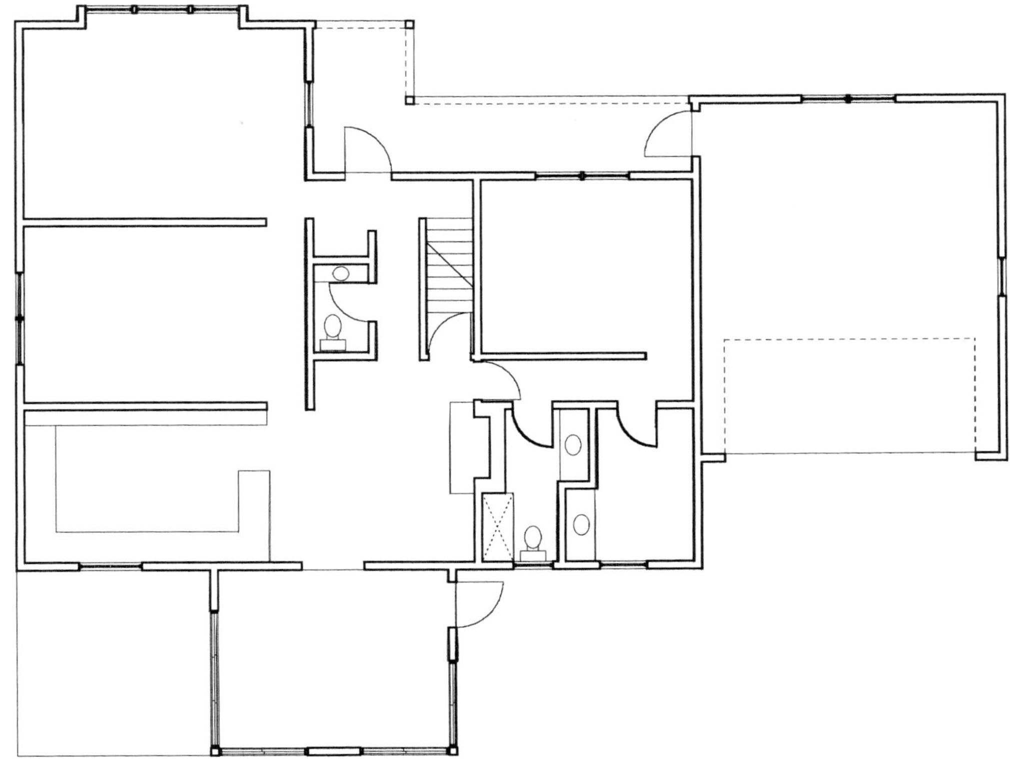

Floor plan before reform

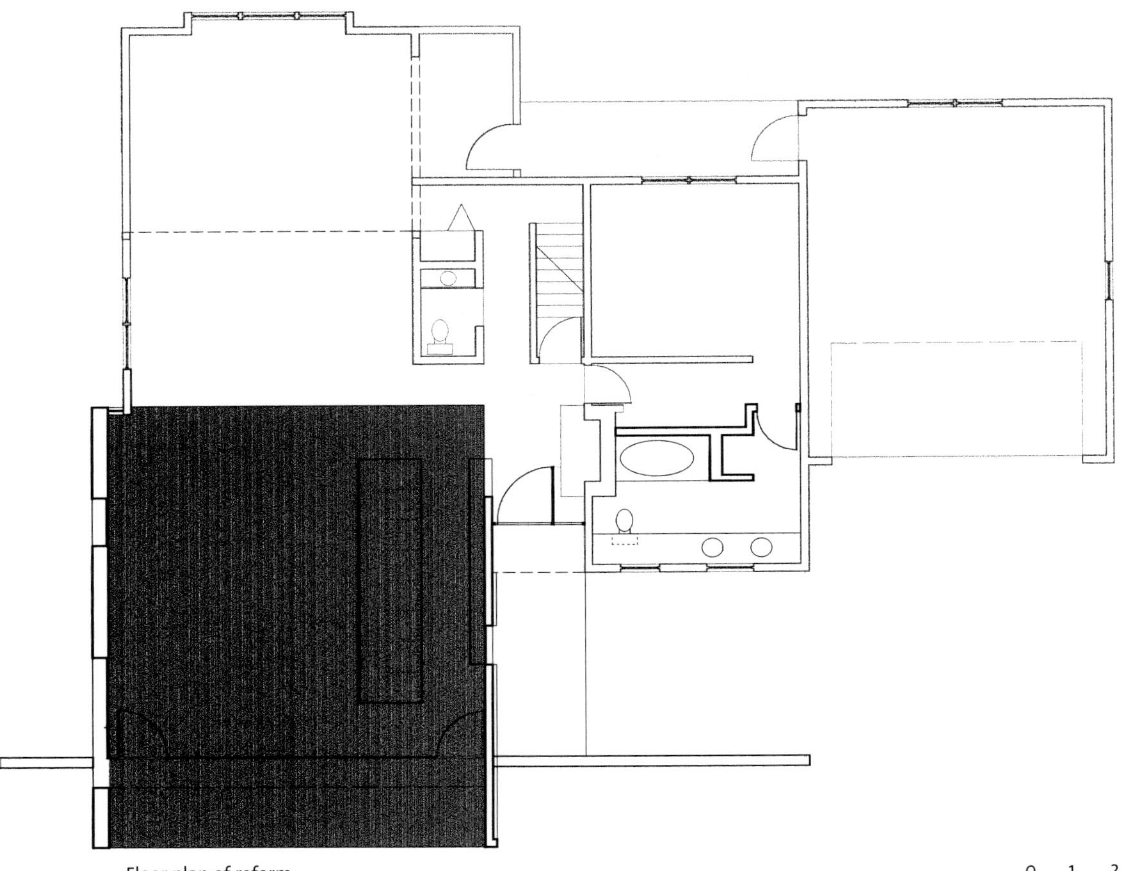

Floor plan of reform

Bad Saarow

Architects: Grollmitz-Zappe Architekten

Photographs © Kristi Kriegel

Location: Bad Saarow, Germany

This house with curved walls was inspired by a rereading of traditional Northern European architecture, a "rara avis" among 1920's building types.

Bad Saarow

During the 1920's the landscape artist Ludwig Lasser worked on the shores of Lake Scharmützelsee, in the small town of Bad Saarow, designing a colony of summer homes for vacation residents from Berlin, which is barely 50 miles (80 km) from the town. The location continues to be as idyllic as it was in that era, since it has not suffered from the sprawl typical of these times. It continues to be a privileged location, an enclave on the sunny north shore of the lake, surrounded by trees and facing a gentle slope that runs to the lake. The house has a basement, ground floor, and two upper levels; daily life takes place on the ground level and in the bedrooms on the upper floors. The basement is constructed of stone masonry, acting as the baseboard for the ground floor, and the rest of the building is wood. Its design shows a peculiar progression in the walls, which curve very gently until they become confused with the roof. Thus, despite its height, the home is gracefully integrated into its surroundings. The remodeling project attempted to preserve the characteristics of the original building, maintaining the natural color of the exterior wood and repainting the interiors of the balconies with a yellow color typical of the region. The layout of the interior was not modified, but the bathrooms were completely renovated and some furniture changed. Only an interior wall on the top floor was removed to enlarge one of the bedrooms.

Elevations

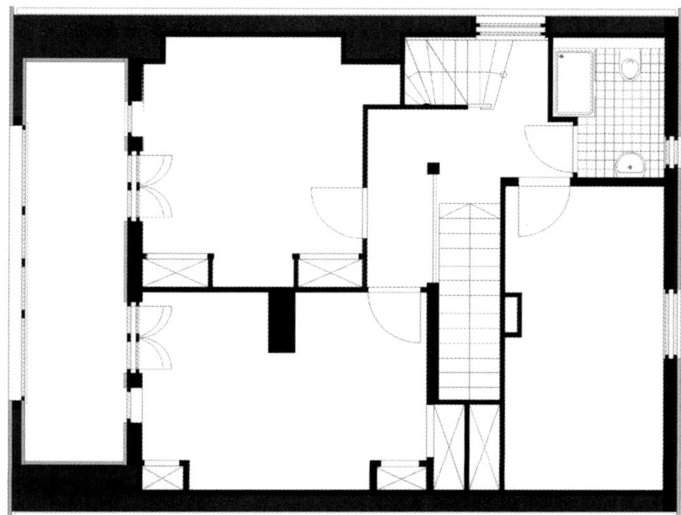

Ground floor

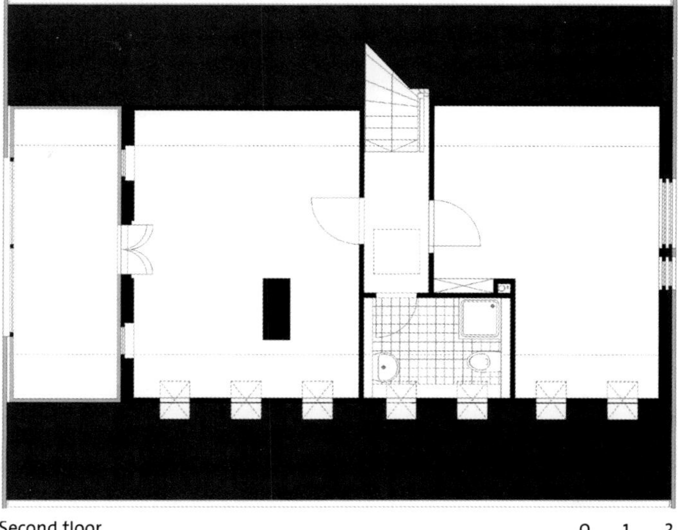

Second floor

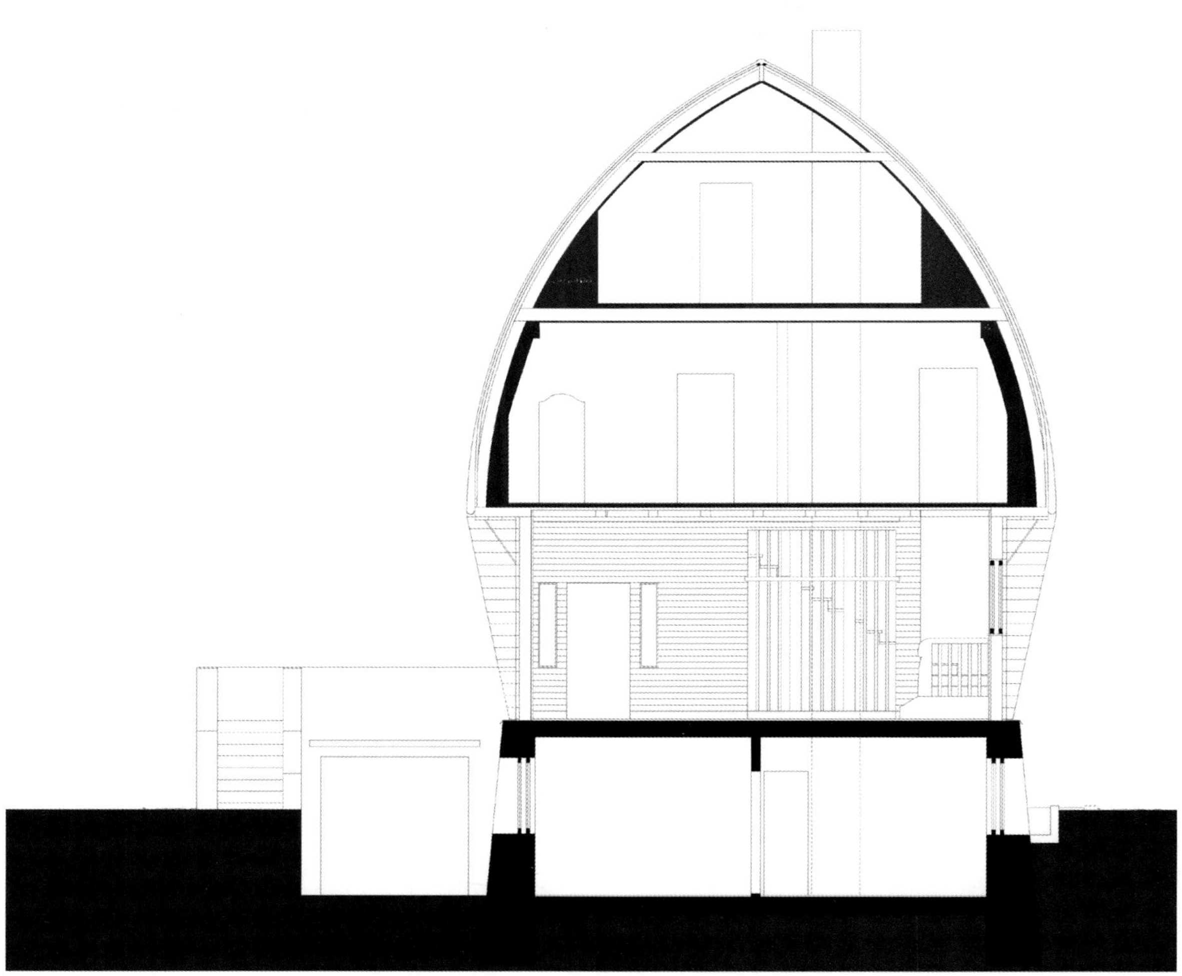

Section

Masnou House

Architects: Jordi Hidalgo & Daniela Hartmann

Photographs © Eugeni Pons

Location: Les Preses, Girona, Spain

THIS HOUSE UNDERWENT BOLD RENOVATIONS IN THE SPACES THAT REQUIRED IT, RESULTING IN A COMBINATION OF THE LOCAL POPULAR ARCHITECTURE WITH CONTEMPORARY BUILDING DESIGNED FOR MODERN LIFESTYLE.

Masnou House

A perforated steel element hidden behind the original volcanic rock walls was the key to this remodeling project. Three half levels that are independent from the existing walls project from the structure and make it possible to combine the rustic flavor of the cabin with the newly designed contemporary forms. This approach allows more light to flow into the ground floor. The system called for lateral bands along the North and South façades, covered with laminated glass panels that provide the space with greater luminosity.

Entry to the cabin is through an exterior staircase, which gives way to the foyer. Another staircase communicates with all the levels of the house. The living room is located on the first floor. Below this floor another level was installed for the kitchen and the dining room, and a level above it for the bedrooms, which are located at the rear, separated from each other by a space that acts as the landing for the stairs and for the bathrooms. The ground floor contains a guest bedroom and a garage.

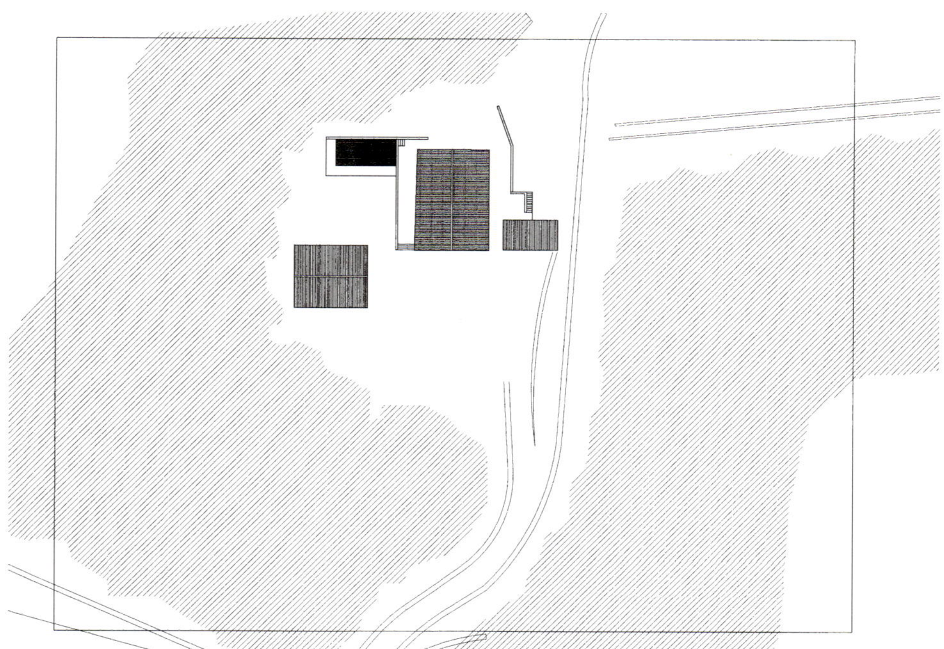

Map of location

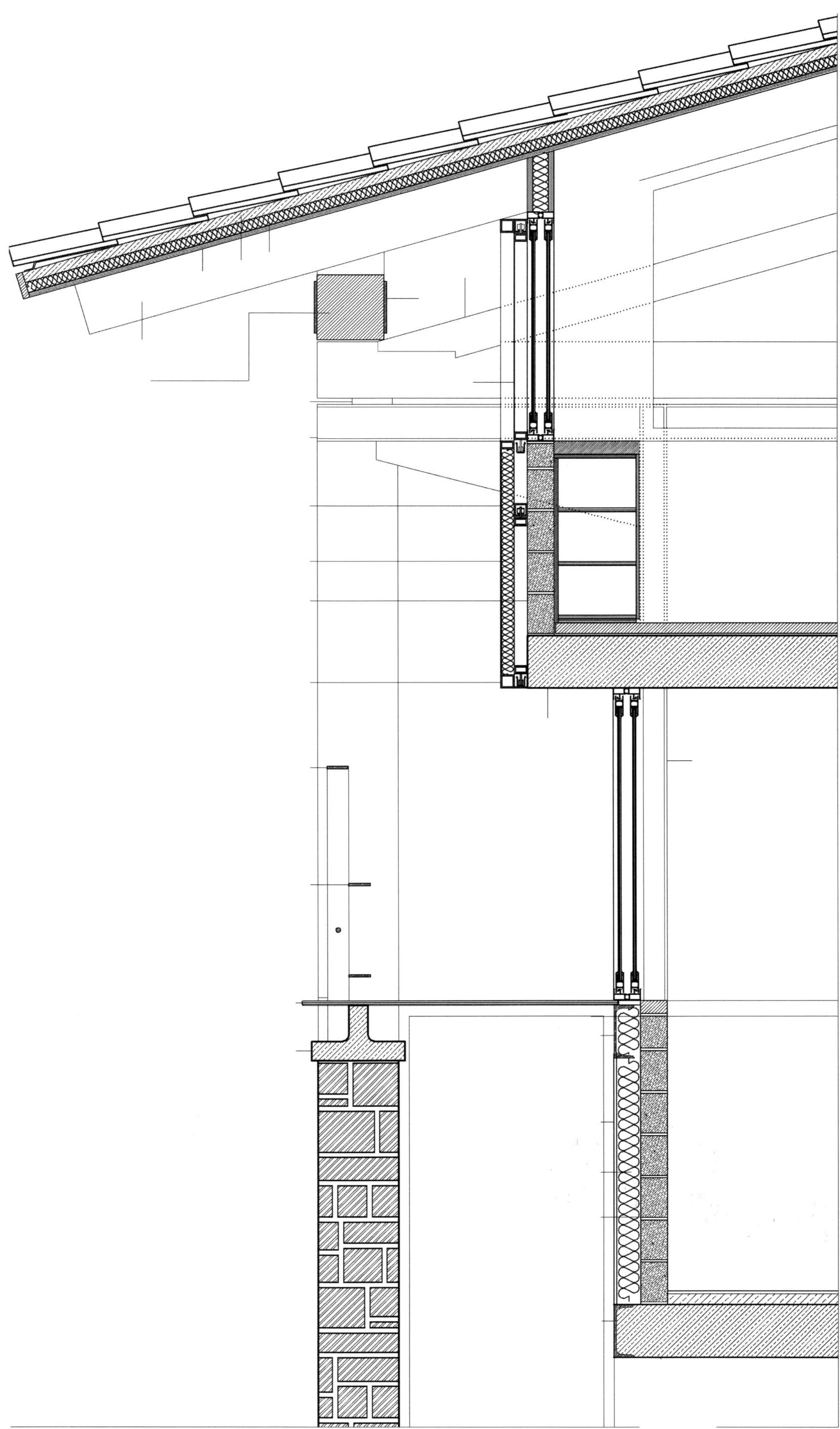

Section

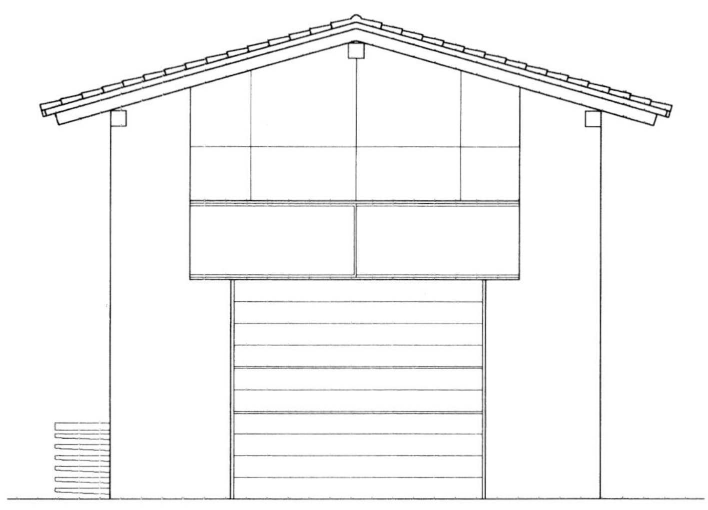

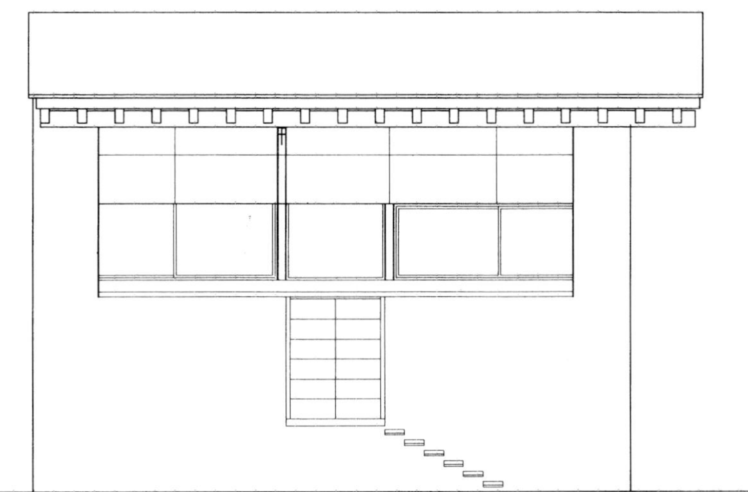

Elevations

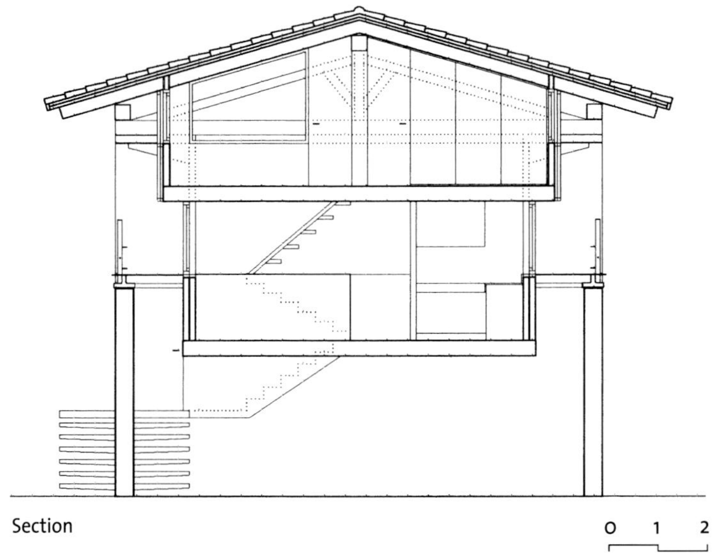

Section

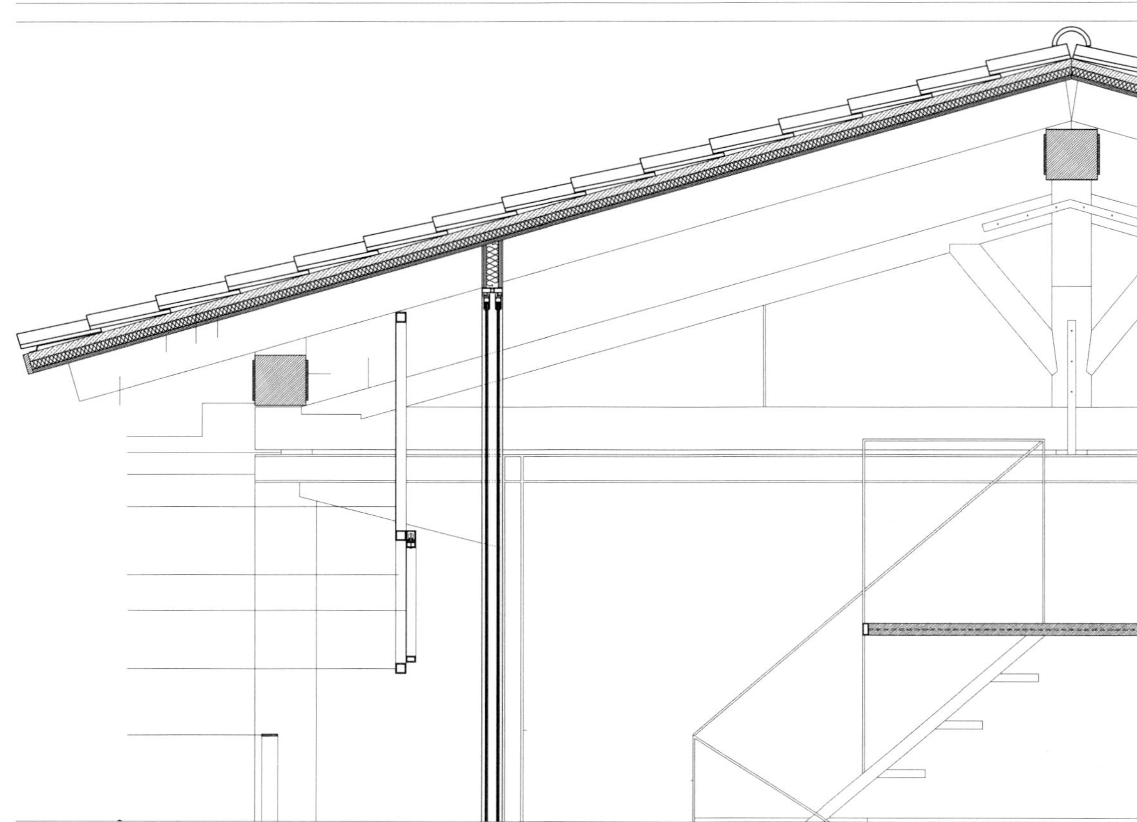

Roof construction detail

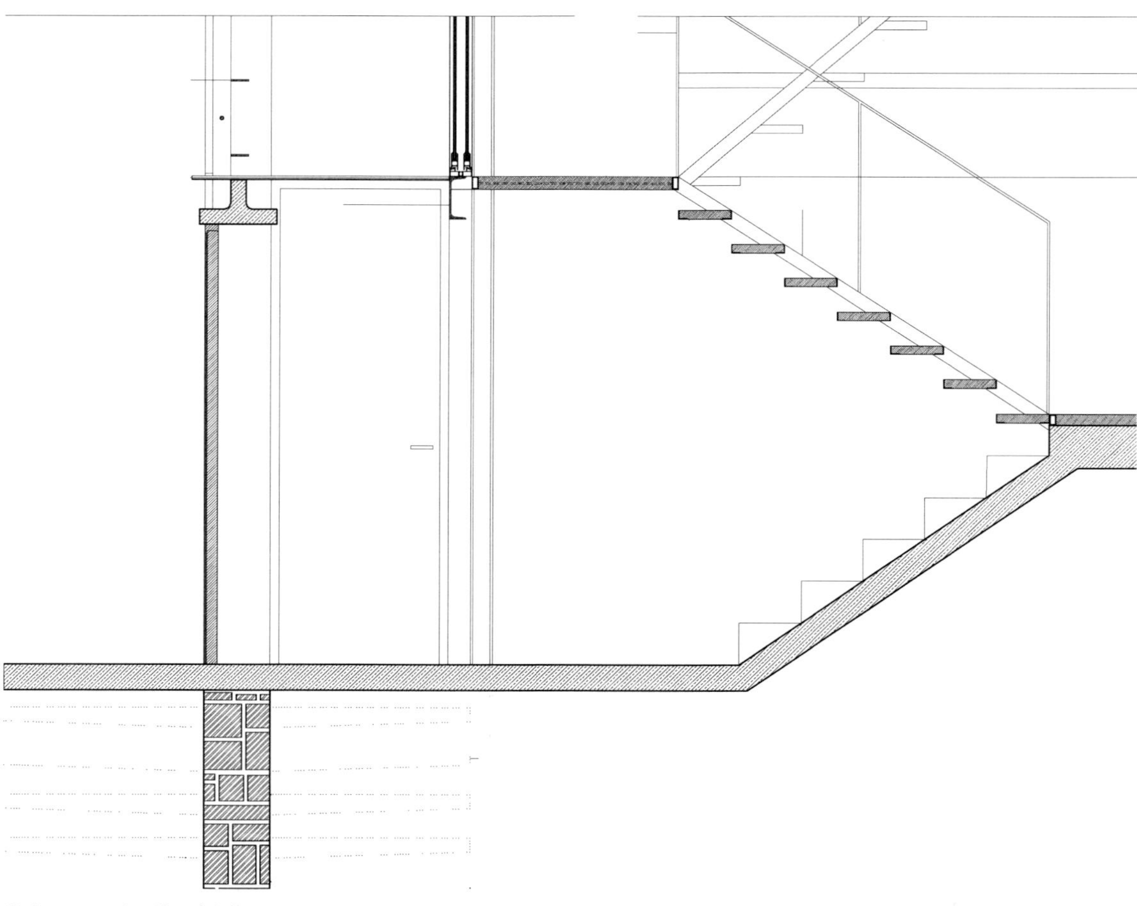

Stairway construction detail

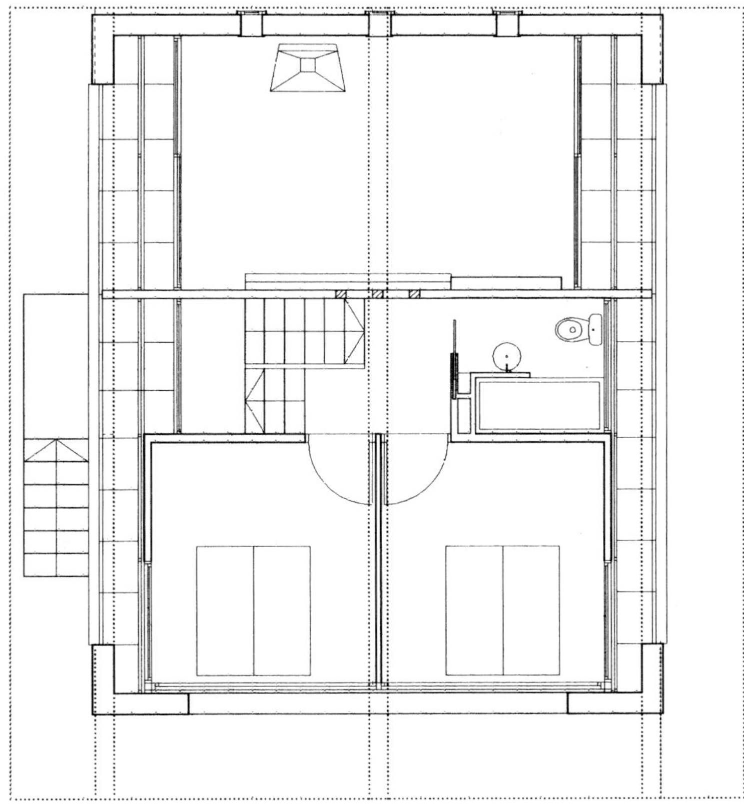

Second floor

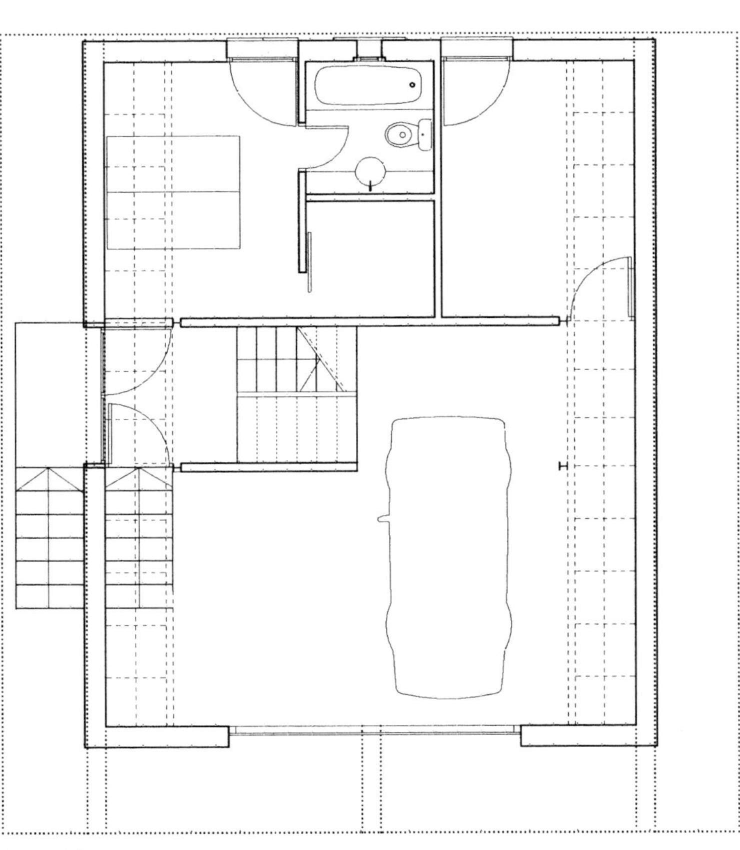

Ground floor

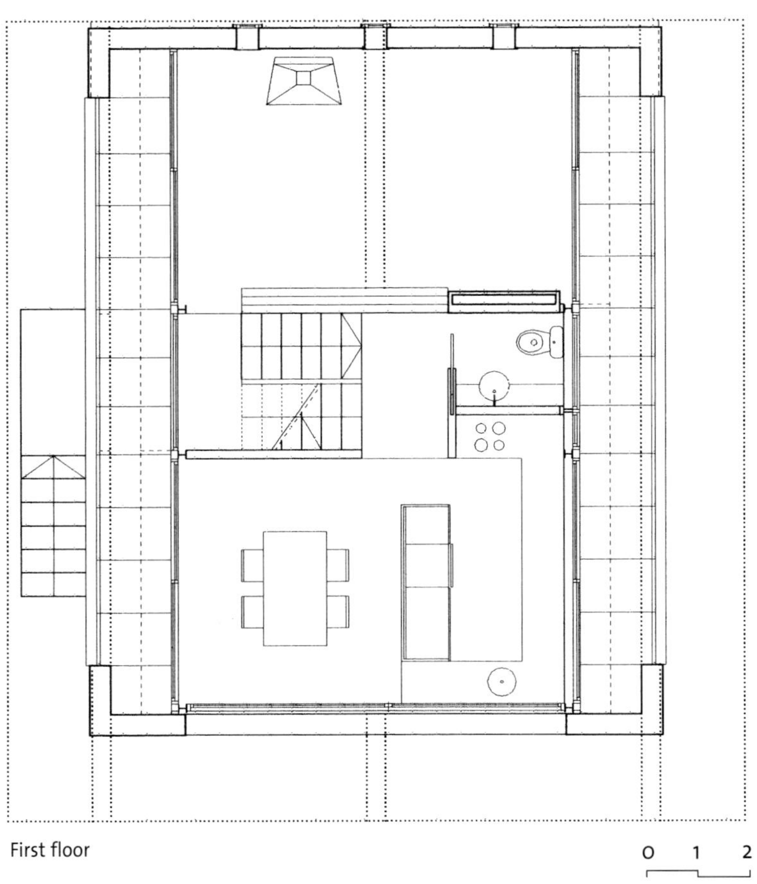

First floor

0 1 2

Barge & Murphy Loft

Architects: Buschow Henley Ltd.

Photographs © Nicholas Kane

Location: London, United Kingdom

Remodeling an entire block of buildings made it possible to create a spectacular loft on the top floor. The industrial image of the old building combined with the modernism of the renovation are reflected in the glass elevator.

Barge & Murphy Loft

The architects Buschow Henley Ltd. took advantage of the opportunity offered by the original structure of this Victorian London building to turn the top floor into a penthouse. After a study of the parameters, they created a new layout in the 2,152 square foot (200 square meter) space and converted it into a loft arranged into two parallel blocks. The most important intervention was the creation of the roof. After analyzing the condition of the original roof, it was determined that this would be the focal point of the project from which the rest of the remodeling would stem. The architects had the idea of replacing the original skylight; to do this they looked at how to design different independent skylights for the roof. Their initial plan presented an ironic view of hanging structures, fences, a lawn, and a garden with a kitchen, as if each skylight encompassed an independent living space with its own yard. However, the final design covered the structure with practical materials such as zinc. This way, the seven skylights of the east wing would open to the south with side views towards the east and west. However, the three semi-independent skylights of the west wing were open to the sky and the west. The group of pavilions was directly connected to the apartments located just below, where the Barge & Murphy loft is located. Inside each one of them, the crystaline transparent cover is highlighted, allowing light to filter in exactly through the center of each plane.

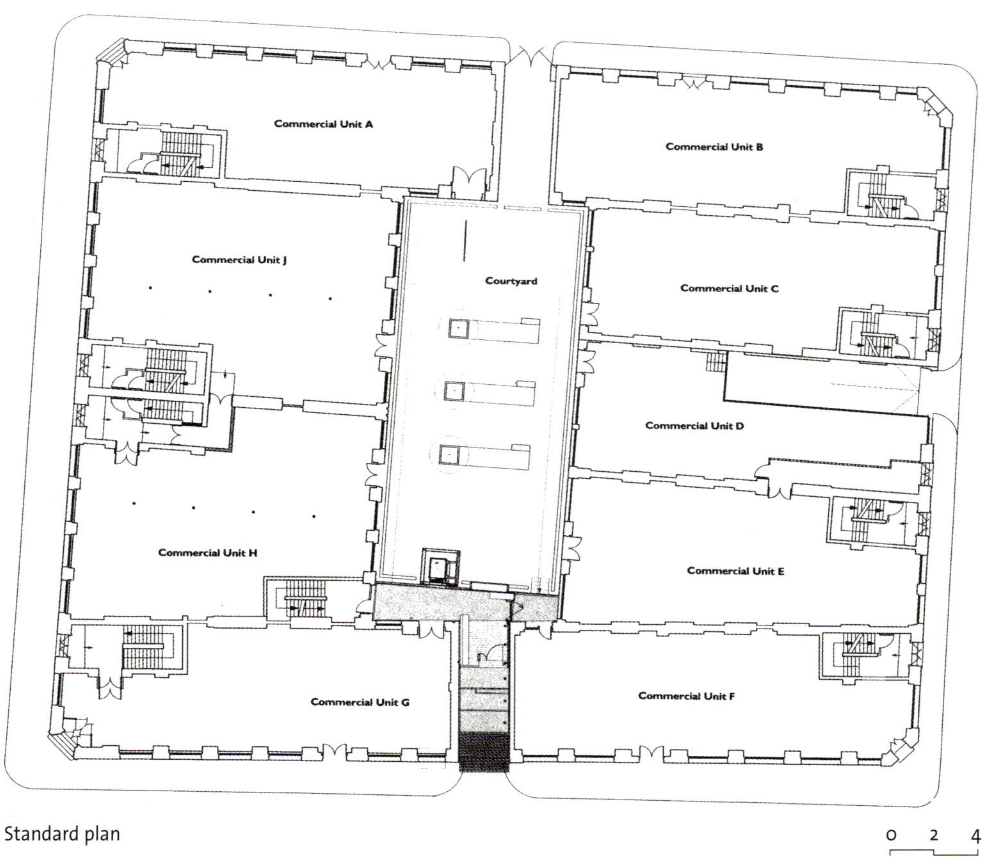

Standard plan

0 2 4

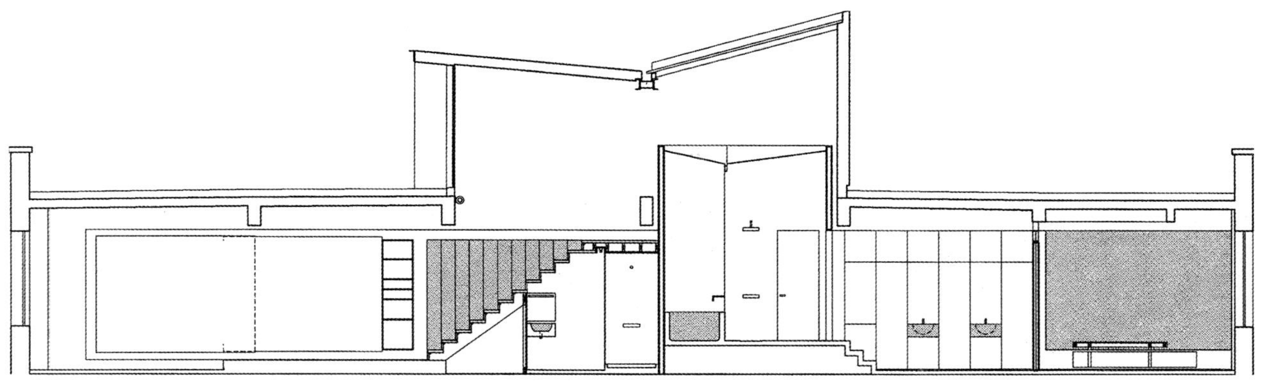

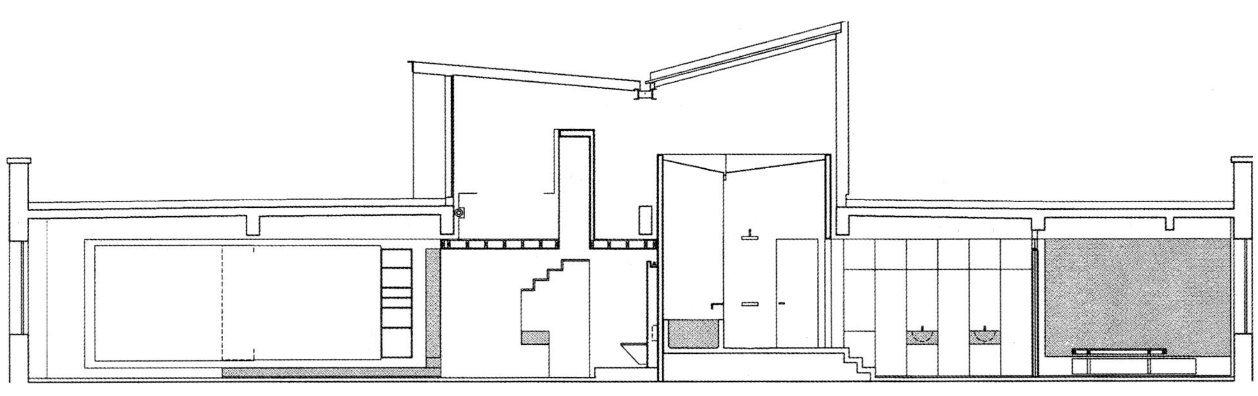

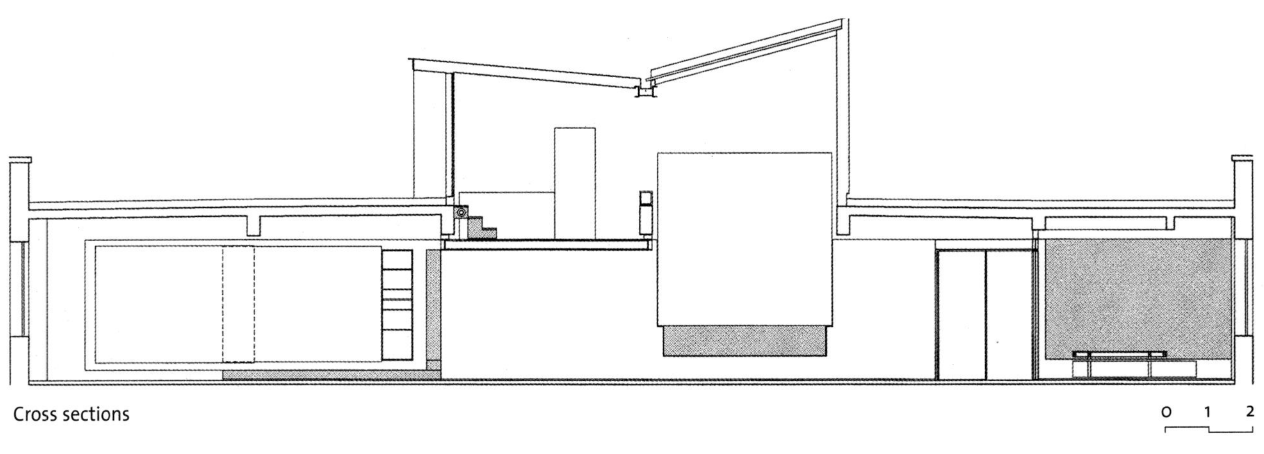

Cross sections

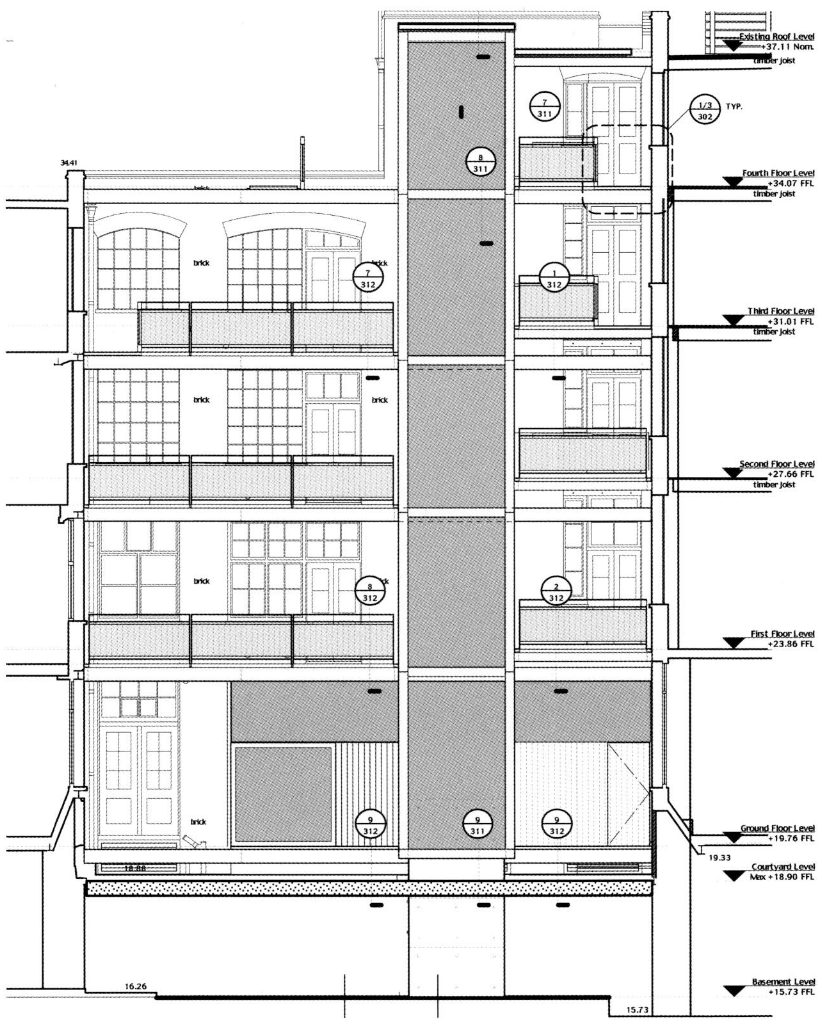

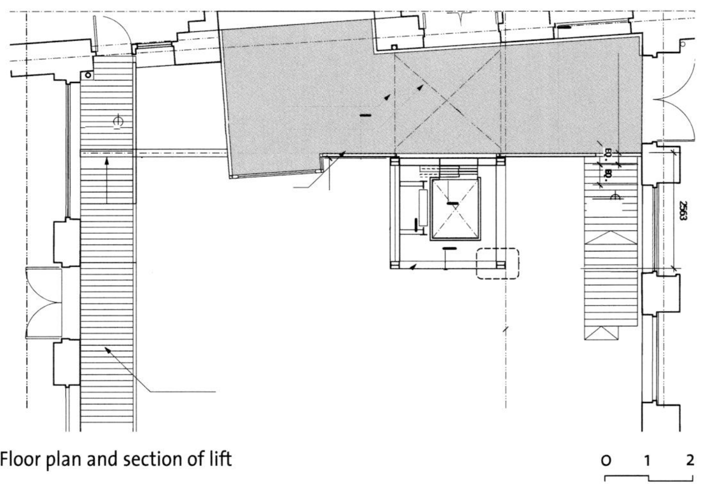

Floor plan and section of lift

The skylights cut through the roof at different points to provide homogeneous lighting to all the spaces from the living room to the bathroom.

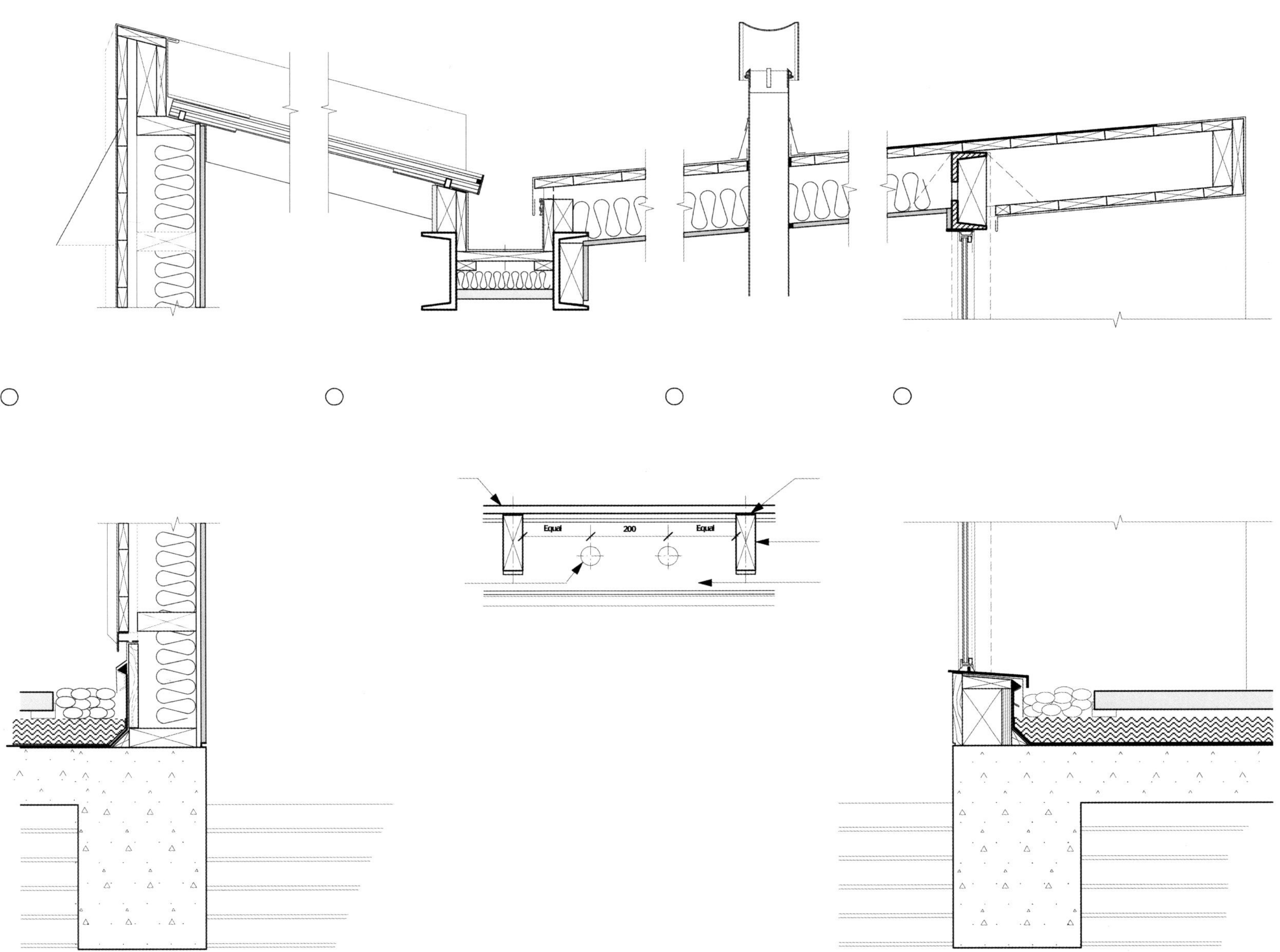

Detail of walls

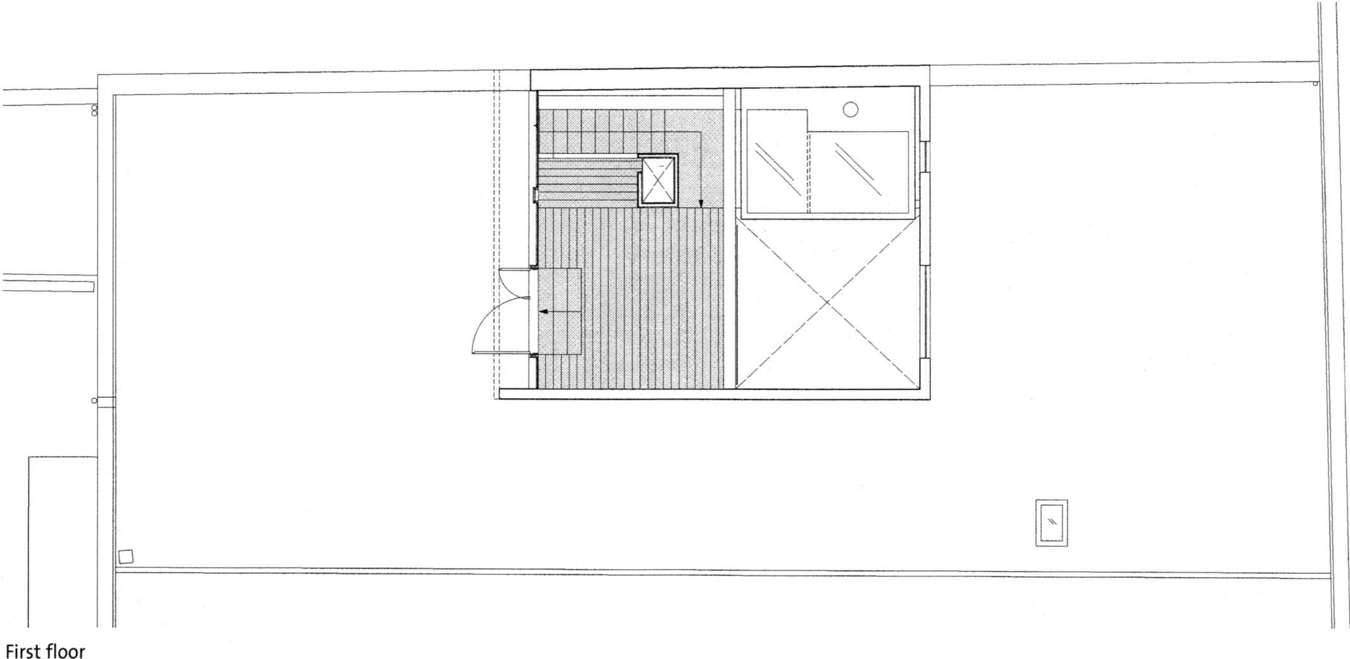

First floor

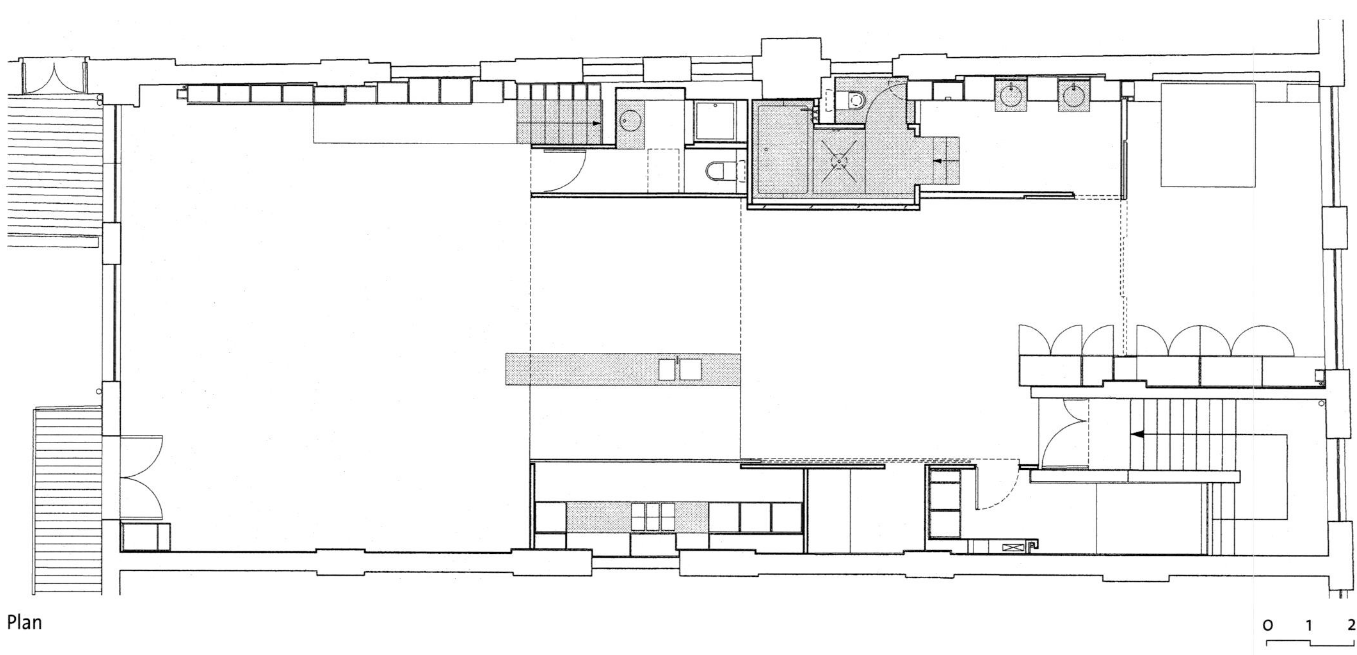

Plan

House with a Porch

Architect: Giampiero Bosoni/GA Architetti Associati

Photography © Matteo Piazza

Location: Serole, Asti, Italy

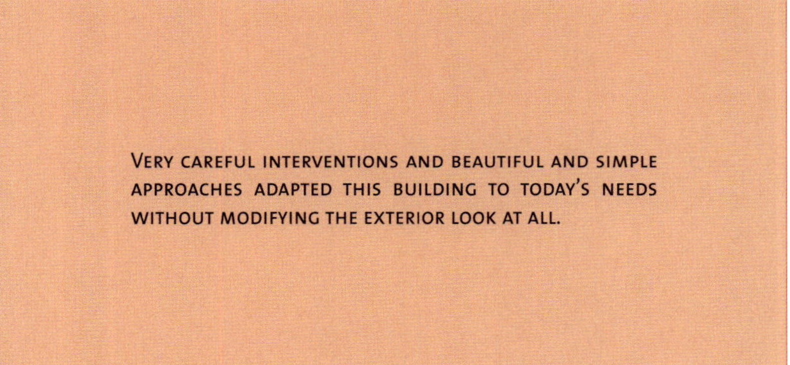

Very careful interventions and beautiful and simple approaches adapted this building to today's needs without modifying the exterior look at all.

House with a Porch

This project encompassed esthetic and functional interventions that did not alter the original structure of the old building, which consisted of two adjacent structures on different levels: a stable and granary in one, and a farmhouse in the other. The final design resulted in harmonious and various relationships between the existing structures and the newly constructed elements, such as the furnace, located in the central area (previously the stable), the windows installed on the west façade, and the iron pergolas that rest on the elevated wooden walkways, which adds a slightly industrial feeling to each of the entrances to the house. Elsewhere, among the remodeling projects were the restoration of the chestnut ceiling in the living room (previously the granary), which was dismantled, cleaned, and replaced; and the terracotta floor in the kitchen that was salvaged from an old building in the area. On the house's exterior the south façade has an impressive visual impact with its three windows on the upper level, each different from the other, and the small windows of the lower level, a typical example of Piedmontese design.

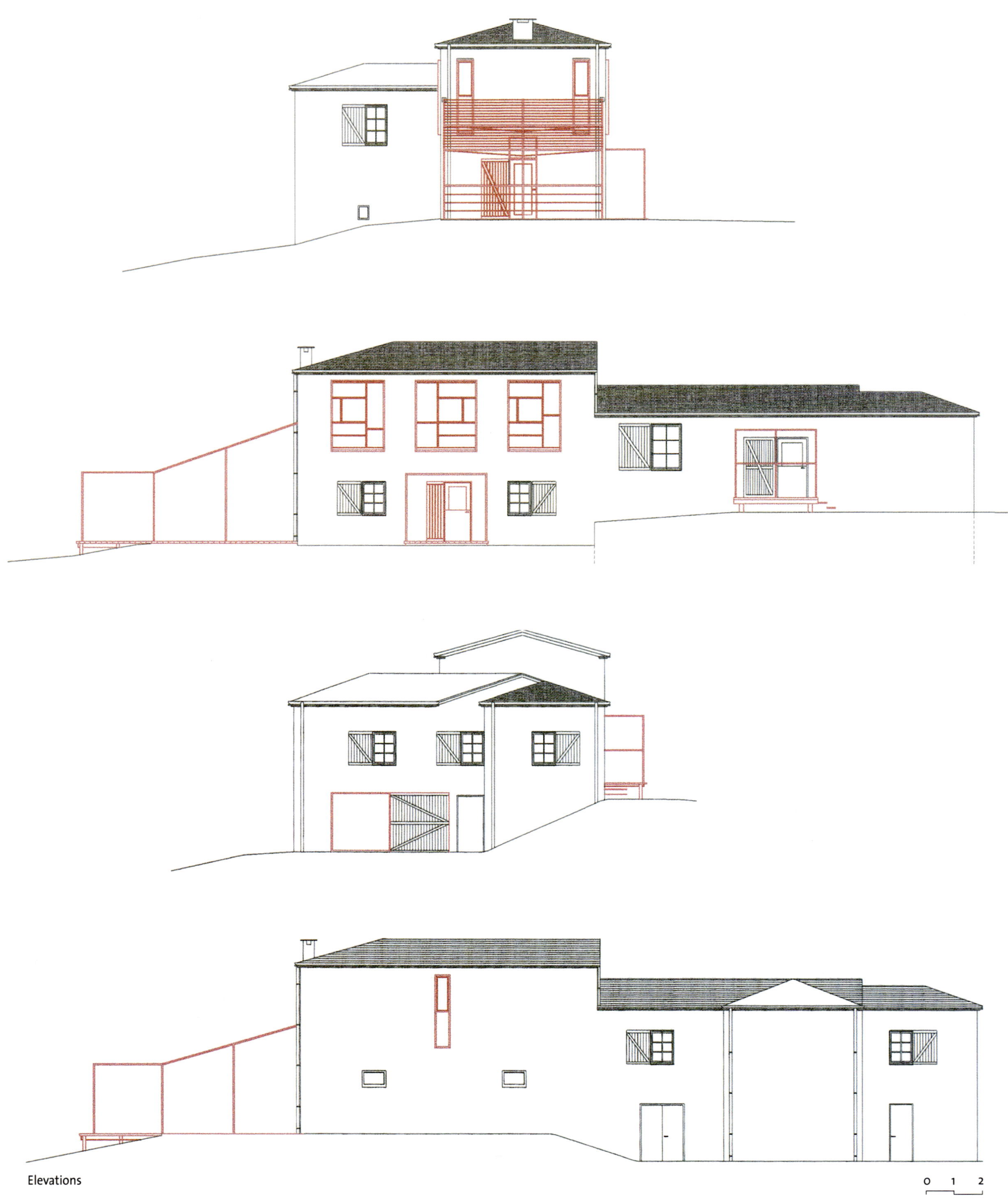

Elevations

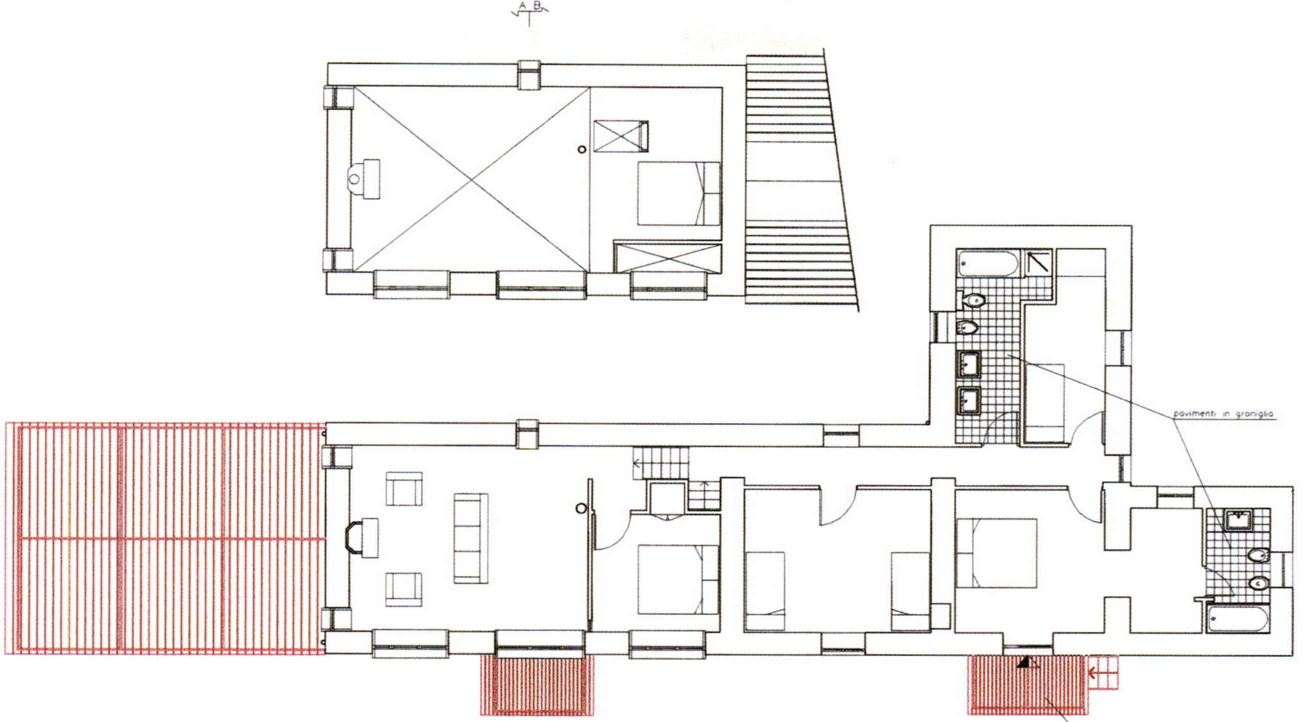

First floor and attic

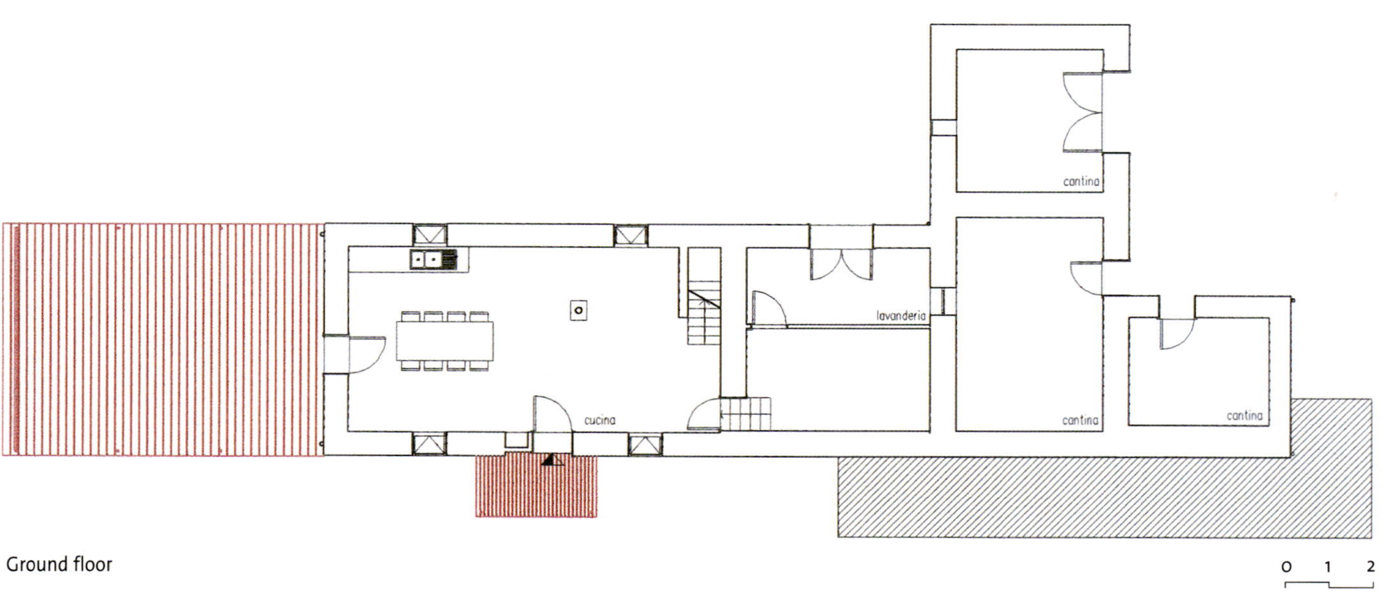

Ground floor

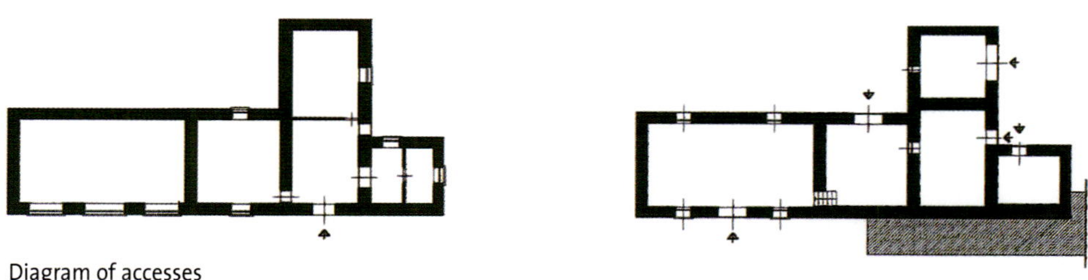

Diagram of accesses

Vertical A-A' section

Horizontal B-B' section

Windows construction details

Sketches of windows

Sketch of vertical windows

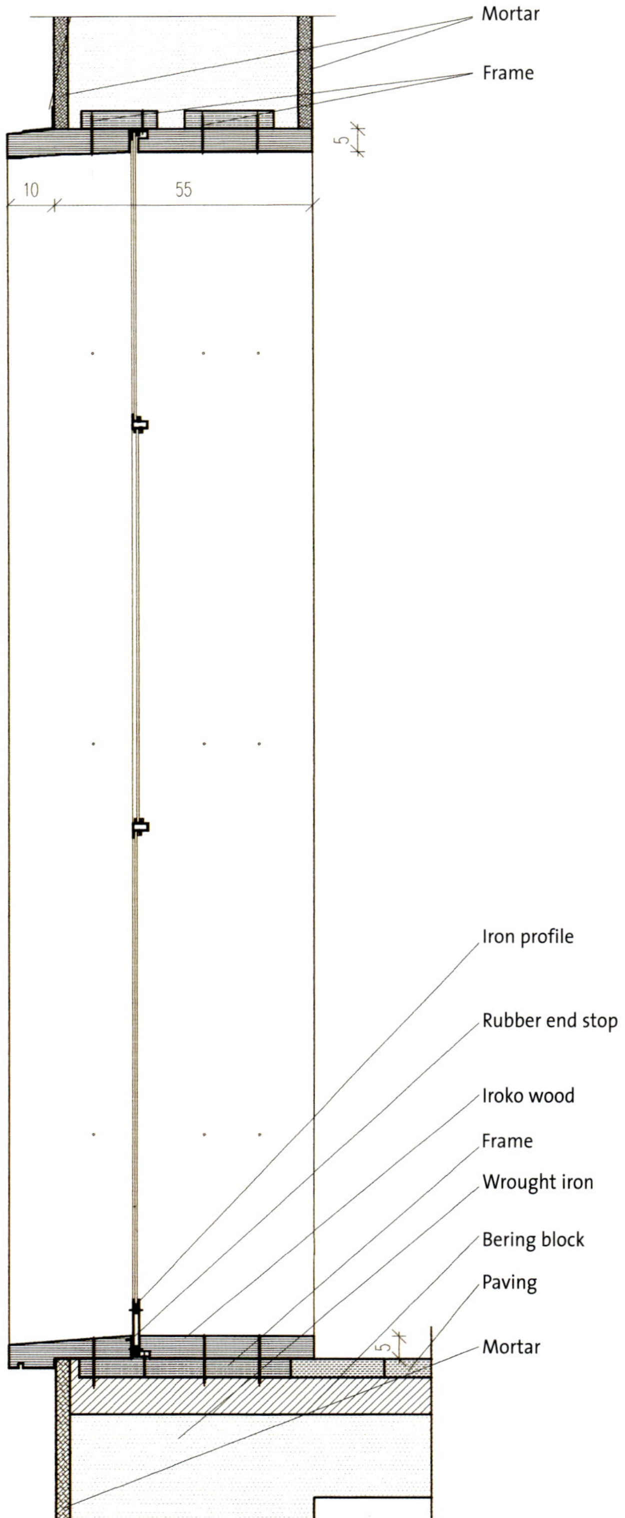

Windows construction detail

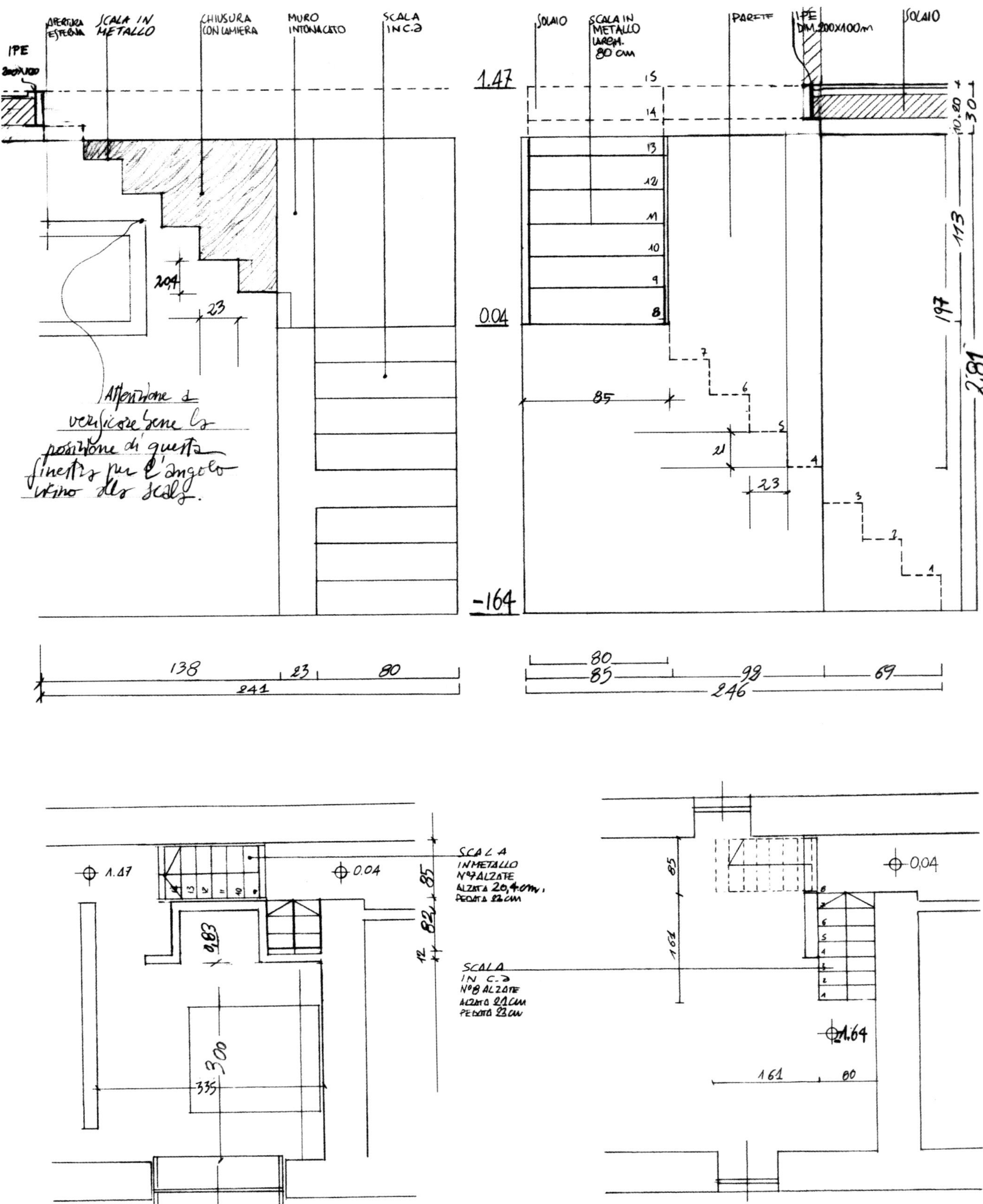

Stairway construction details

Crepain Loft

Architects: Jo Crepain Architects

Photographs © Jan Verlinde, Ludo Noël

Location: Antwerp, Belgium

THE LARGE GLASS PANELS TAKE FULL ADVANTAGE OF THE VIEWS OF THE CITY, WHILE FLOODING THE INTERIOR WITH LIGHT. THE VISUAL CONNECTION WITH THE TERRACE CONTRIBUTES TO THE FEELING OF LUMINOSITY AND SPACIOUSNESS OF THE MAIN AREA OF THE LOFT.

Crepain Loft

This project preserved the five-story warehouse structure, while the office building of 1930 was demolished to build in its place a garage and an interior garden that provides access to the residence and offices. The latter were designed as well-lit spaces with movable partitions that occupy 8,800 square feet (820 square meters) of the first four levels: from the basement to the third floor. The fourth and fifth floors, which are connected by a spiral staircase, were reserved for a 3,660 square foot (340-square meter) living space. On the fourth floor is a multifunctional space of 1,076 square feet (100 square meters) designated as exhibit and conference rooms. The living areas as well as the offices are articulated around a structure —previously occupied by a feight lift— that houses the elevator and the utilities. The architect made use of the original elements with a clear industrial character, such as the beams, the load bearing cast iron columns, and the vaulted masonry ceiling. From the outside it can be seen that the new structure was covered with aluminum panels, a feature that contrasts with the rest of the walls, which are painted gray.

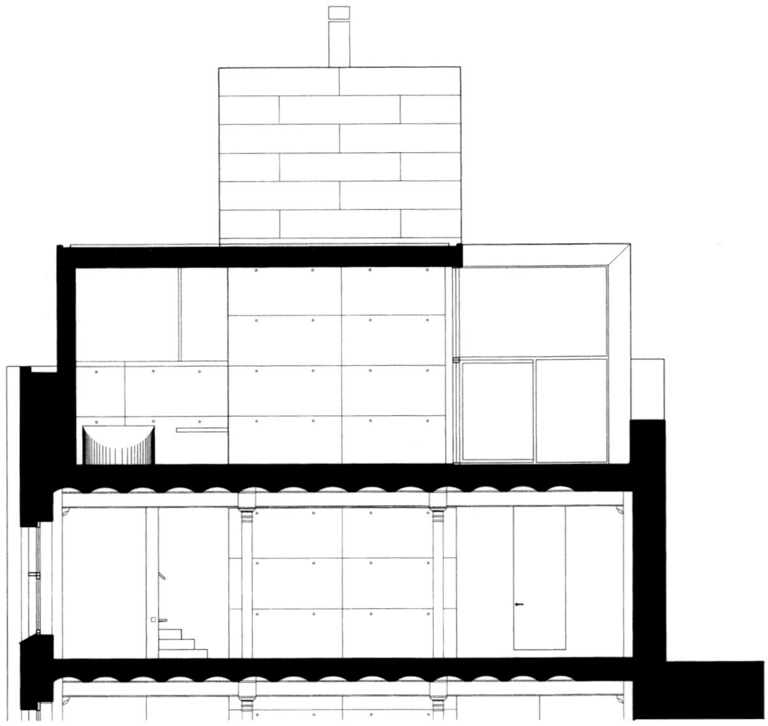

Cross section

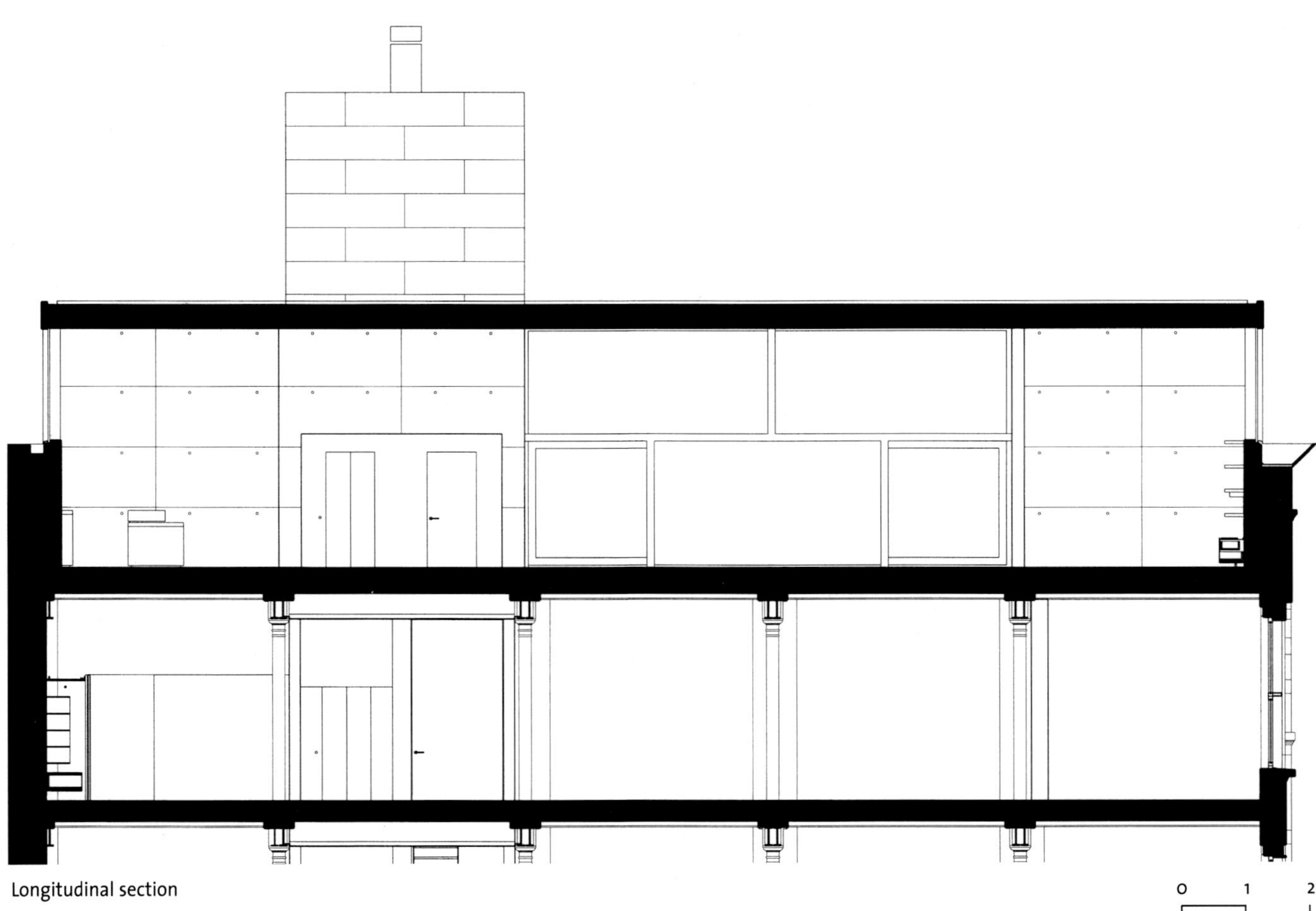

Longitudinal section

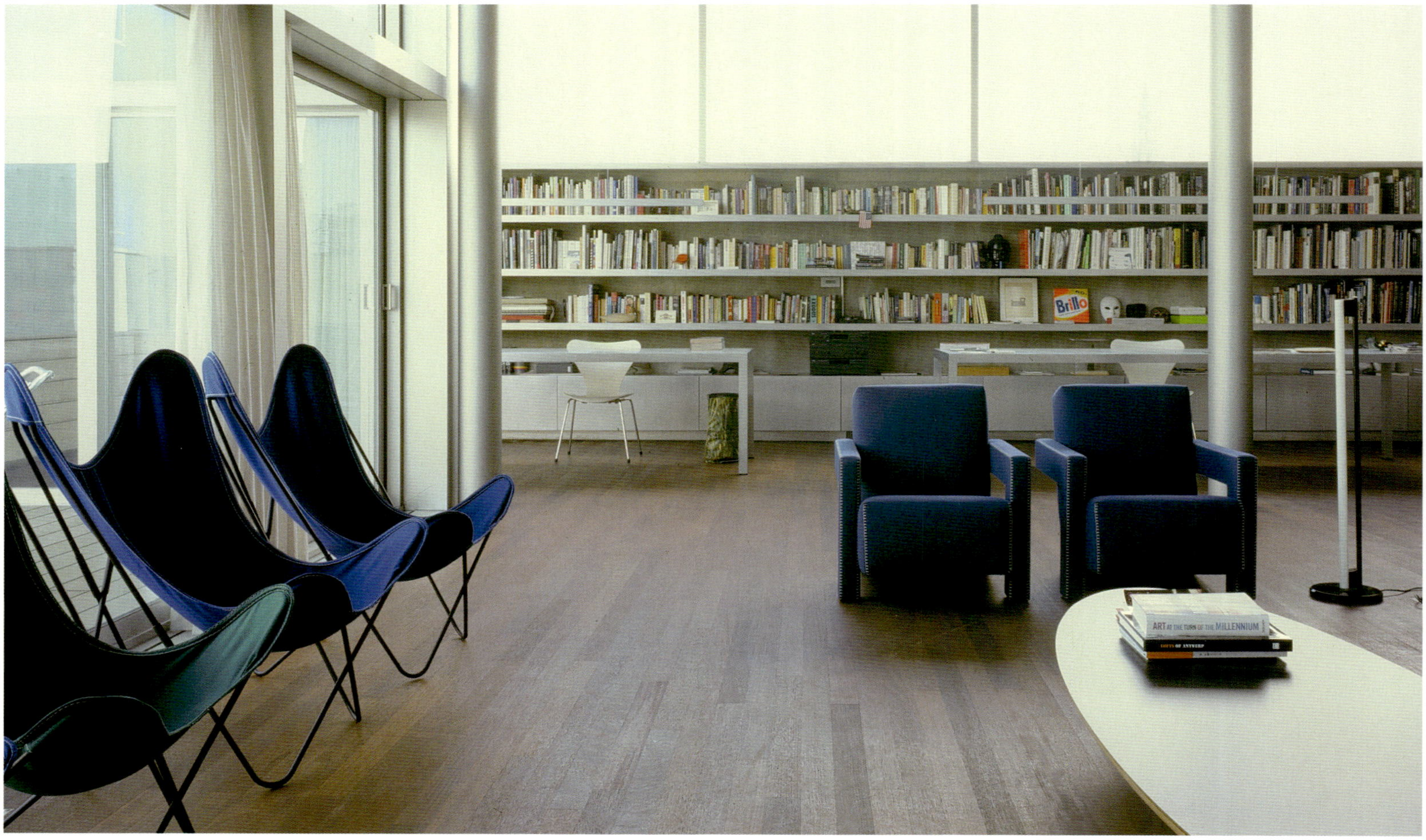
Brillo
ART AT THE TURN OF THE MILLENNIUM

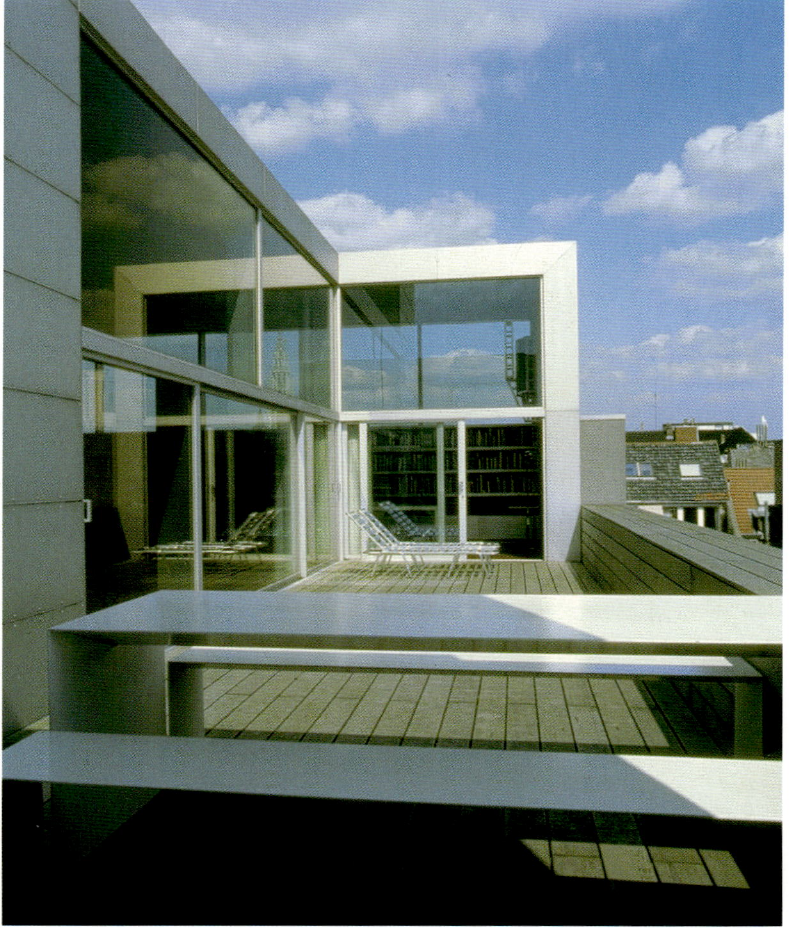

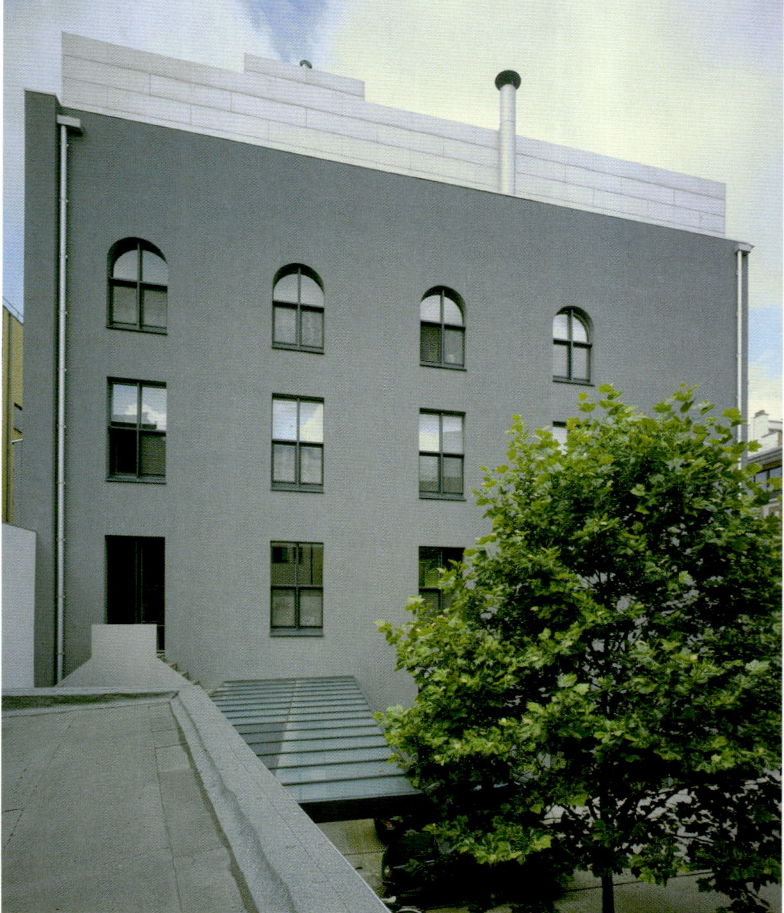

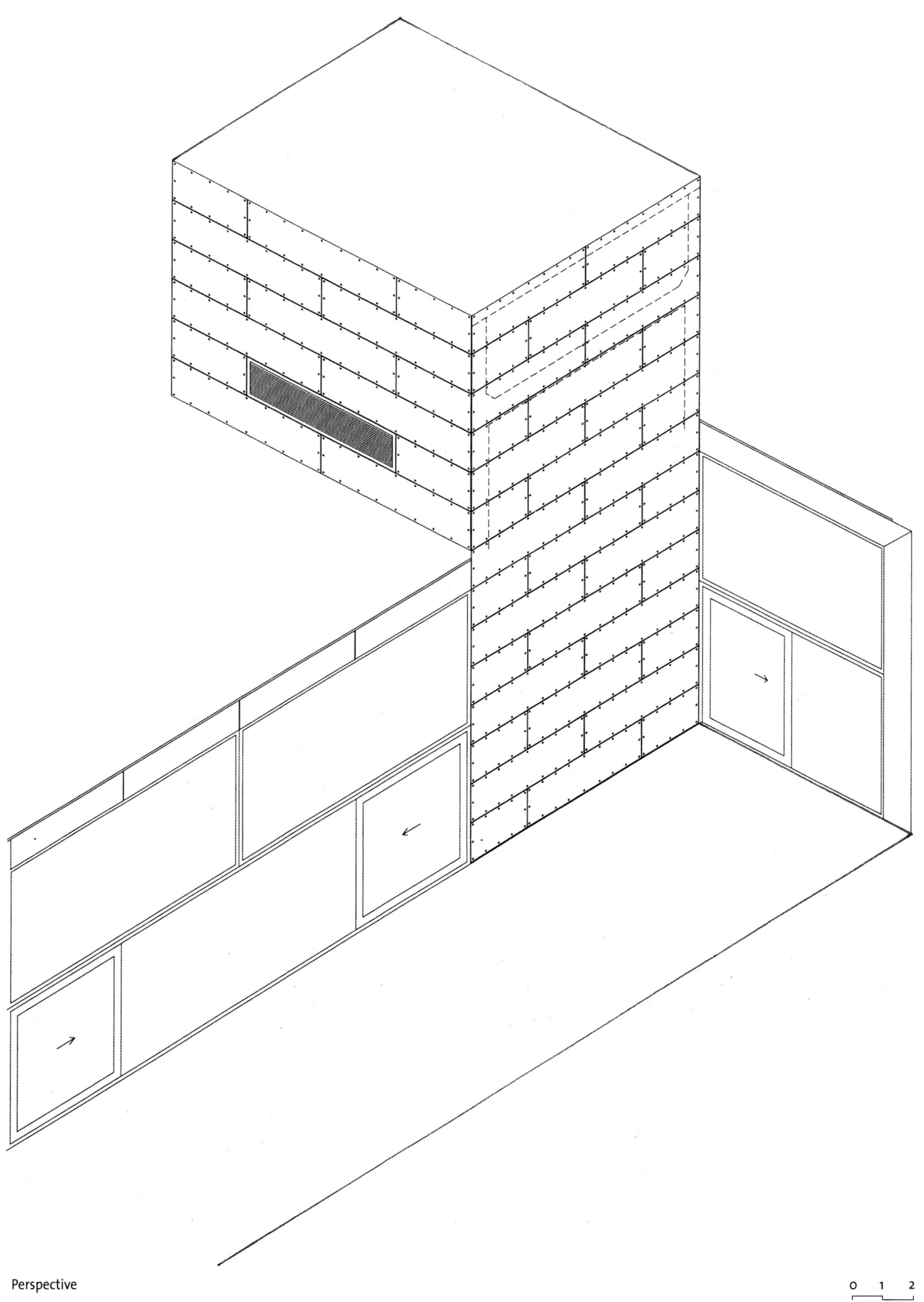

Perspective

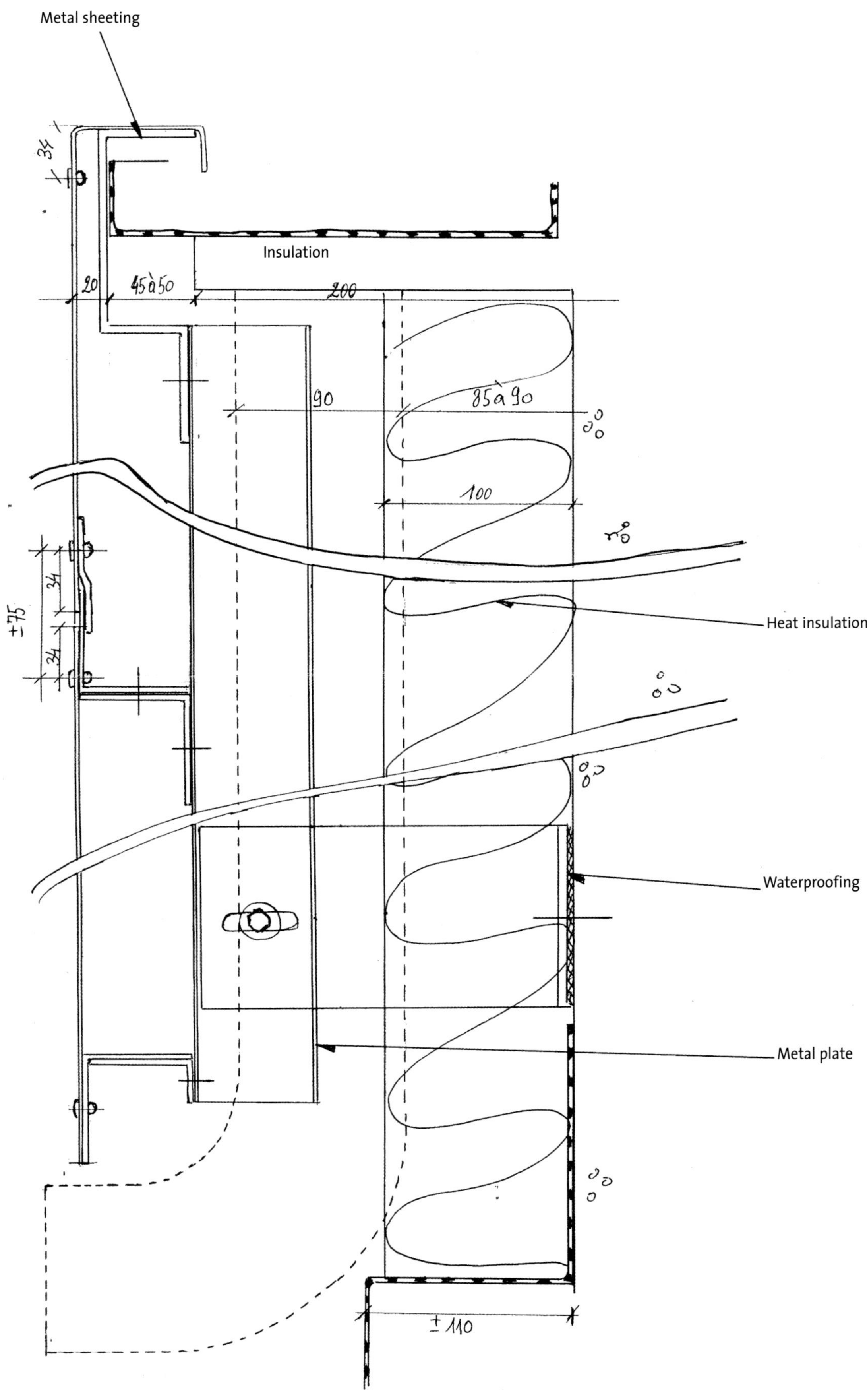

Detail of façade and roof

Ground floor

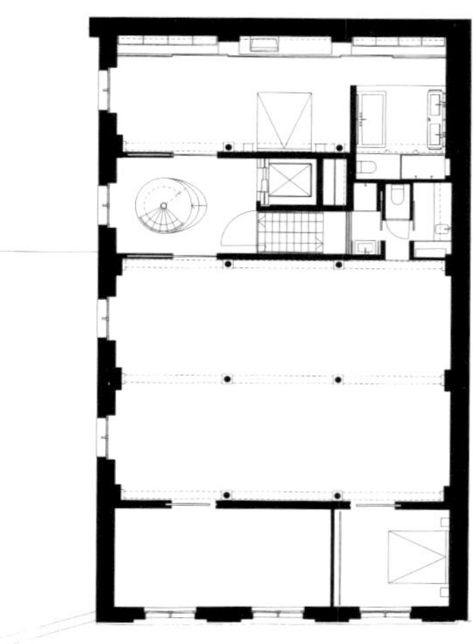

First floor

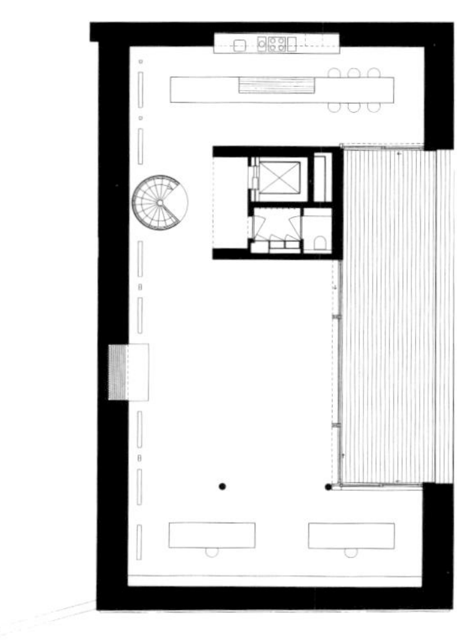

Second floor

0 1 2

Temple of Love

Architect: Dirk Jan Postel/Kraaijvanger

Photographs © Christian Richters

Location: Burgundy, France

The delicacy and beauty of this house is appropriate to the landscape that surrounds it. Its structure, made exclusively of glass, respects the romantic image of the ruin with all its beauty.

Temple of Love

This peculiar design for using the building and the magnificent natural surroundings of the area stemmed from the accidental discovery of a domed room inside an old railroad station destroyed during the war. This robust masonry building has two levels, one at the height of the river's edge and the other at the level of the old road. The domed room could only be entered from the upper level through a small hatchway, which was not appropriate for a residence. Therefore, an opening was created at the lower level to provide access, light, and views of the river from this space that houses the bedroom and the living room. The plan for the upper level included a very peculiar room that is in direct contact with nature while causing minimum visual impact. Because of the location, the roof was designed to be supported by laminated glass panels whose function was to provide a 360-degree panoramic view. The glass panels fulfill a structural function, supporting the nearly two-ton roof thanks to the small size of the space, the strength of the material, and to four panels also made of laminated glass placed perpendicular to the glass walls to act as buttresses. Outside a glass bench whose supports are reminiscent of train rails reflects the overhanging trees and part of the building; it is tinted a light green, like a pond. The glass wall that faces this bench conceals functioning doors that have neither pull handles nor visible hinges.

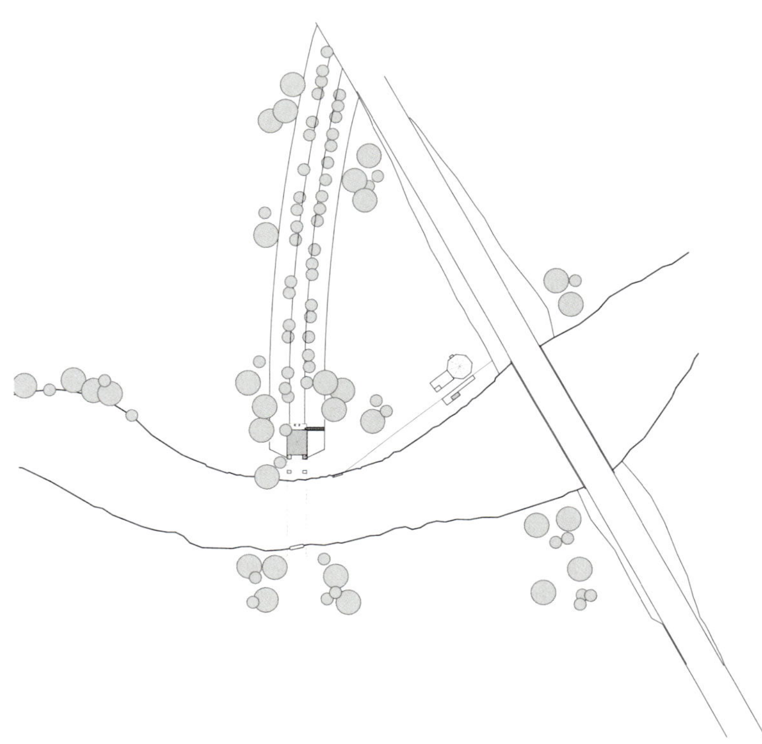

Map of location

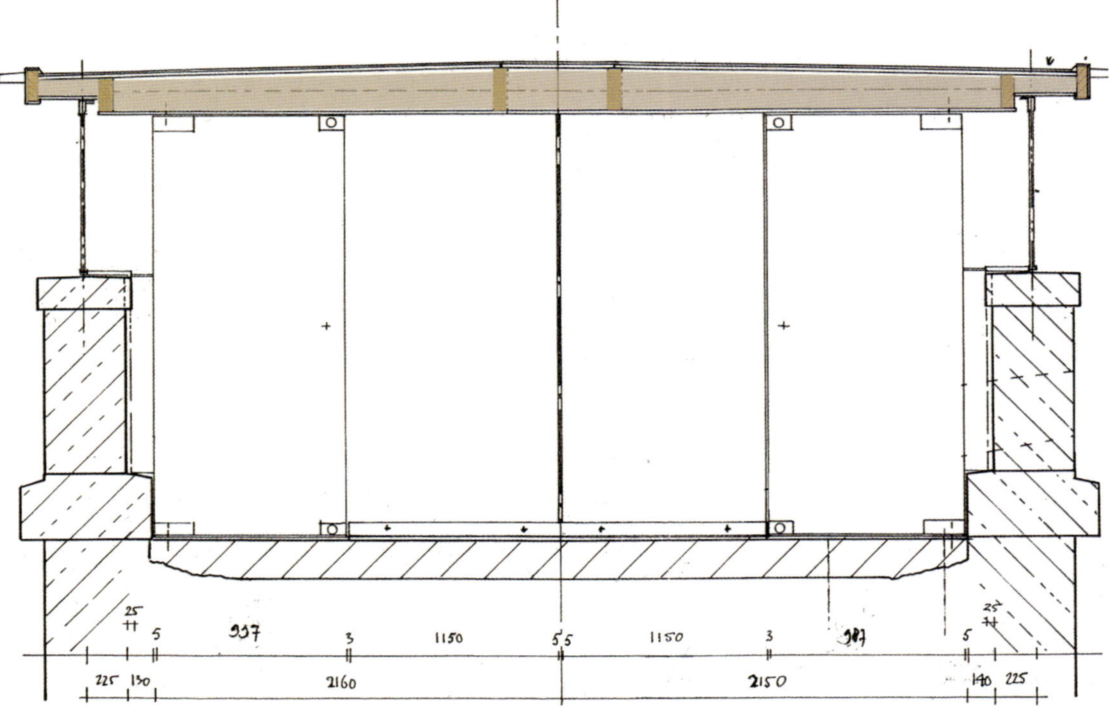

Detail of section

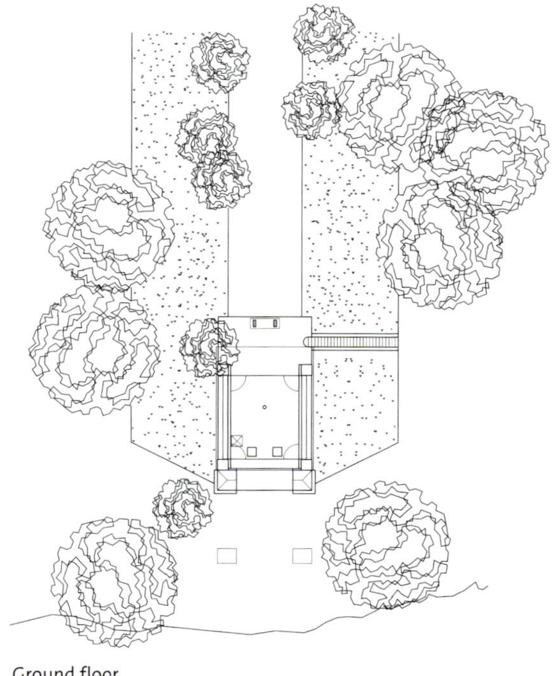

Ground floor

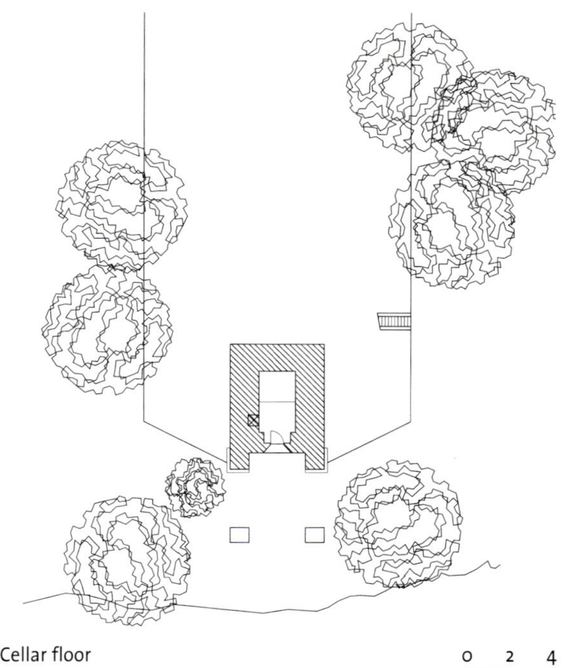

Cellar floor

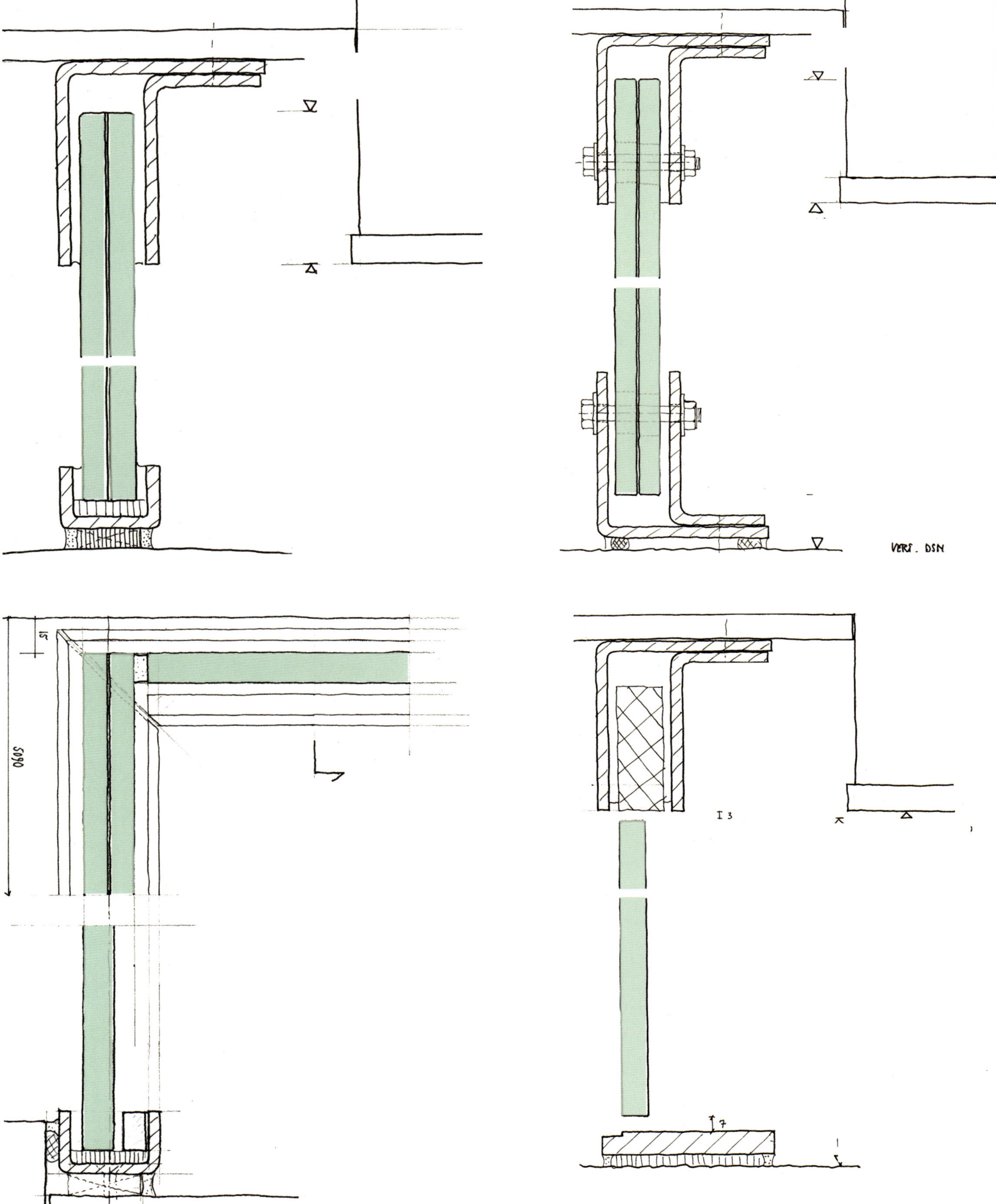

Detail of glass walls

Ca la Mostera

Architects: Iñaki Alday & Margarita Jover Biboum

Photography © Jordi Bernadó

Location: Monells, Girona, Spain

MAKING USE OF PRACTICAL SOLUTIONS AND DISTANCING ITSELF A LITTLE FROM THE NATURAL ENVIRONMENT, THIS REMODELING PROJECT IS A COHERENT EXERCISE TYPICAL OF THESE TIMES, AND VIEWS THE REMODELING AS A NEED FOR CREATING A COMFORTABLE RESIDENCE FOR YEAR ROUND USE.

Ca la Mostera

This construction was designed as a residence for year round living, specifically avoiding the latest trend in the Empordà for making weekend houses with large porches and no views.

This reform consists of adapting of an old agricultural building, using local materials, and does not pursue a rural inspiration with rustic undertones. Therefore, they used galvanized steel sheet, cool tones on the façade, and plaster in the interior to protect it from humidity and seepage.

One of the problems that had to be resolved was the lighting in the semi-basement, where the stables and the cellar were originally located, which had no windows. Several tapered boxes made of galvanized sheet steel were incorporated into the walls, making it possible to pierce through the wall slightly without the need for reinforcement. These pieces allow a lot of light into the interior while they can barely be seen from the outside since they are 11,5 x 23 inches (20 x40 cm) on the outside and 44 x 20 inches (110x50cm) on the inside. Another solution was to place a window inside the old fireplace, so that it would function as a source of indirect light for the entire floor without losing its original function, thanks to a new flue that was installed inside the chimney.

The entire project is a series of solutions that make this old farmhouse inhabitable. It avoids rustic clichés and passé images trying to look authentic in favor of an approach that is more aligned with the reality of the moment, whether it is a matter of practical solutions for living or esthetic lines.

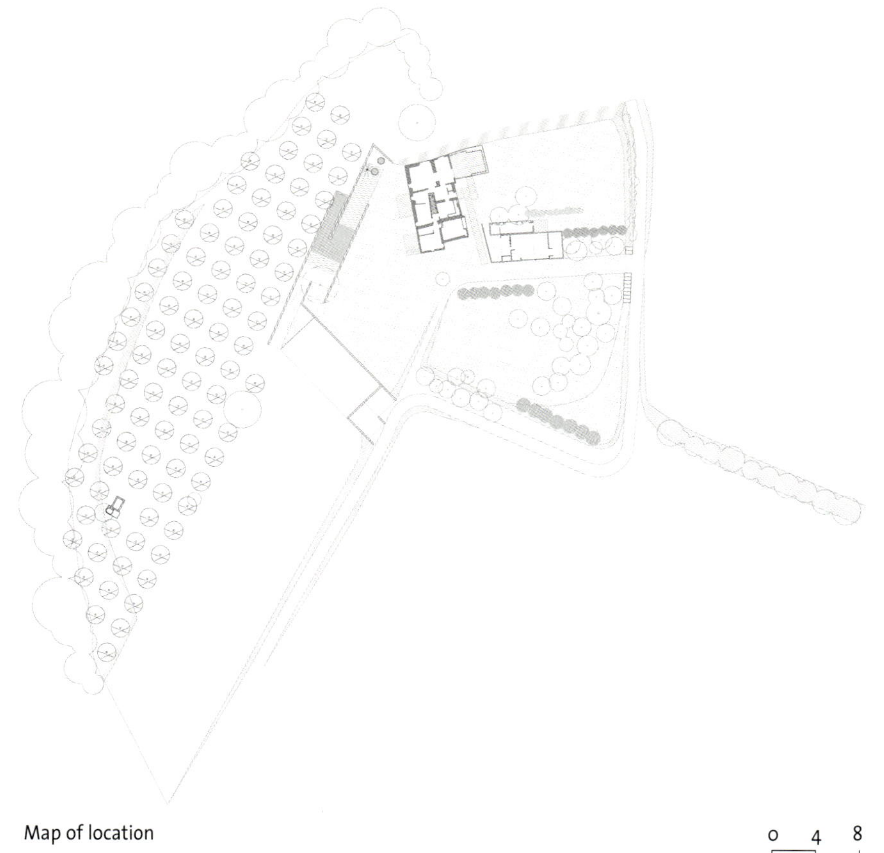

Map of location

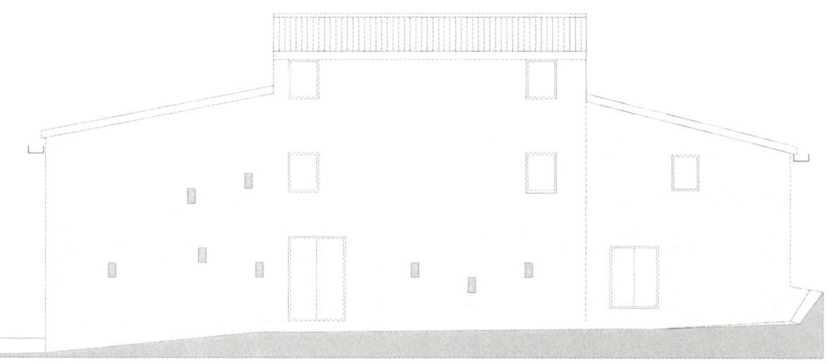

Elevation

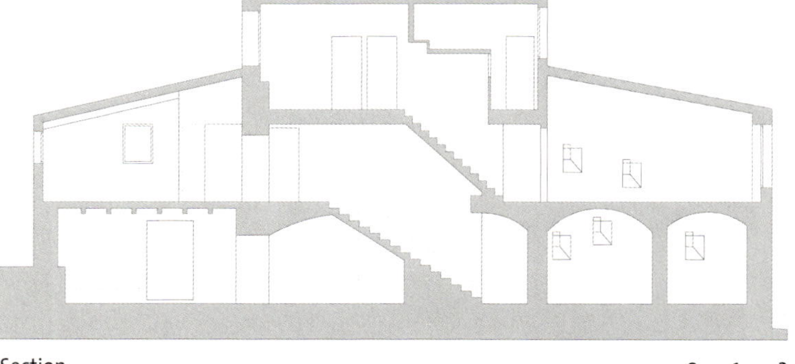

Section

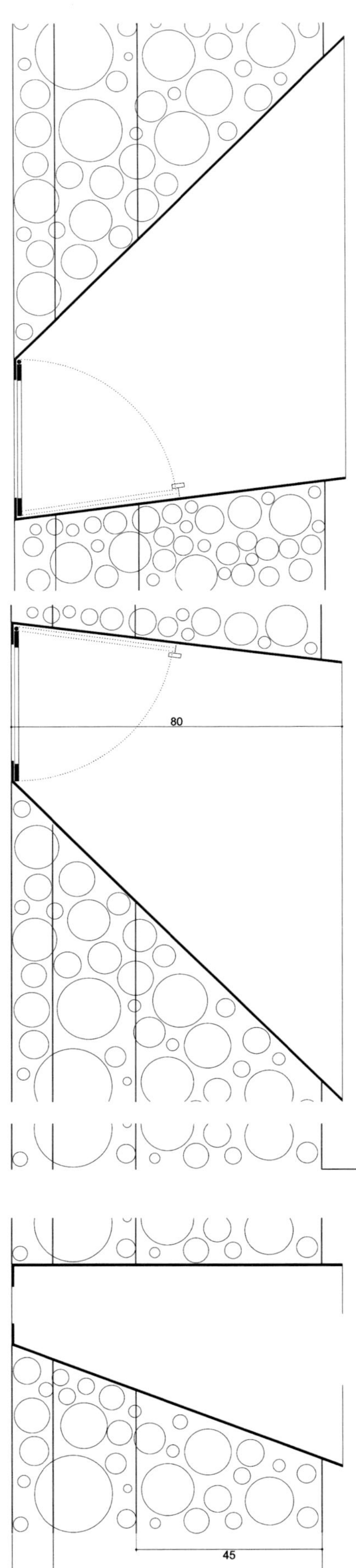

Detail of floor plan of windows

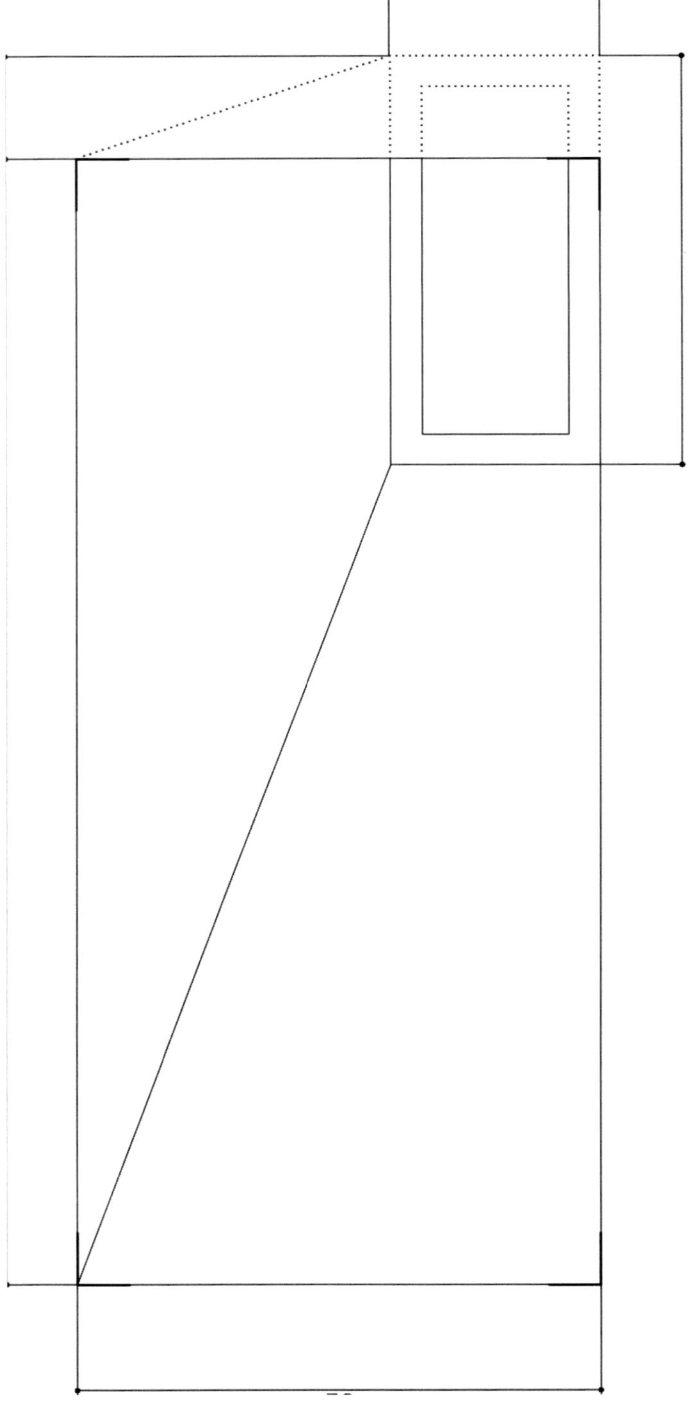

Detail of side view of windows

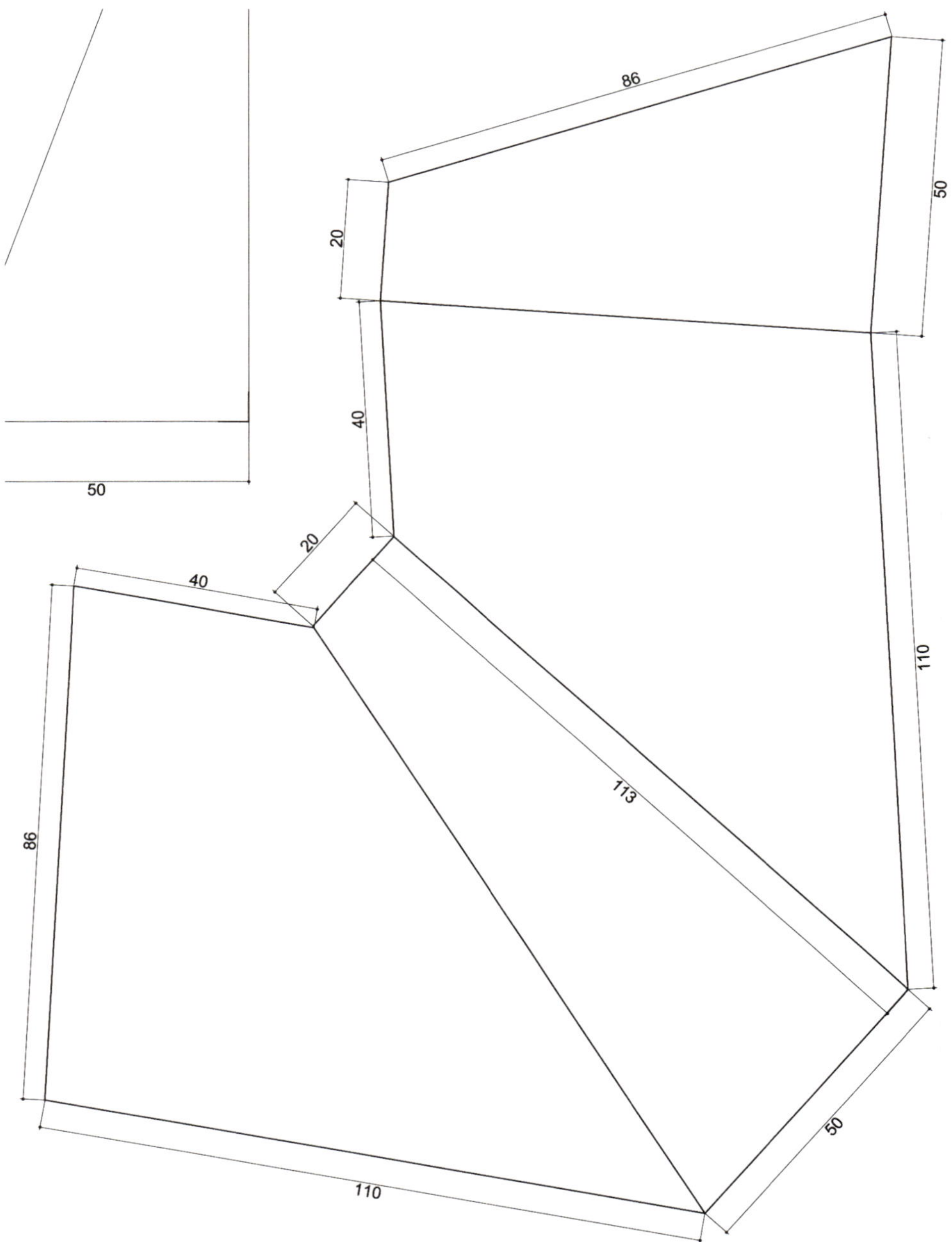

Layout of galvanized steel sheet

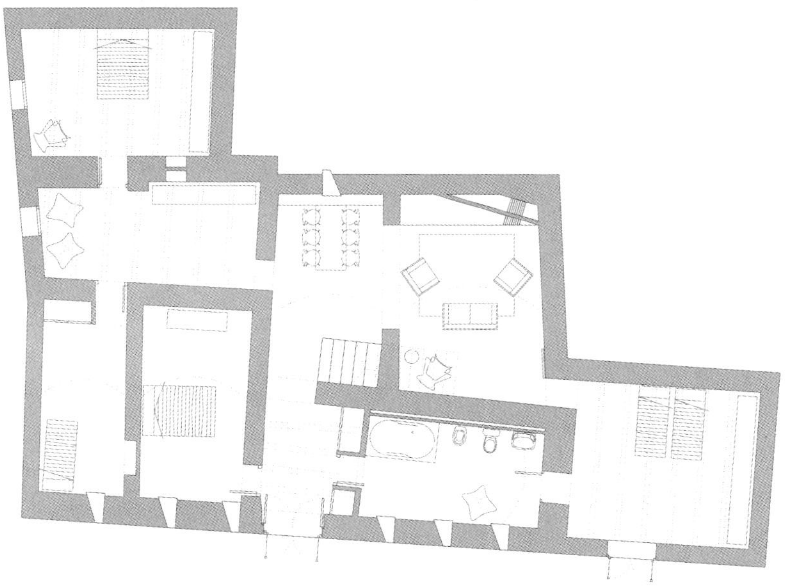

Ground floor

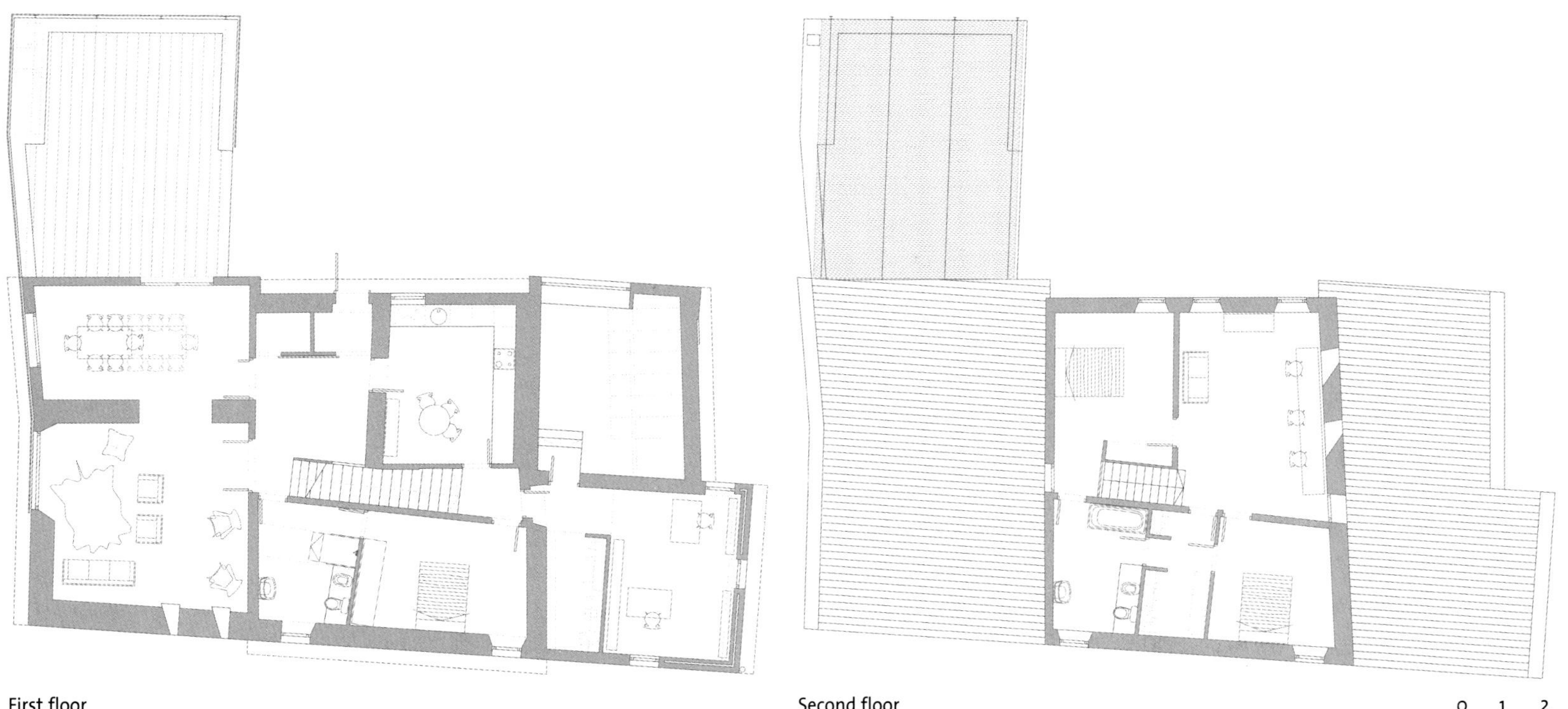

First floor

Second floor

Sketch

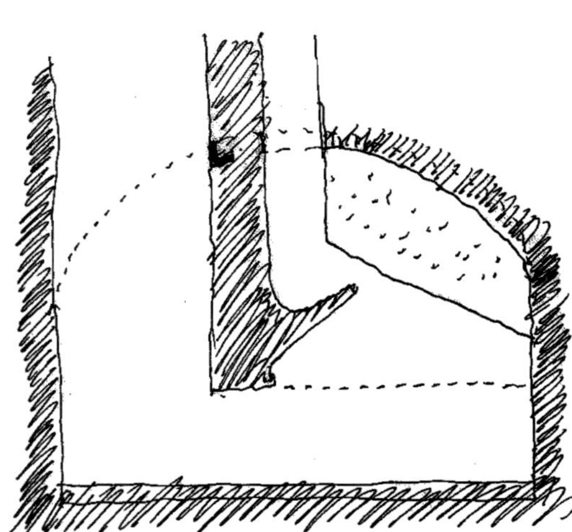

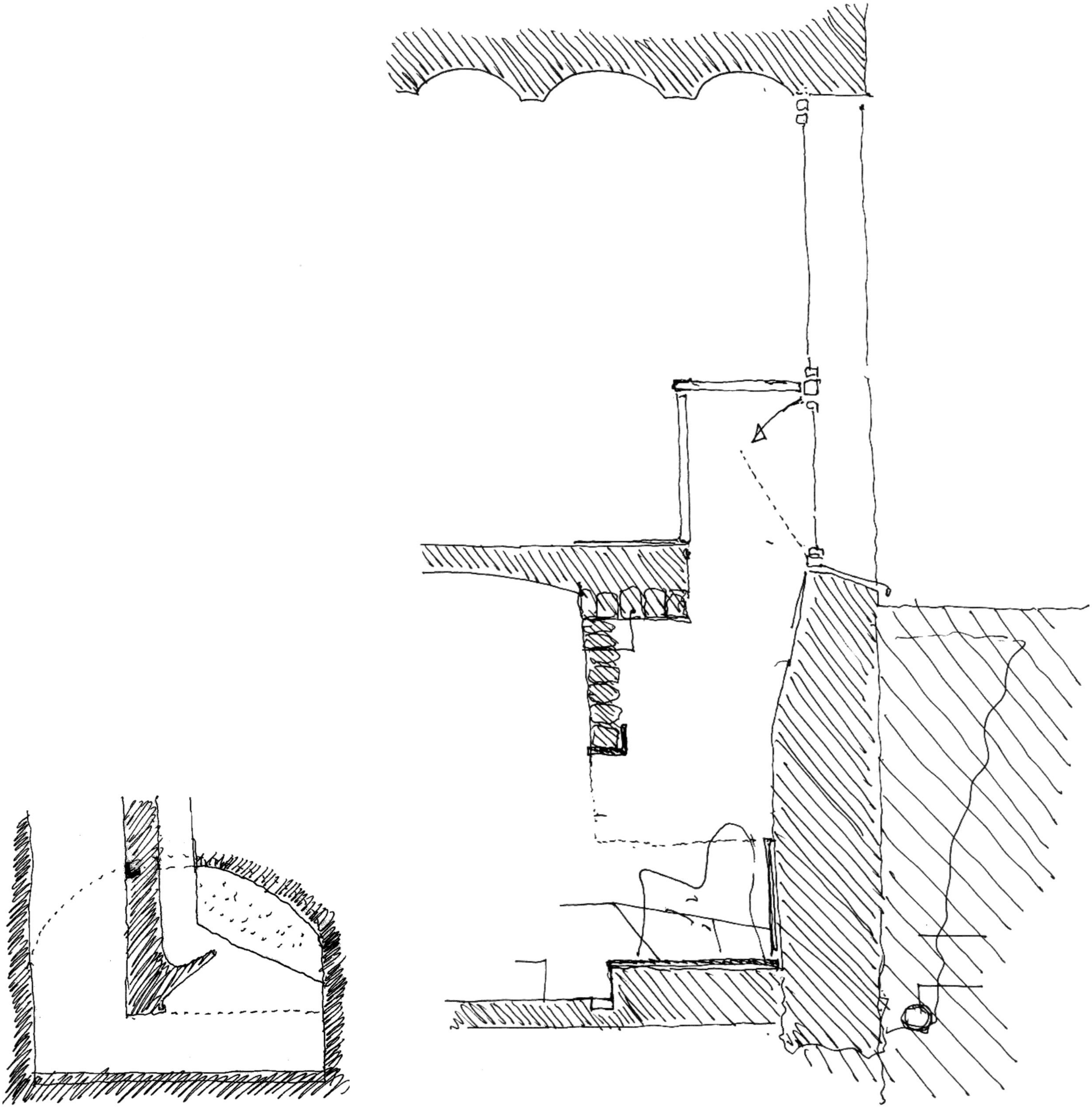

Sketches of sections

1 House + 1 House = 1 Bedroom

Architects: Enric Miralles & Benedetta Tagliabue

Location: Barcelona, Spain

The removal of the ceiling to create a bedroom of double height is one of the most daring ideas of this project. The design of the new skylight and the old beams offers a very beautiful and well-balanced space.

1 House + 1 House = 1 Bedroom

The project, which was awarded the FAD (Promotion of Decorative Arts) Prize in Interior Design in June 2000, consisted of converting two small houses located in the Barcelona neighborhood of La Clota into a single house. One of the dwellings was specifically reserved for domestic activities; the lower level includes the living room, the dining room, and the kitchen, and the second floor houses three bedrooms. The second dwelling underwent a much more dramatic change: the central framework of the floor and the roof were partially removed and a catwalk and a skylight were installed. Here were located a two-storey library/study and a vestibule open to the living room. The catwalk was designed to reach the highest shelves of the library, and it also connects the bedrooms with the bathroom. Since one of the main goals of this project was to preserve the spirit of the old building, the beams, the ceilings, the walls, and some of the different layers of paint accumulated over time were left exposed. The architects themselves designed a large number of the furniture pieces.

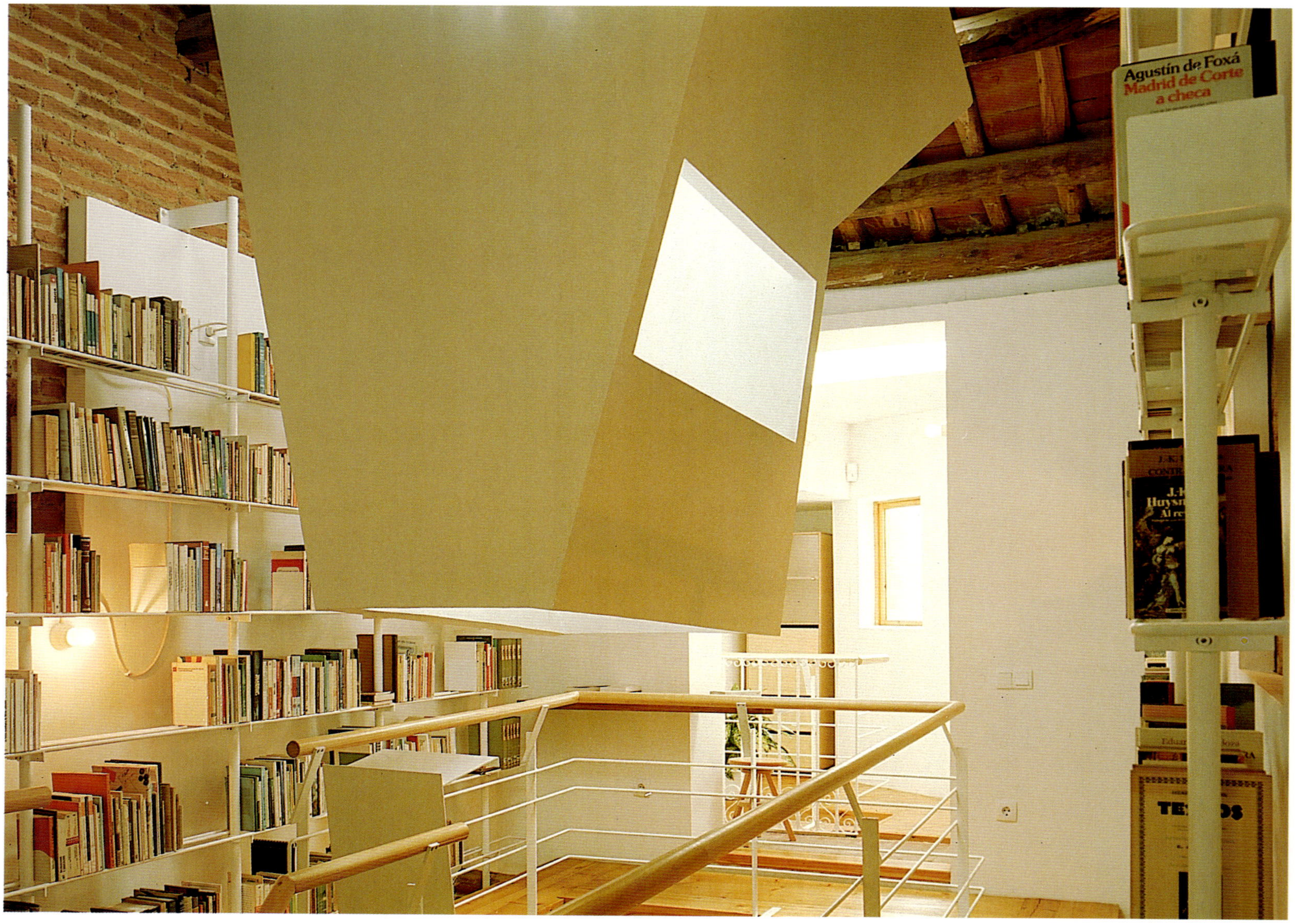
Agustín de Foxá
Madrid de Corte
a checa

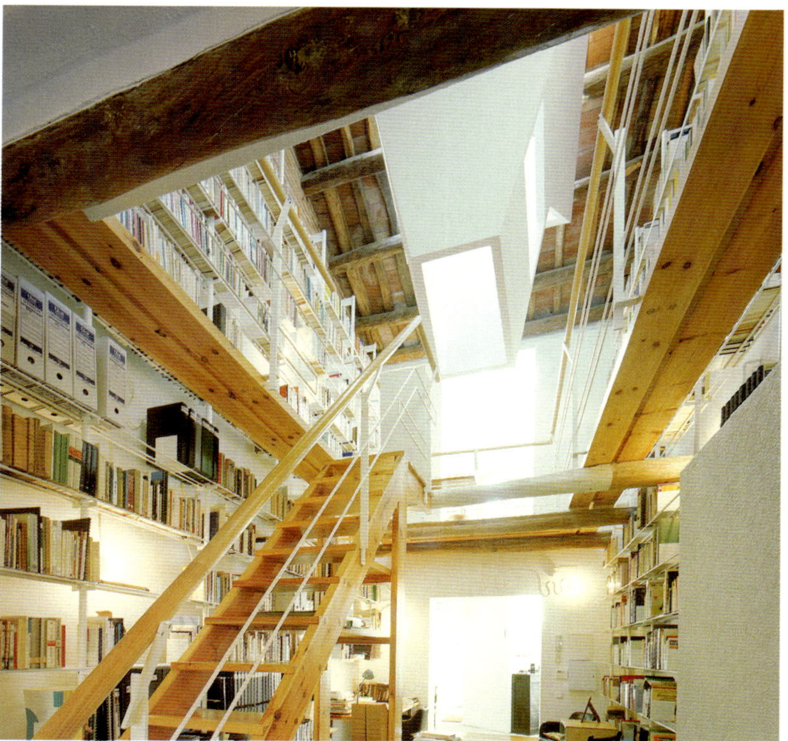

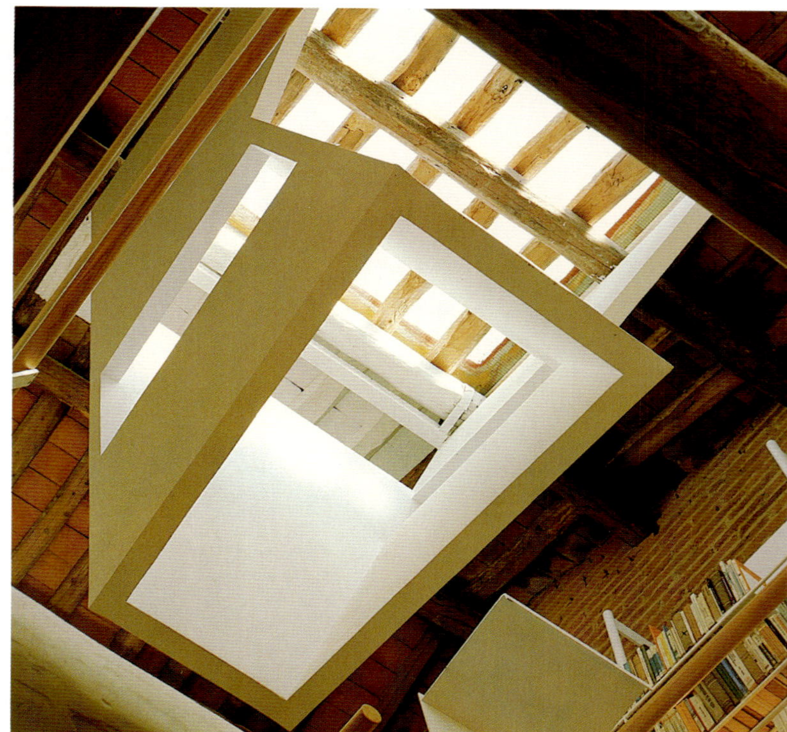

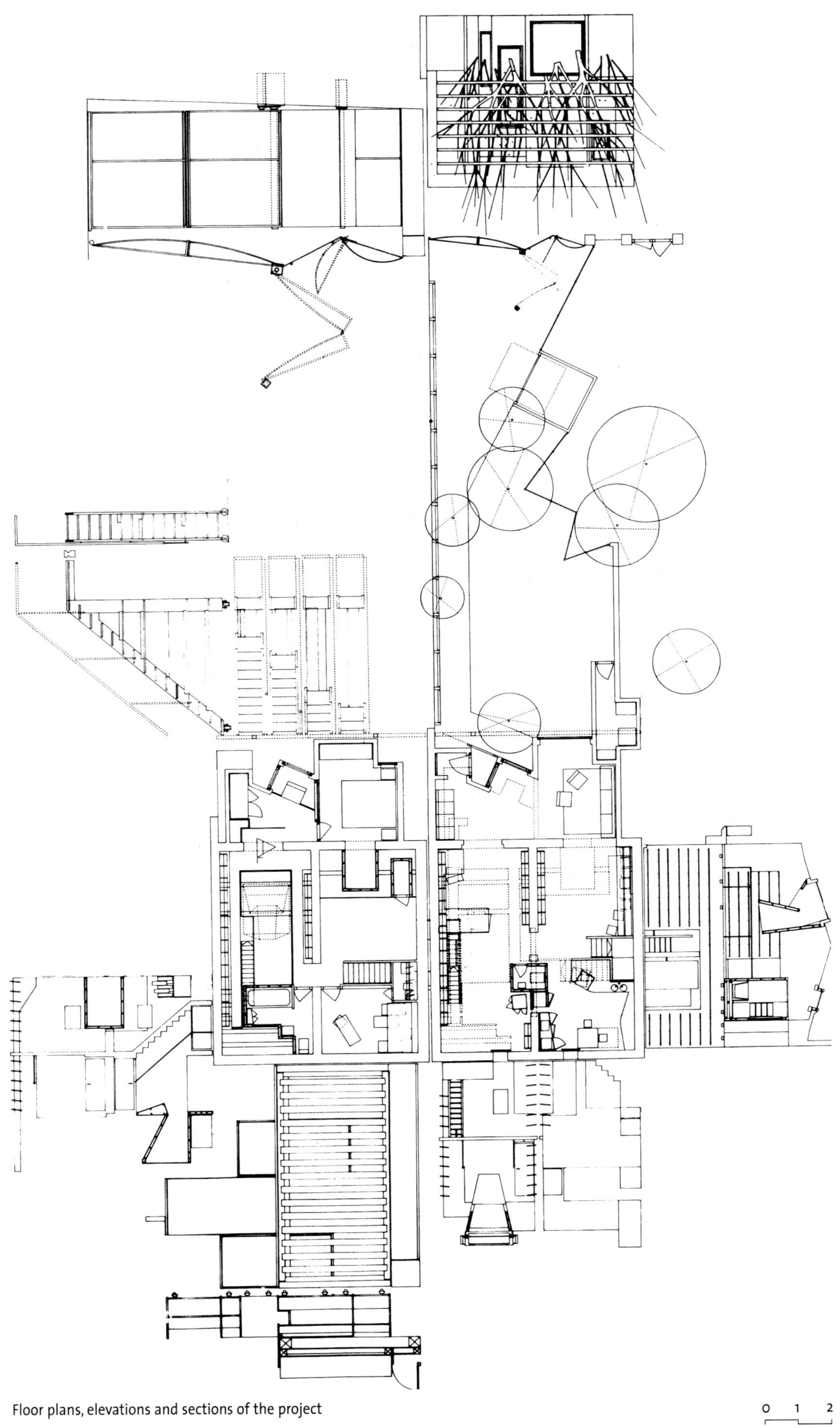

Floor plans, elevations and sections of the project

0 1 2

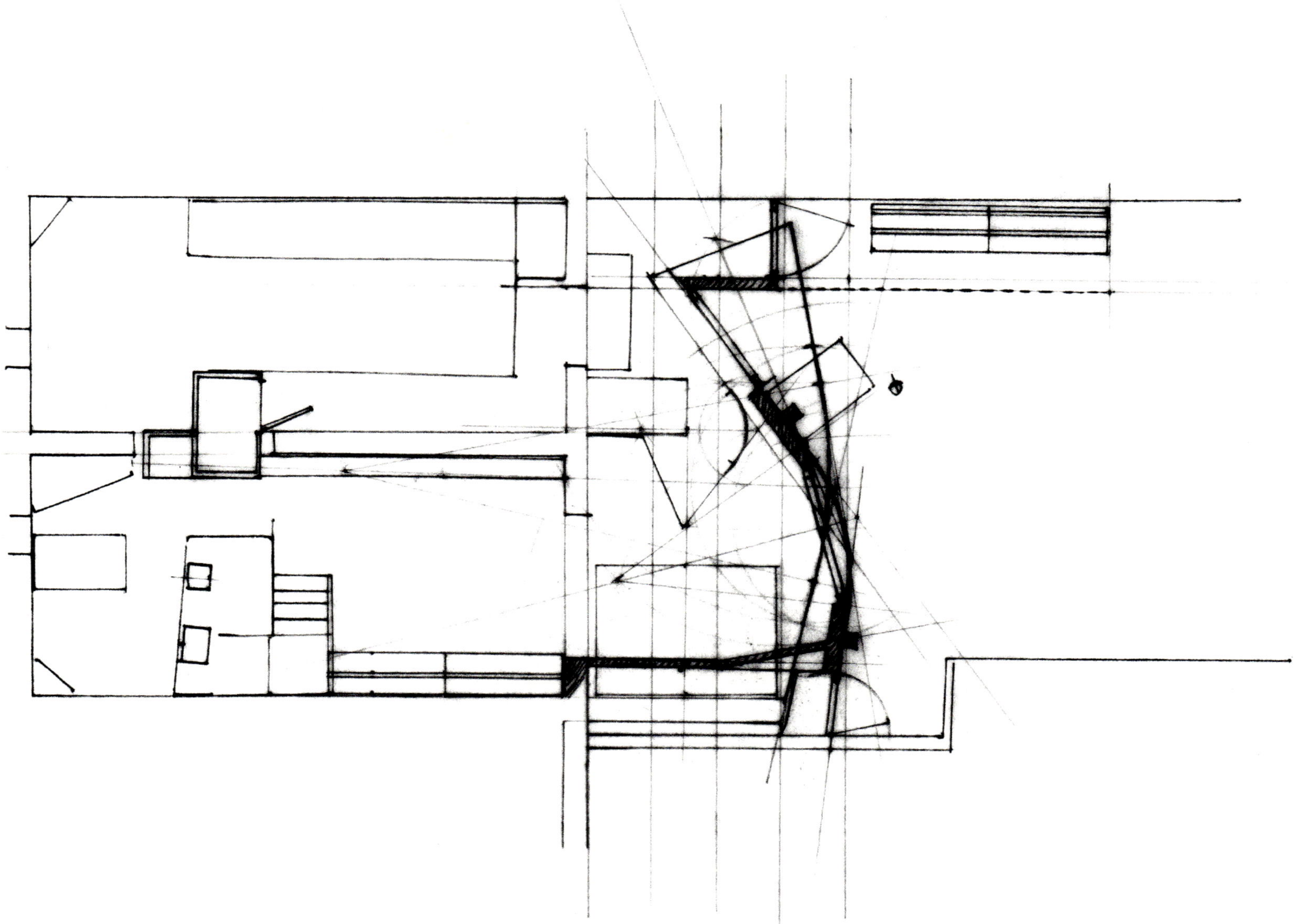

Detail

Model

0 1 2

Mas Cantallops

Architect: Miquel Capdevila

Photography © Jovan Horvát

Location: Olot, Spain

Mas Cantallops is an example of a remodeling project that respects its setting by using construction techniques typical of the area. This project consisted of converting a farmhouse into an attractive rural tourist house surrounded by the beauty of a natural reserve.

Mas Cantallops

This project consisted of remodeling a masía (farmhouse) in the volcanic area of Garrotxa Natural Park and it included two different phases: the transformation of the old granary into a new house, and the renovation of the masía into a rural lodging house for tourists. The intervention had to closely adhere to the strict regulations of the park as well as to the views that it offered. The southeastern façade of the masía enjoys a lot of sunlight and beautiful views, therefore it is here where the daytime areas, consisting of a large dining room with two levels on each floor, were installed. The lower level connects with the garden through a porch, which also serves to preserve the privacy of the viewing areas of both floors since the second floor connects to a gallery that is open in two directions with the house's best views towards the southeast and the northeast. The interior layout is based on a long central hallway flanked by several bedrooms, connecting them all to the entrances located in the northeast wall of the top floor and the southeast façade on the lower level. This solution, together with the inclusion of a kitchen on each level, makes both levels completely independent and able to function as separate apartments. The old granary had the opportunity to enjoy the views of the surrounding fields and woods, therefore a decision was made to cover the previously open façade with a glass wall. This way every bedroom is in direct contact with nature and enjoys the changing light throughout the day.

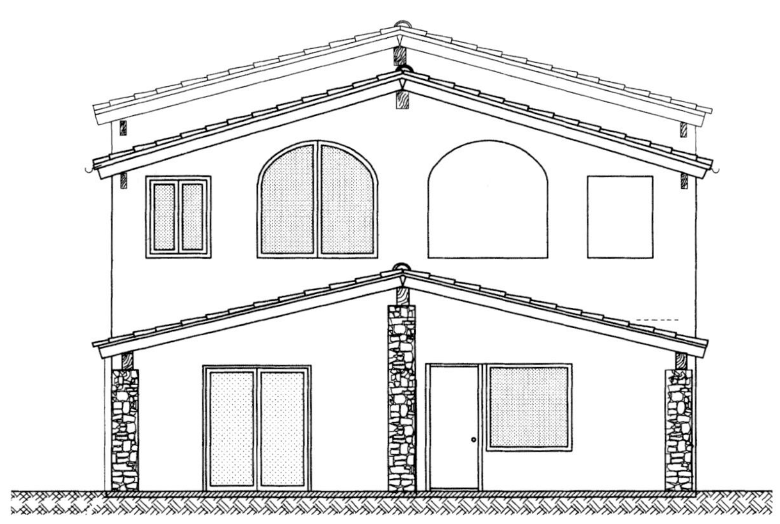

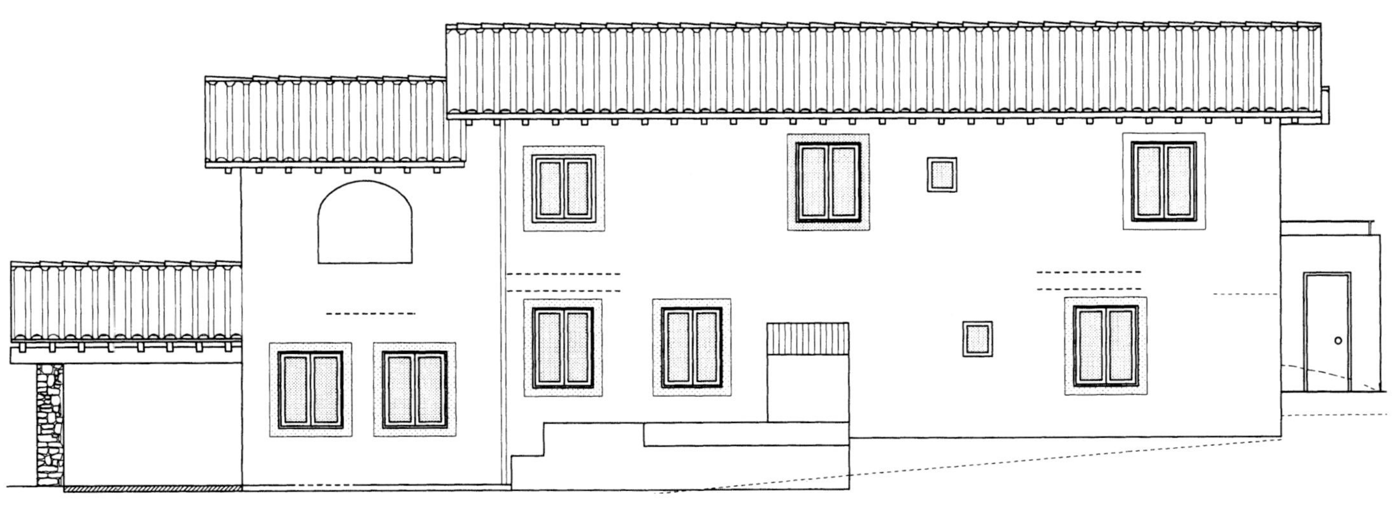

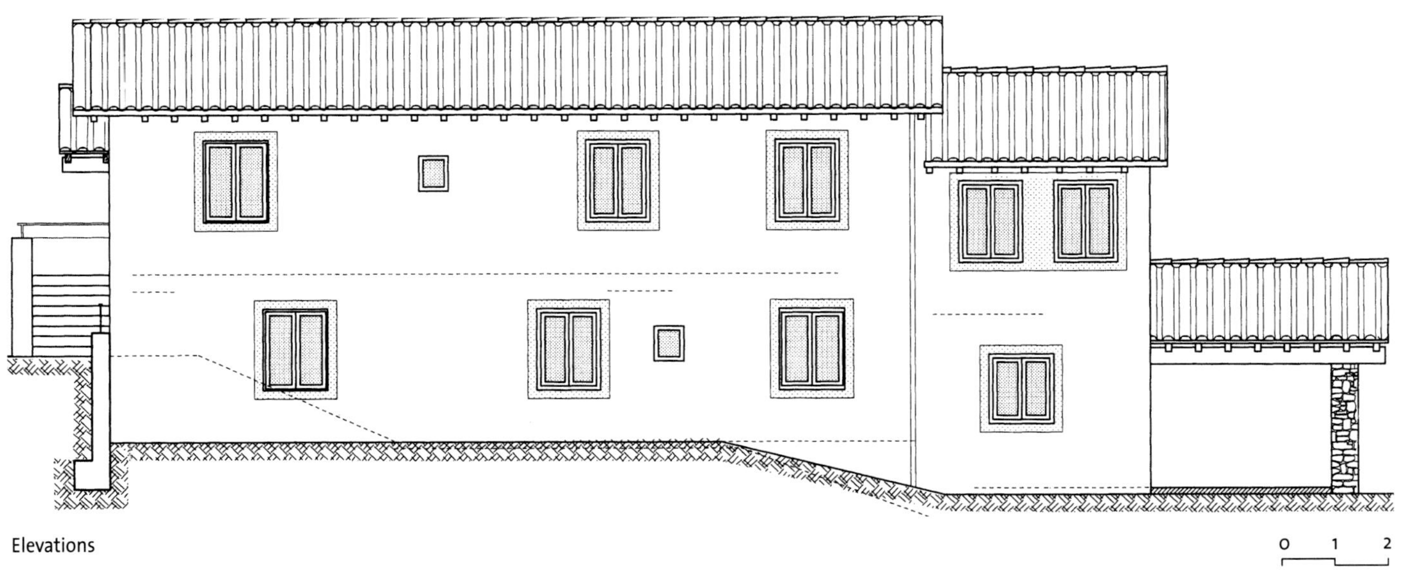

Elevations

Longitudinal section before reform

0 1 2

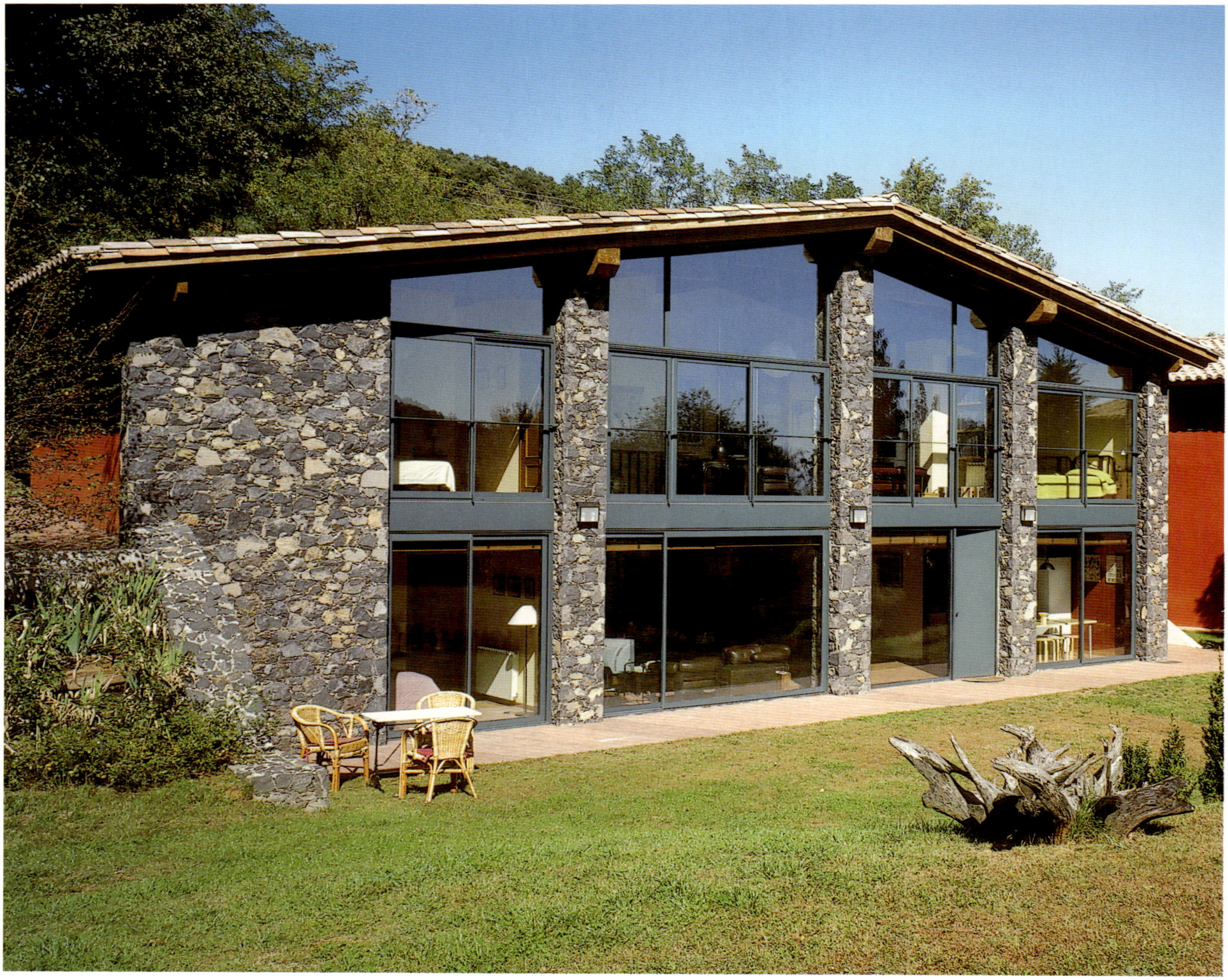

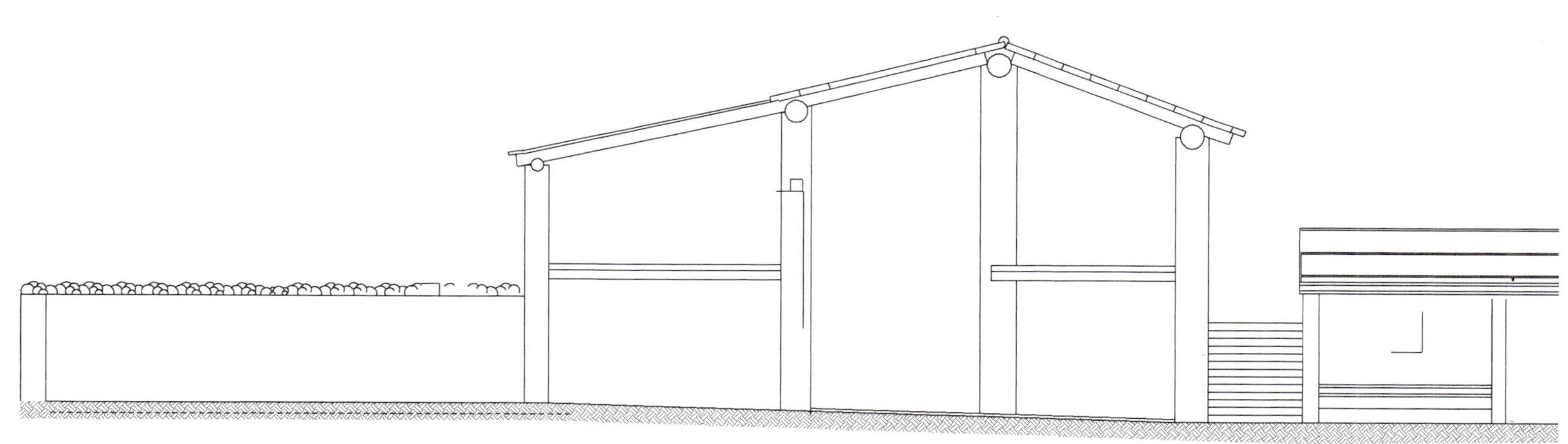

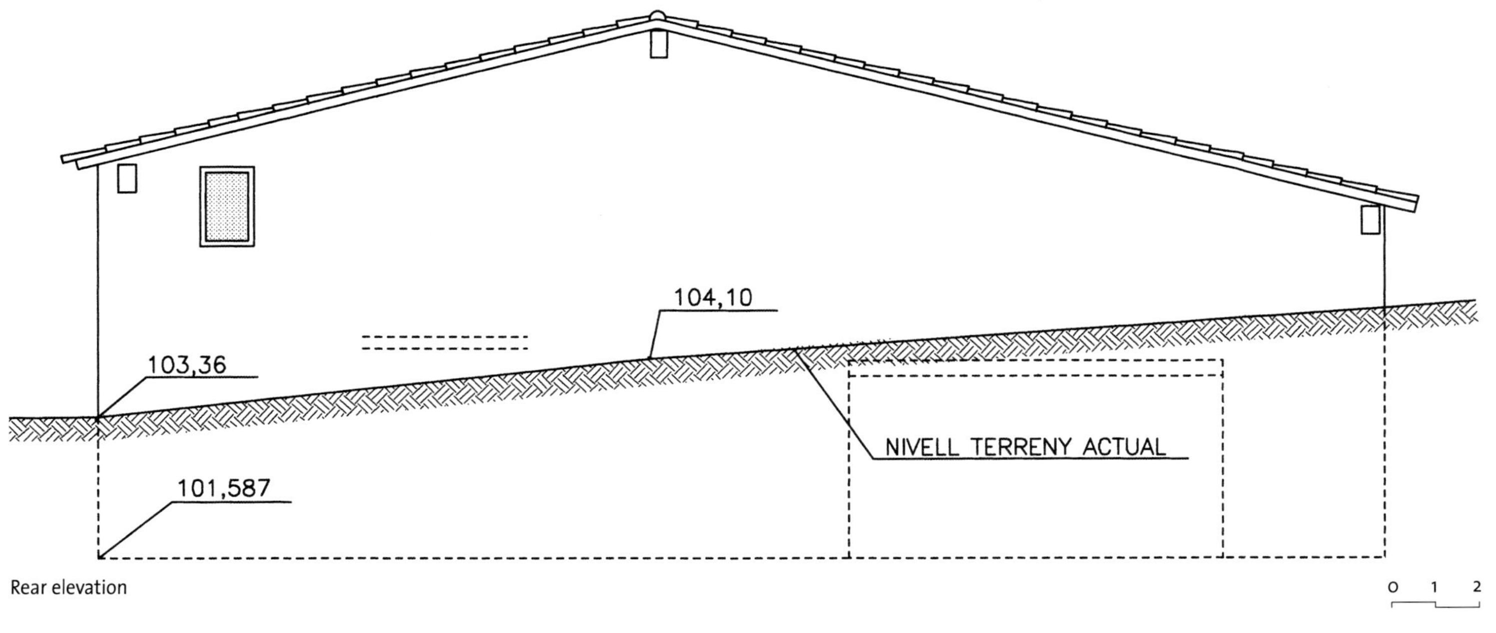

Rear elevation

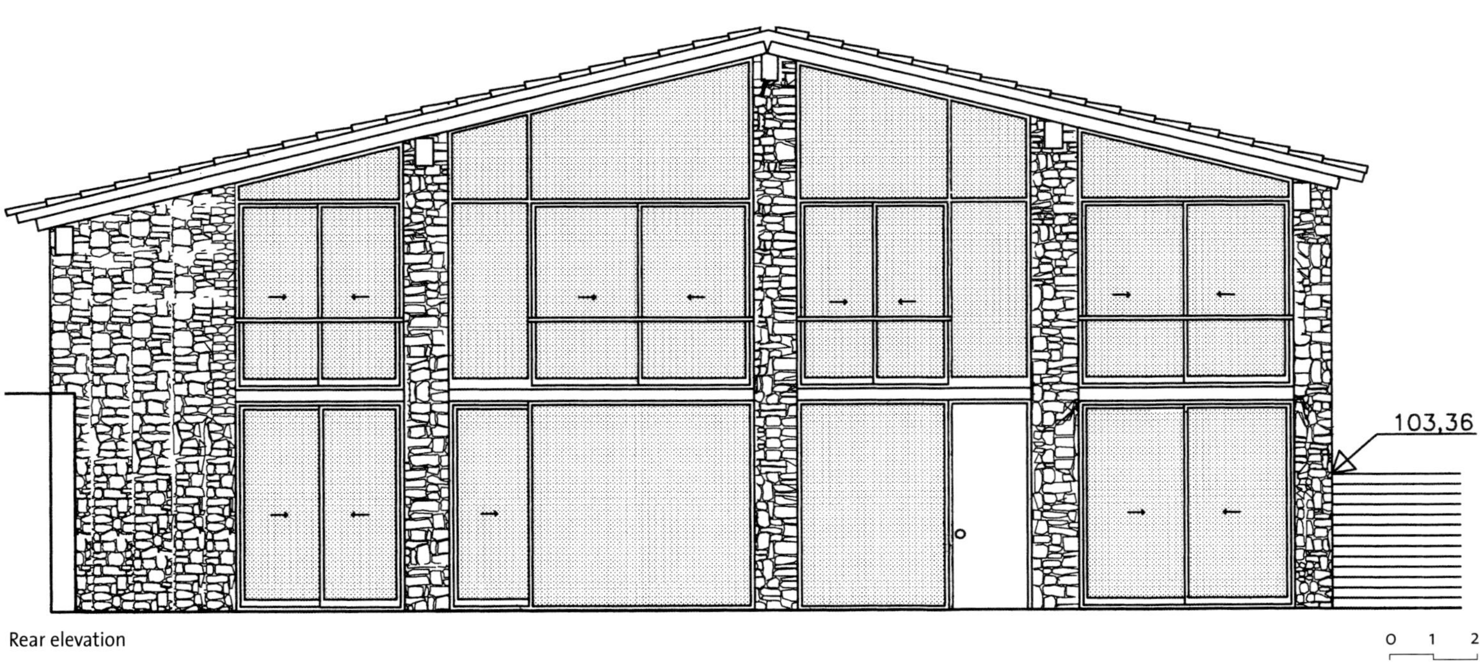

Rear elevation

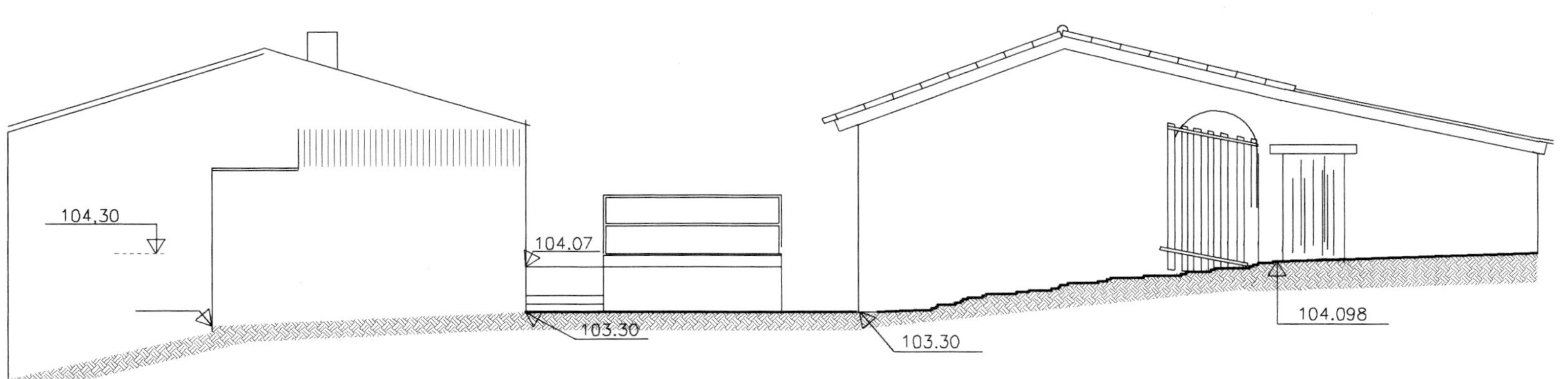

Section of buildings before reform

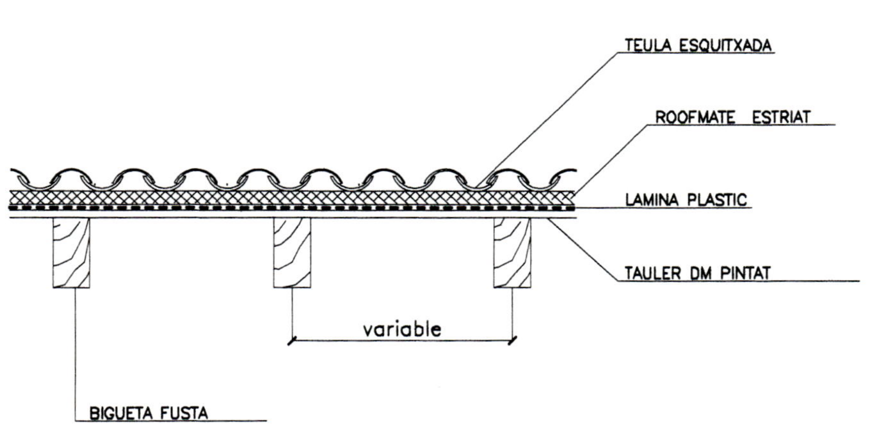

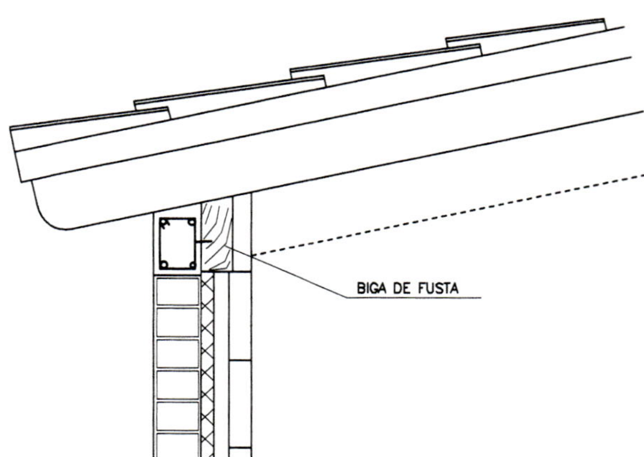

Details of roofs

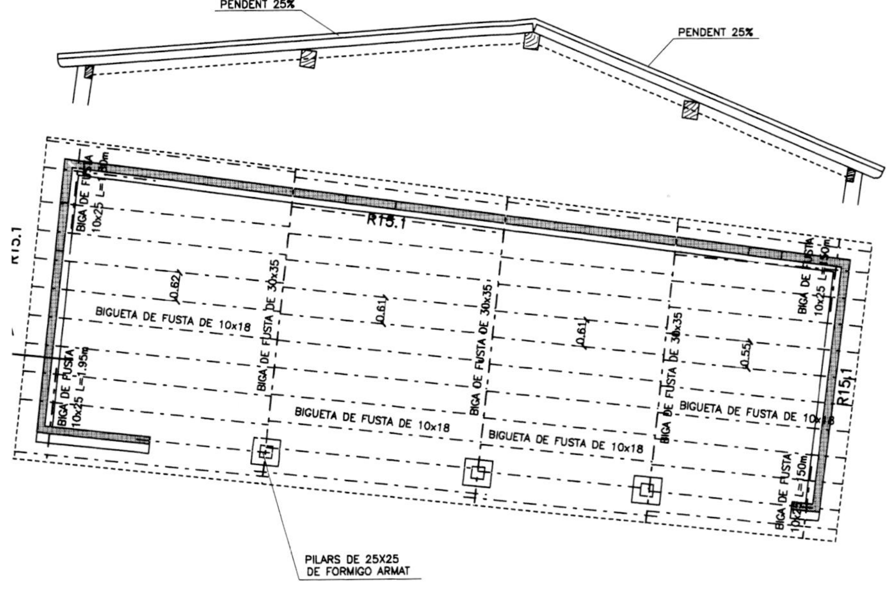

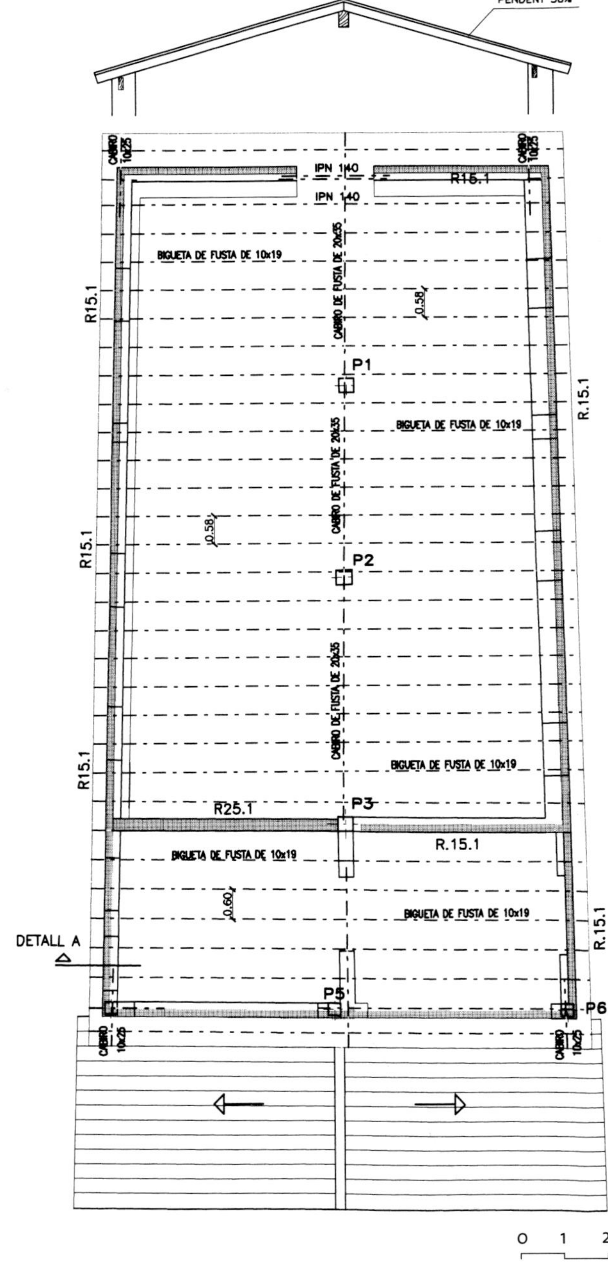

Plan of structures

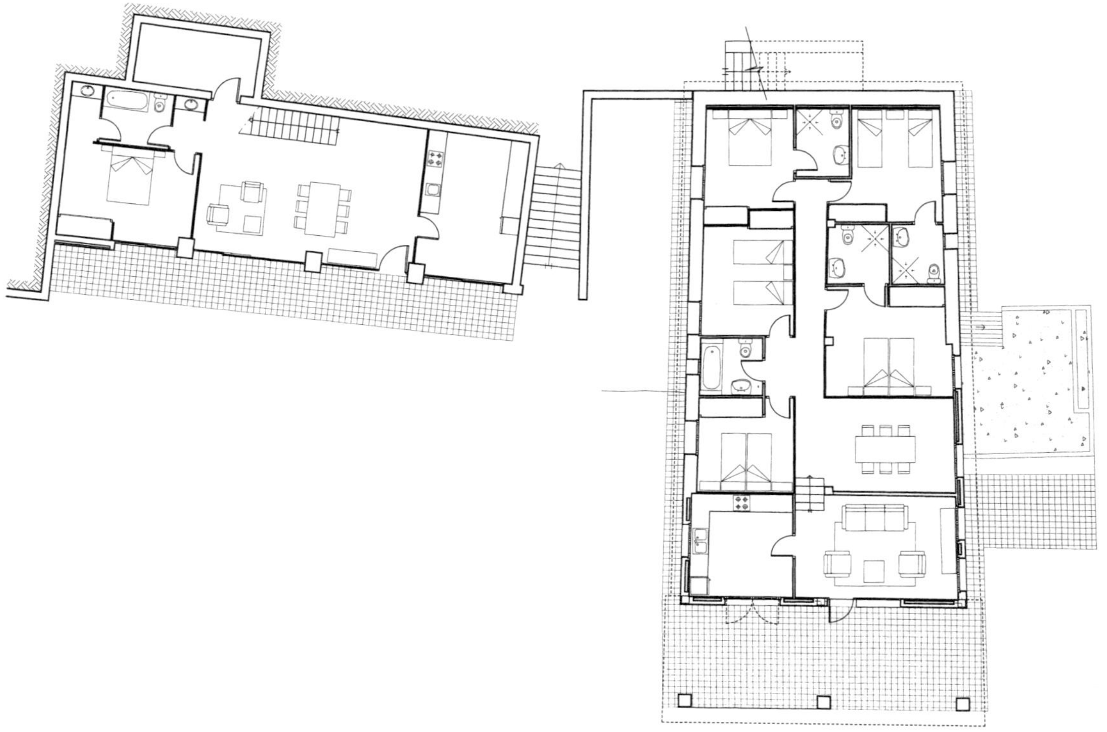

First floor

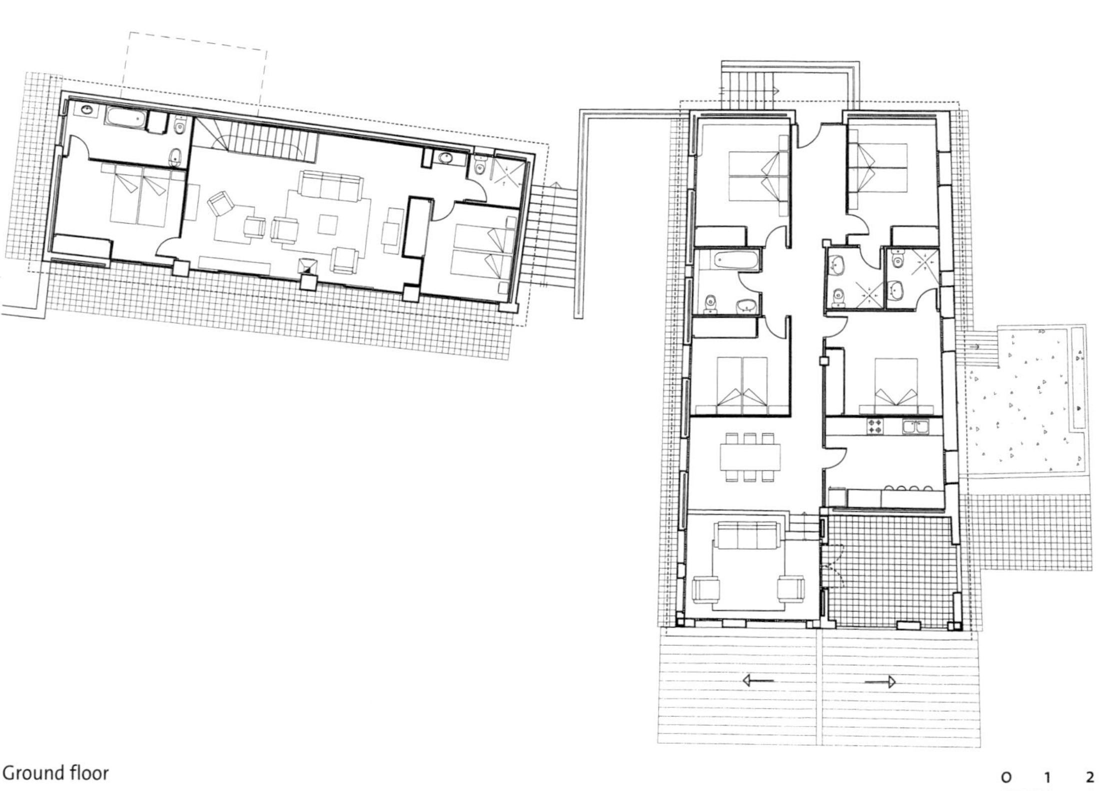

Ground floor

Jote Apartment

Architects: Andrade Moretin Arquitetos Associados

Photography © Nelson Kon

Location: São Paulo, Brazil

A STRIKING APPROACH THAT IS STILL ALWAYS RESPECTFUL OF THE ORIGINAL CONSTRUCTION ADAPTED THIS HOUSE TO THE NEW USES AND NEEDS OF ITS RESIDENTS, WHO EXPRESSED THE DESIRE TO PRESERVE THIS LANDMARK BUILDING.

JOTE APARTMENT

The Prudencia building is one of the examples of the architectural quality of the modern movement in Brazil. It was built at the end of the forties in one of the residential neighborhoods in downtown São Paulo. Updating one of its 4,800 square foot (450 square meter) apartments for a couple and their two children was based on a plan to redefine the communication between the spaces in an attempt to make them more fluid, but at the same time allowing a space to be separated from the others if desired. With this in mind, a new design was createded for the hallway. The square footage of this space was expanded and a large bookshelf was installed, hanging from an L-shaped beam structure that runs along ceiling around the entire perimeter. This solution gives this room a feeling of importance, and it also confers a strong sense of continuity. The structure stands out like a piece of furniture that enters and runs through the entire house, and transforms the hallway into a space that is something more than a passageway. In addition, it gives the bedrooms privacy because it highlights the doors to the kitchen and the dining room and disguises the entryways to the private areas. Besides fulfilling a structural function, the beams make it possible to easily channel all the electrical installations and at the same time facilitate indirect lighting by concealing the various light sources.

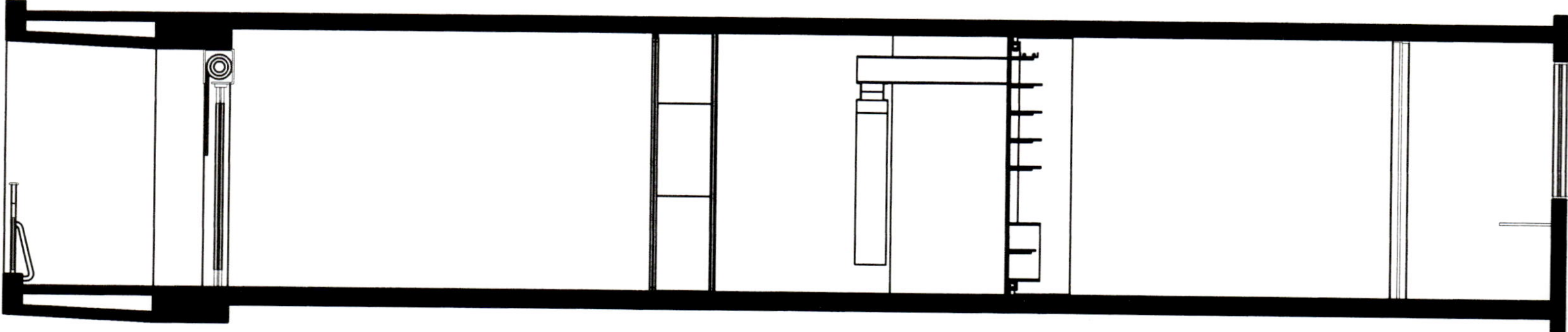

Cross section

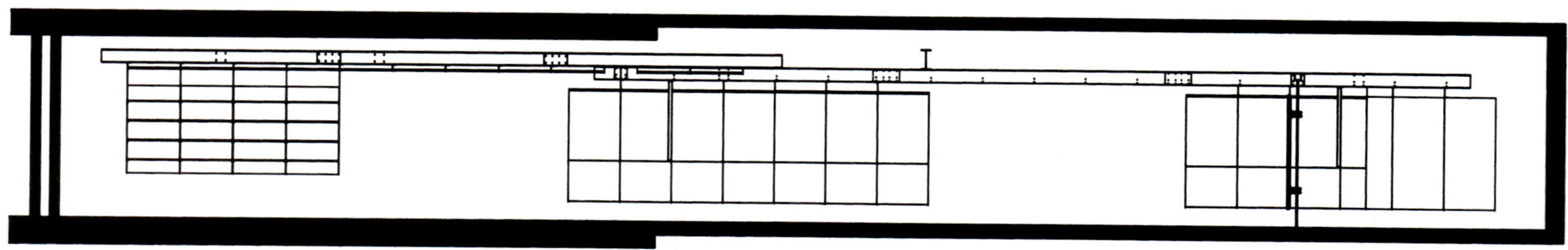

Longitudinal section

0 1 2

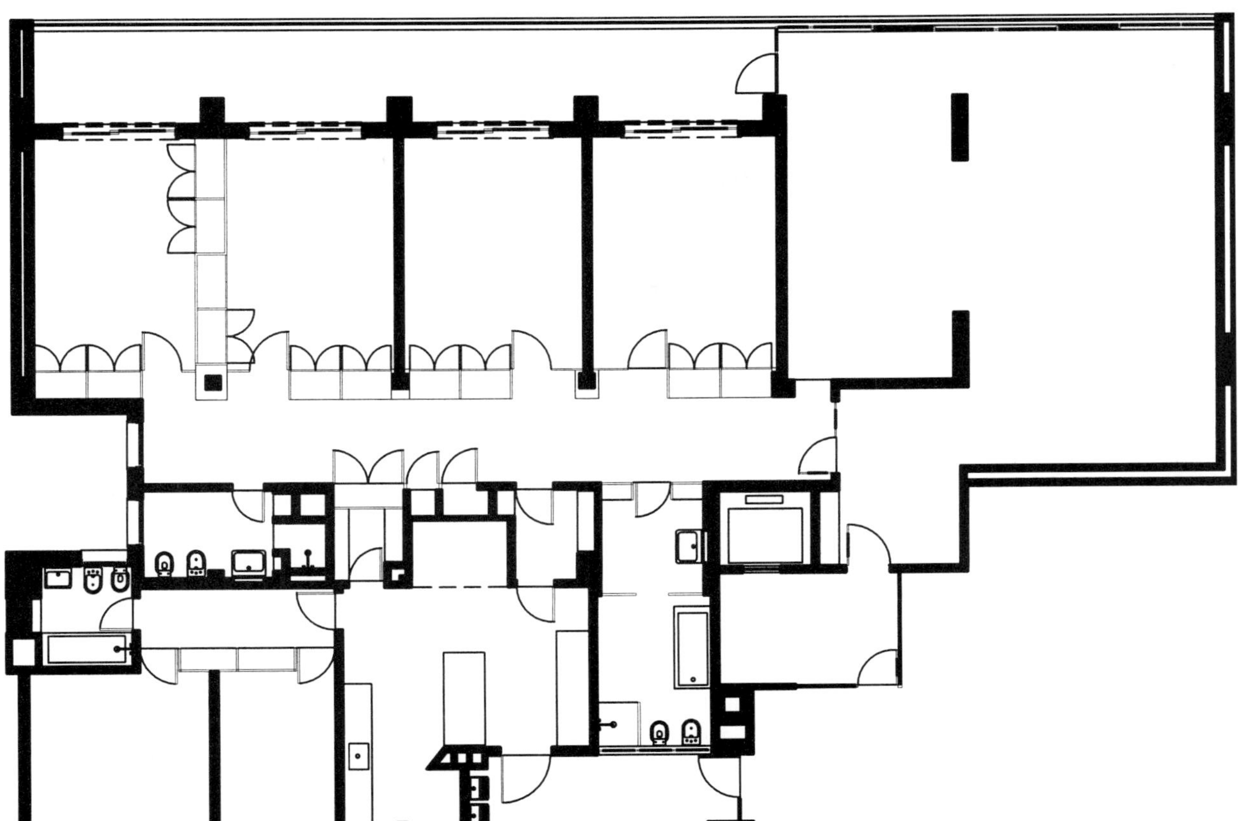
Original floor plan

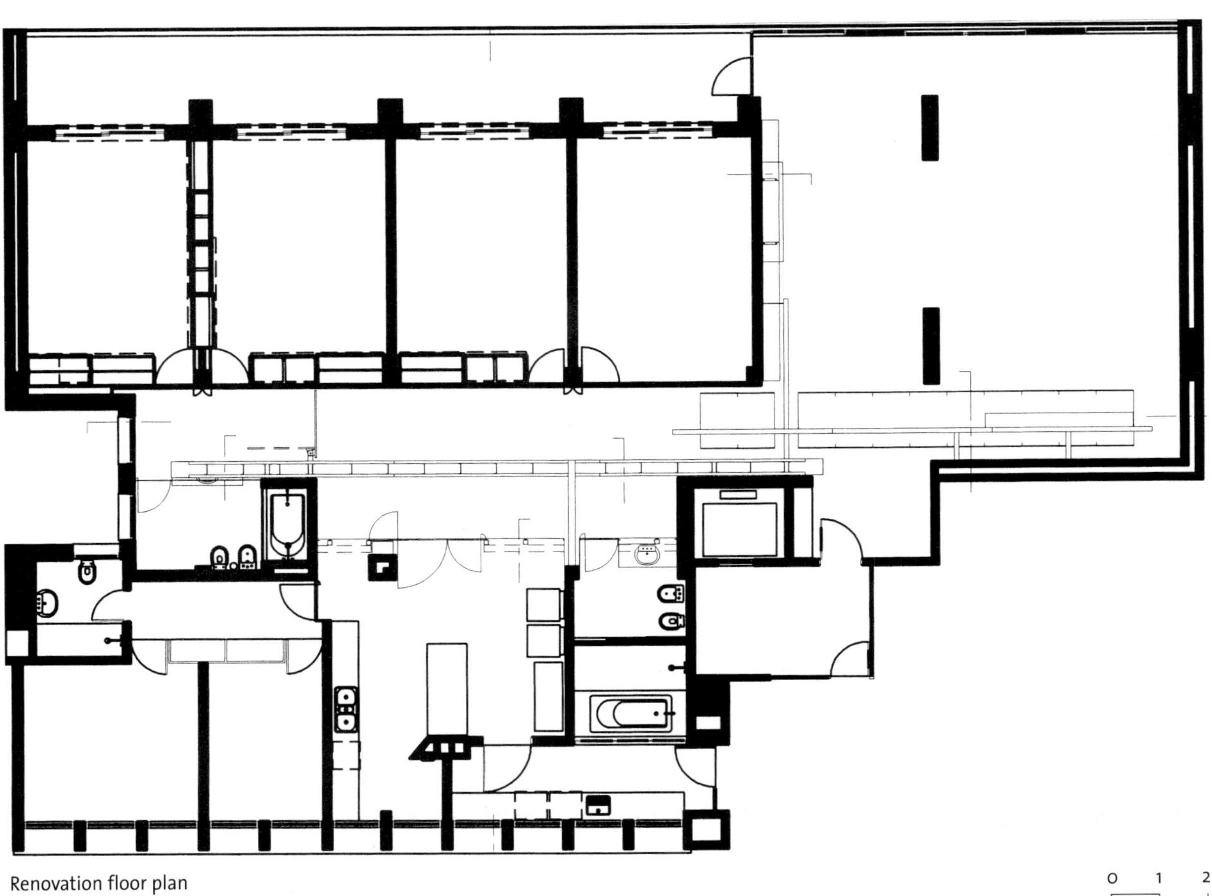

Renovation floor plan

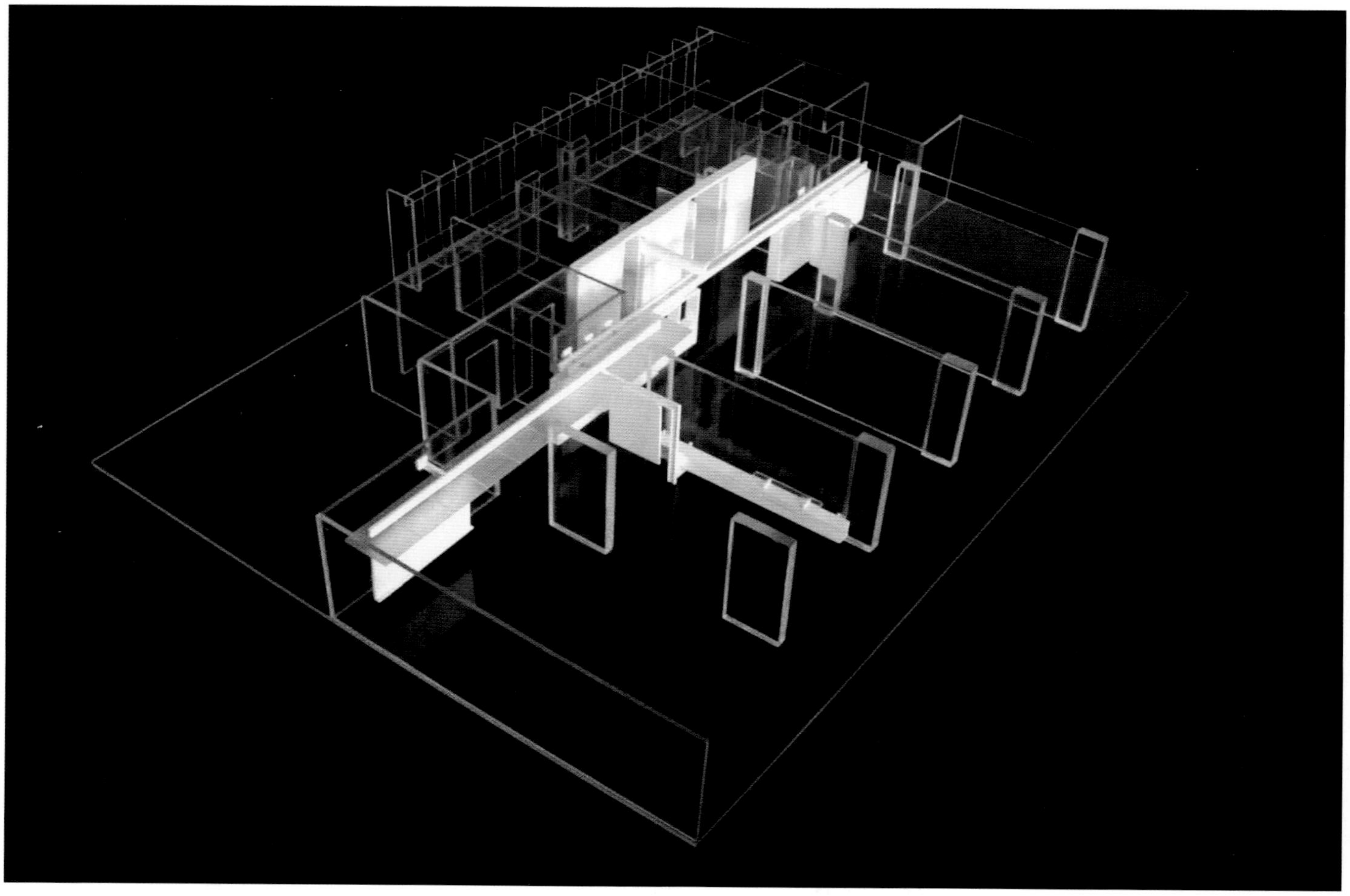

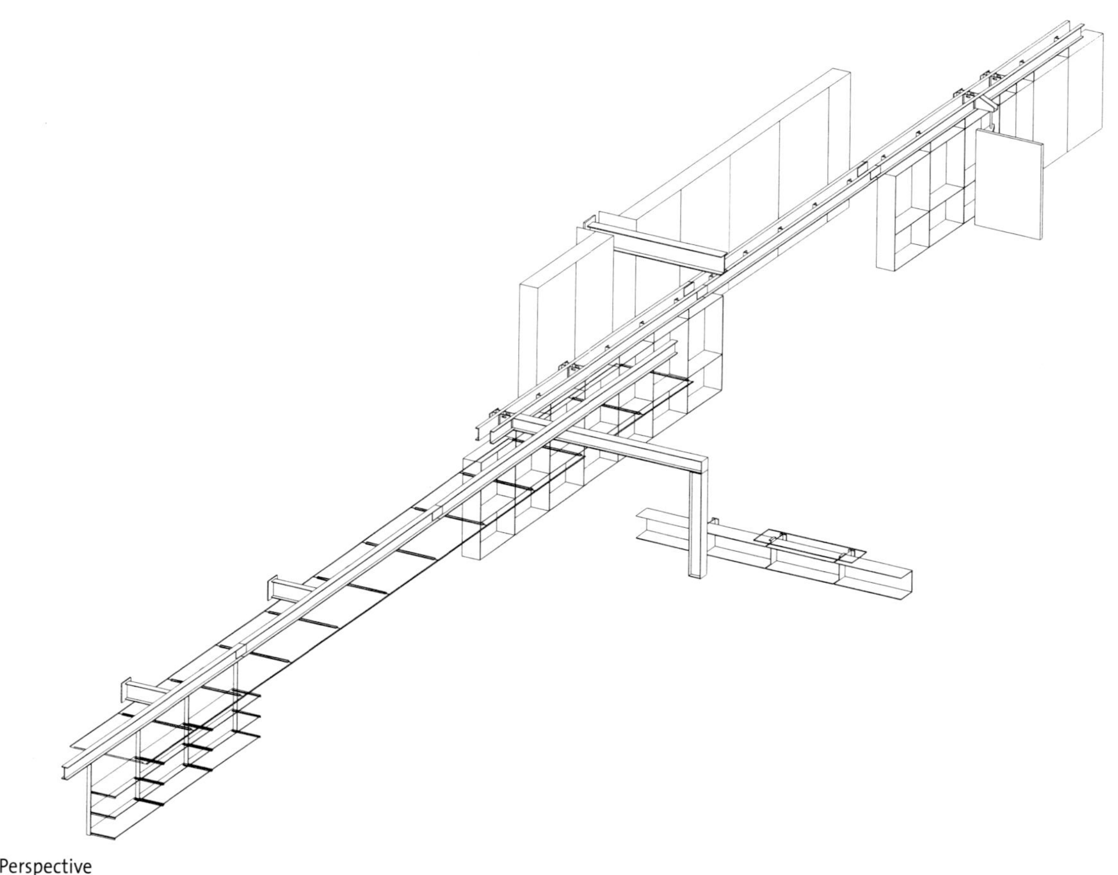

Perspective

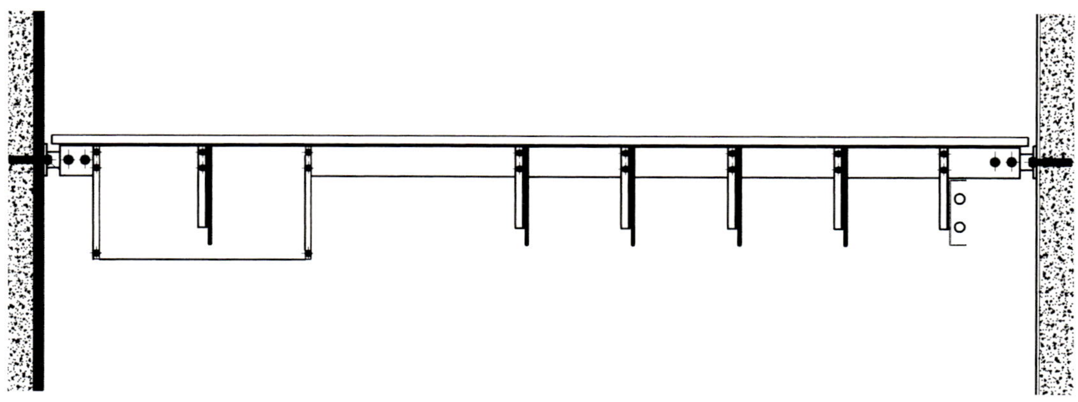

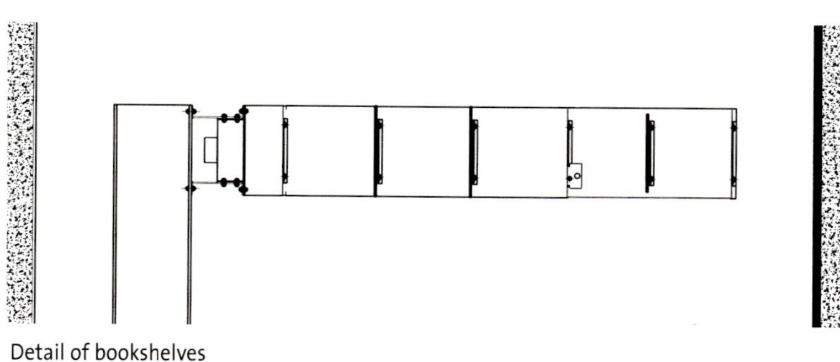

Detail of bookshelves

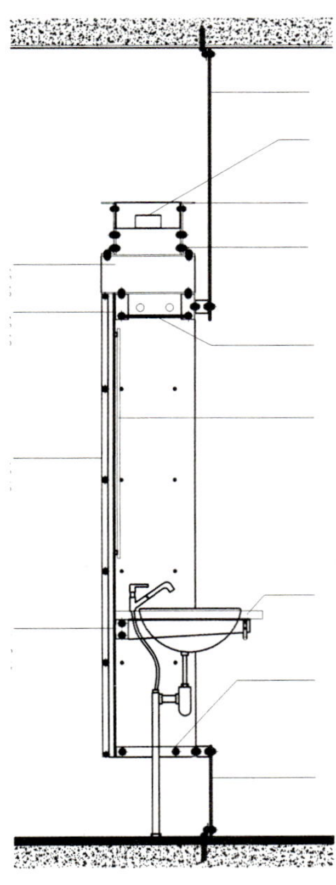

Detail of bathroom

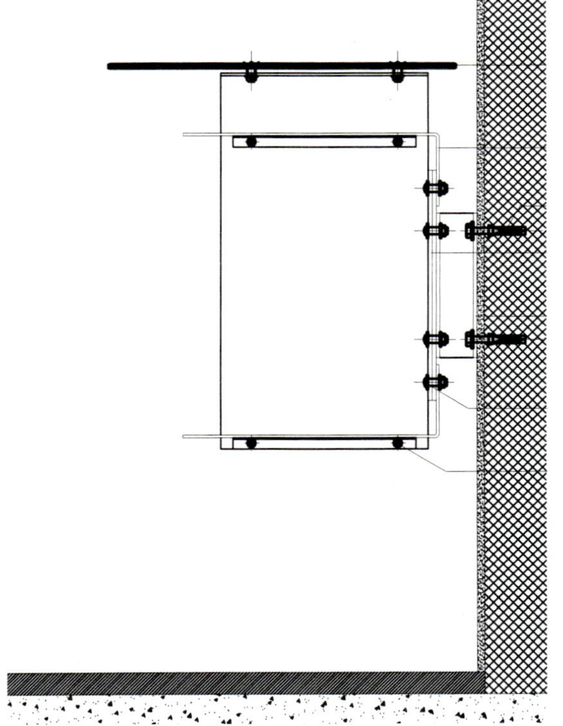

Detail of cabinet

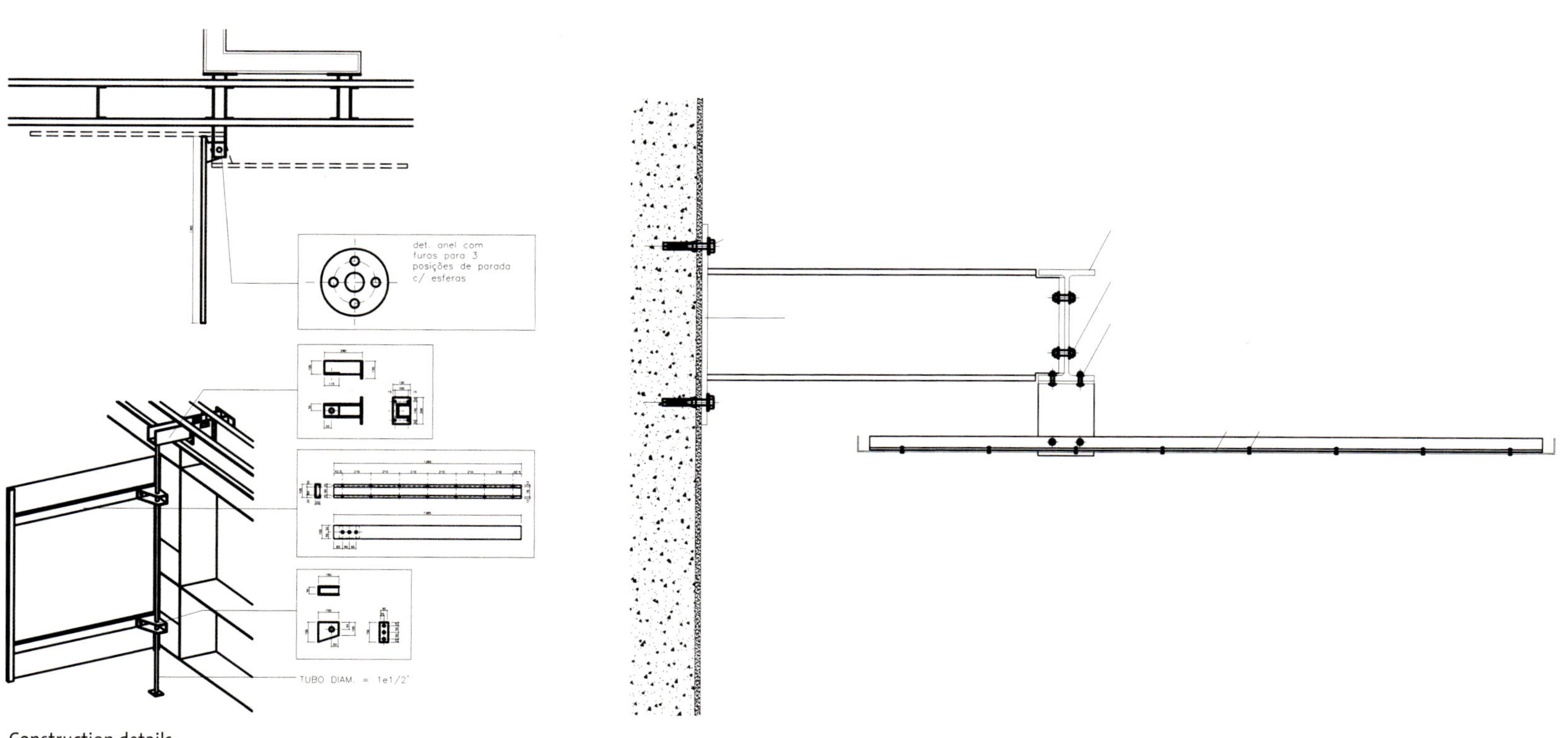

Construction details

O House

Architects: Atelier Matador

Photographs © Sven Everaert & Jean Pière Legros

Location: Mons, Belgium

The evolution of an industrial society into a service economy in the last fifty years has led to an increase in the number of old factories that have been converted to residential use, changing the old industrial zones into part of the urban fabric.

O House

Transforming this old glass factory into a single-family home required a lot of thinking about the layout of the approximately 2,700 square foot lot that was quite deep. The old factory was located at the rear of the lot, and three of its four walls had no openings to the outside. It was entered through a patio that was in very bad condition. In addition to the plan to use the existing factory building, it was decided to transform this intermediate space into a true patio that would be the hub for the rest of the house and one of its main rooms. The need for natural light in the existing building played an important role in making this decision, and the patio is now a source of light and communication. A new pavilion was built parallel to the garden to connect the façade with the rear. It is a very large undefined space that can be used for many types of activities. The strategic placement of the large windows means the entire house faces the patio and does not sacrifice the privacy of its residents since the remodeling plan took into consideration its placement away from the neighboring houses and garages.

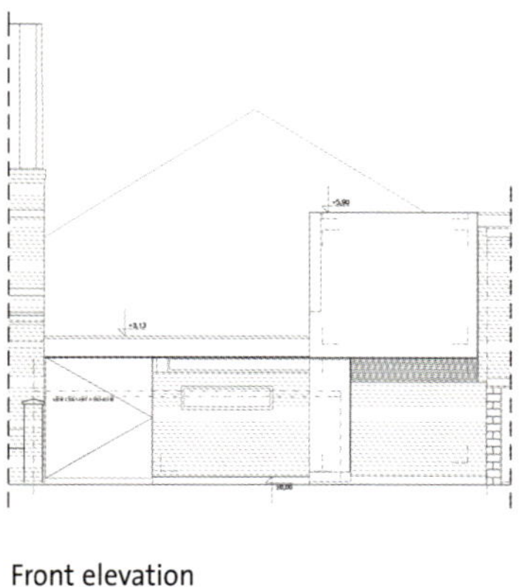

Front elevation

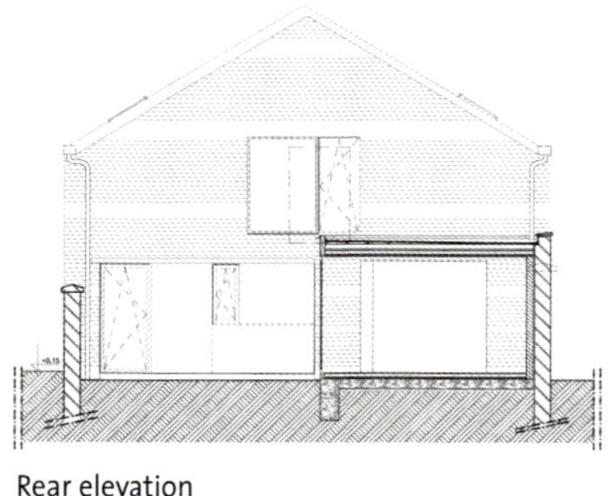

Rear elevation

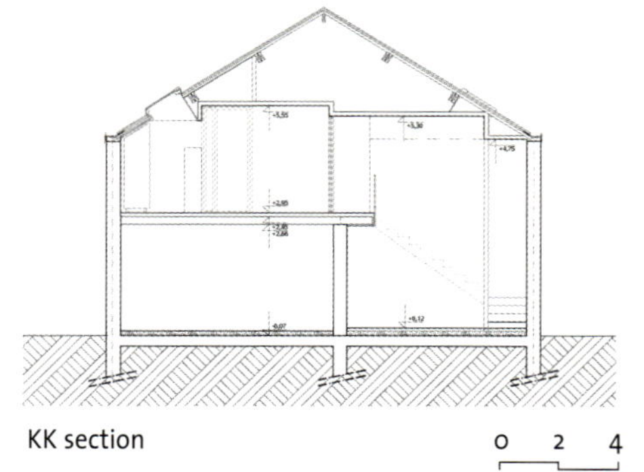

KK section

0 2 4

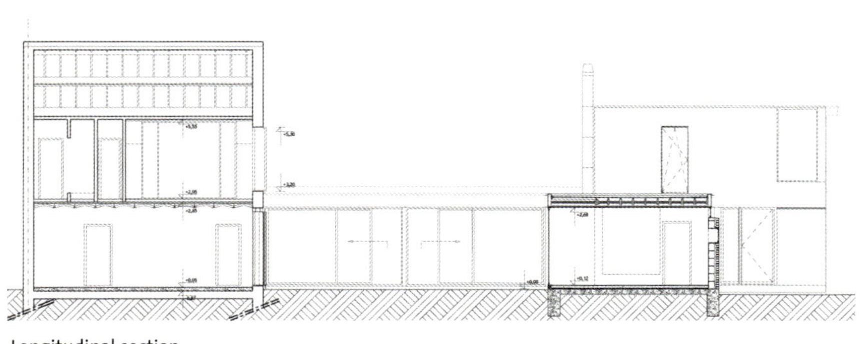

Longitudinal section

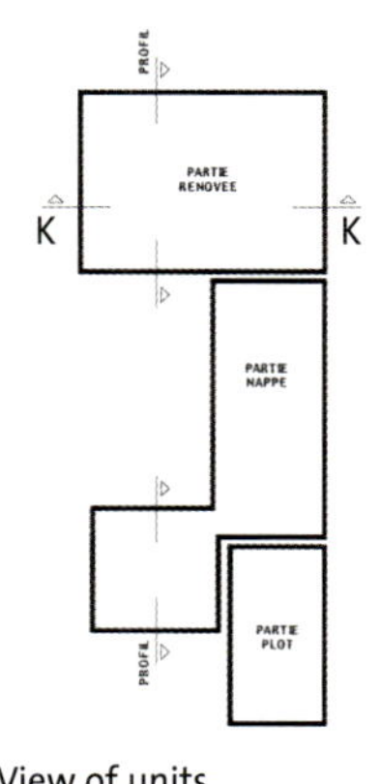

View of units

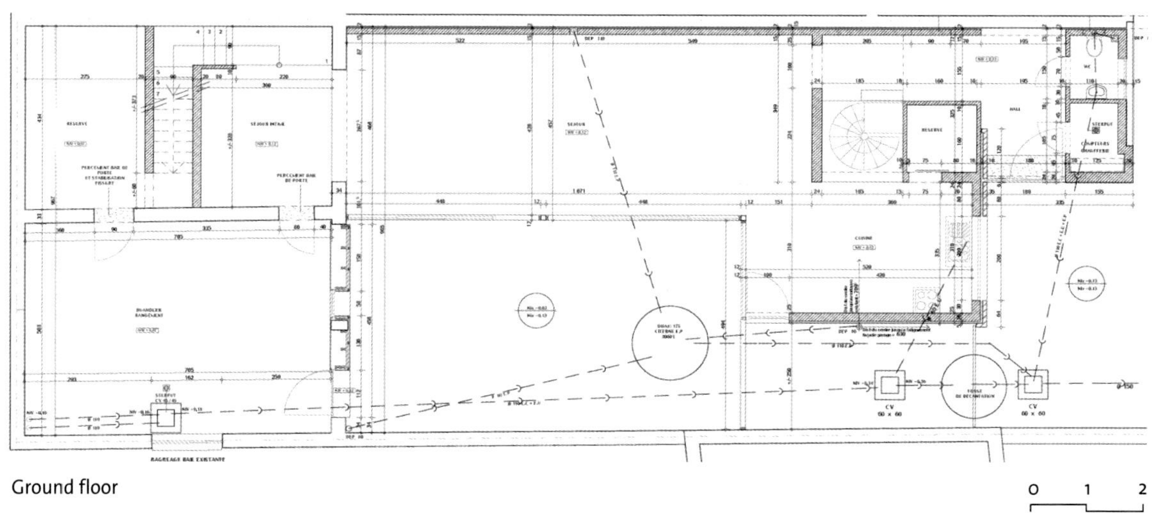

Ground floor

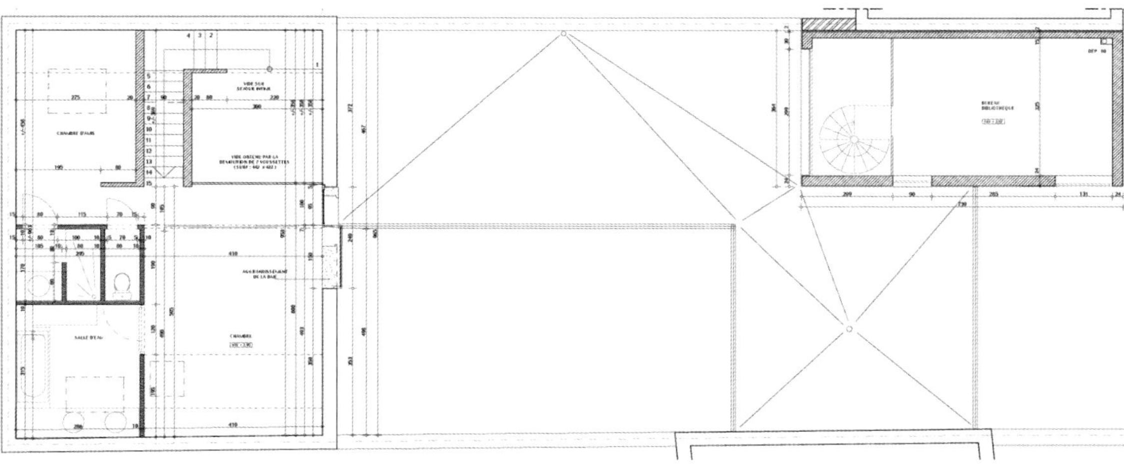

First floor

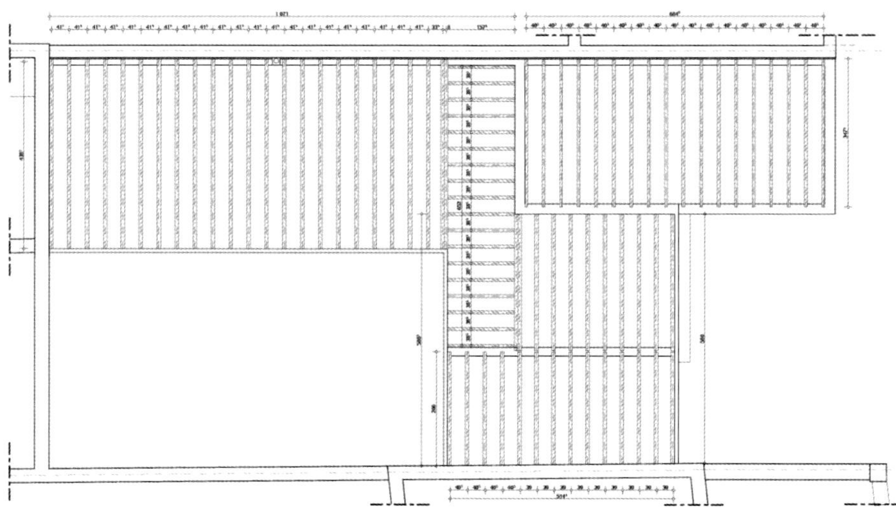

Plan of structures

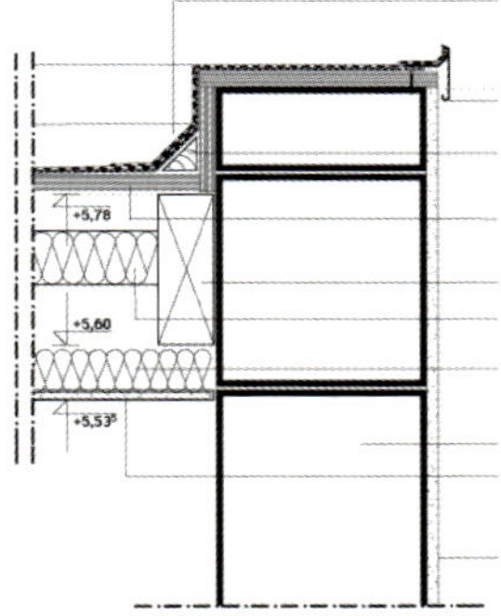

Detail of intersection between roof and façade

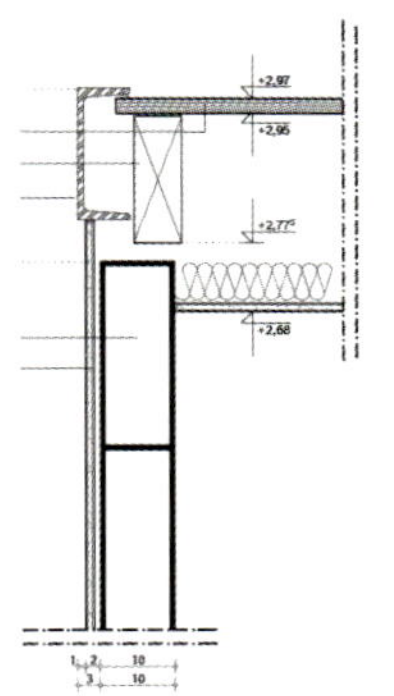

Detail of mezzanine

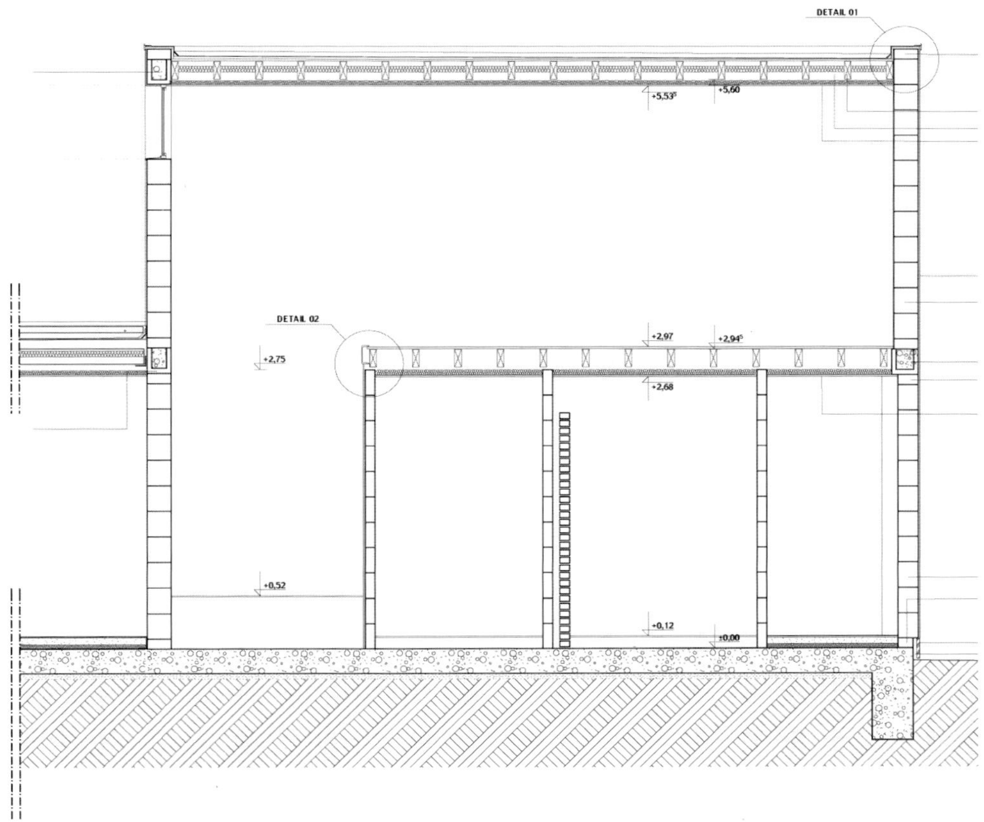

Section of multifunctional block

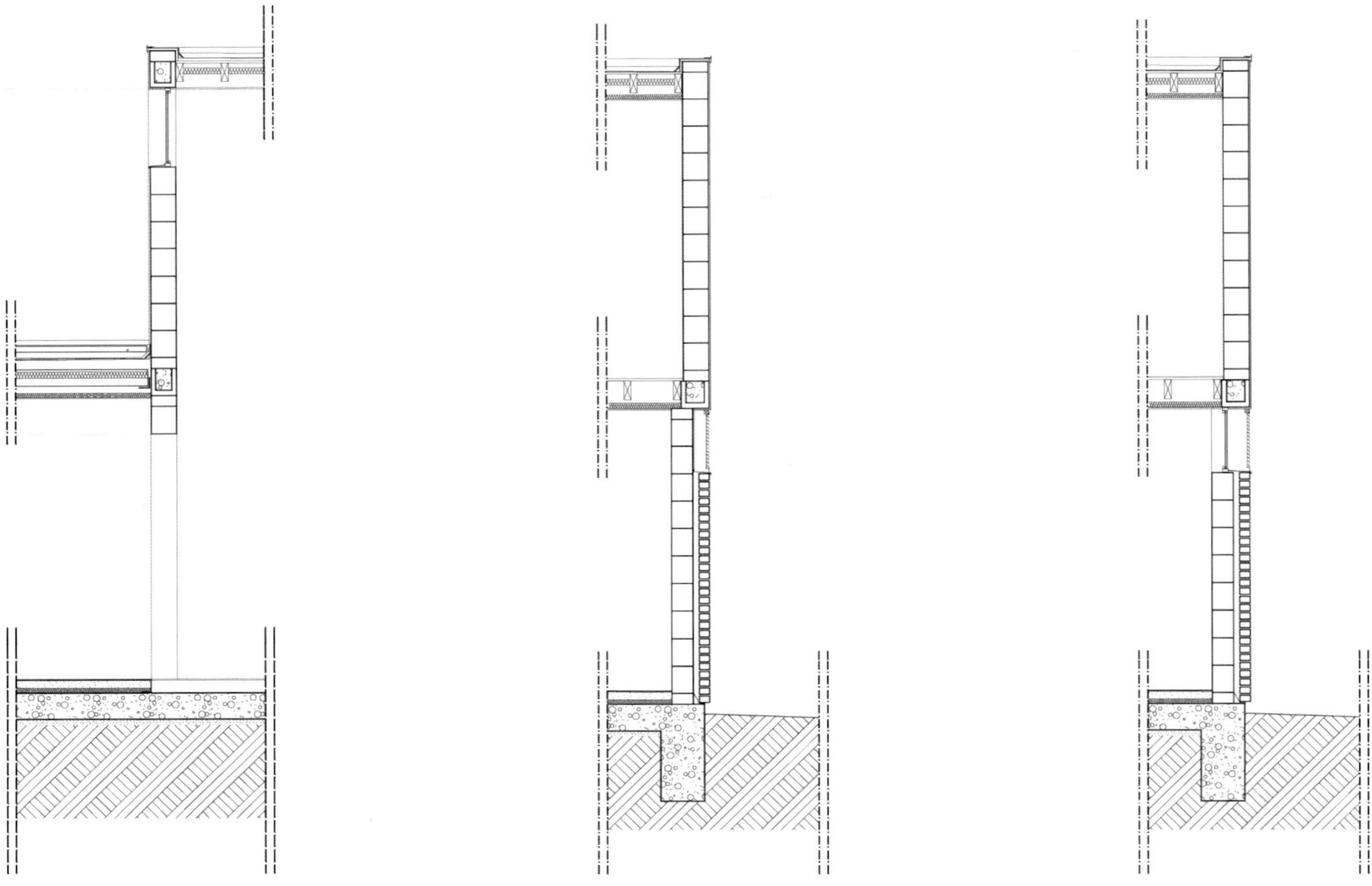
Sections of façade construction detail

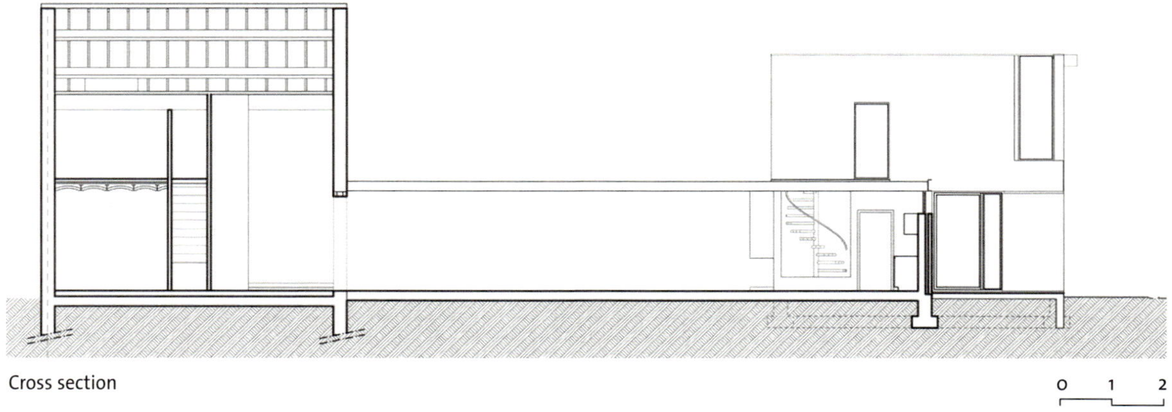

Cross section

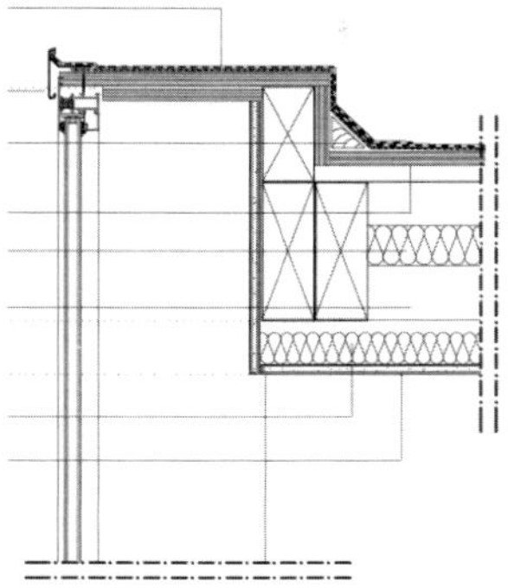

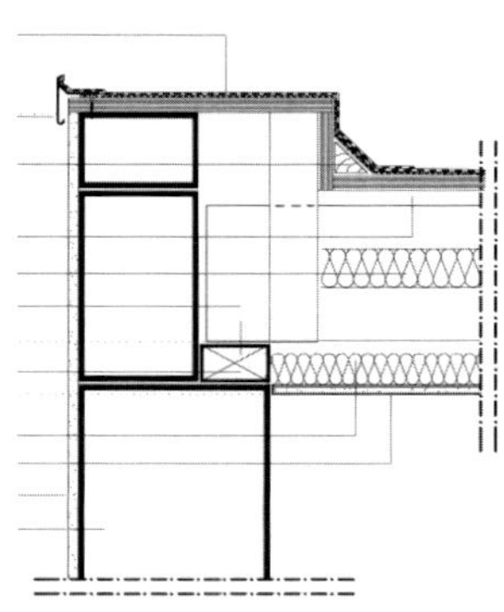

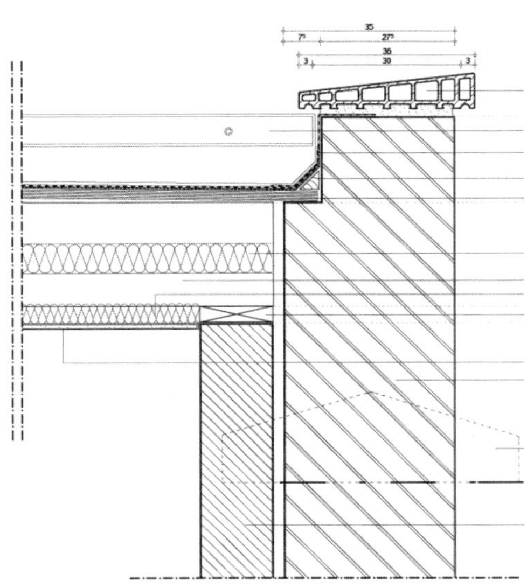

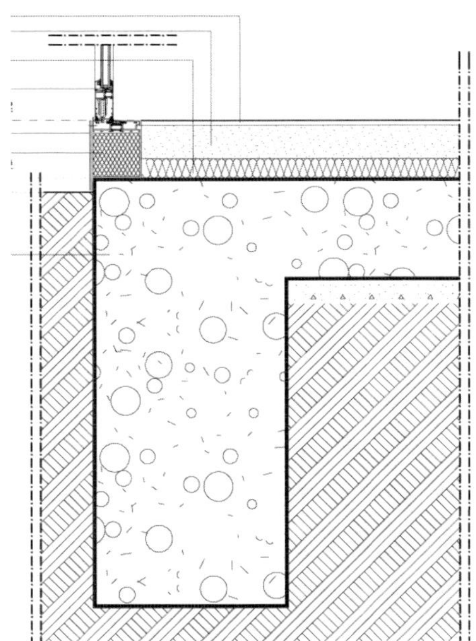

Construction details

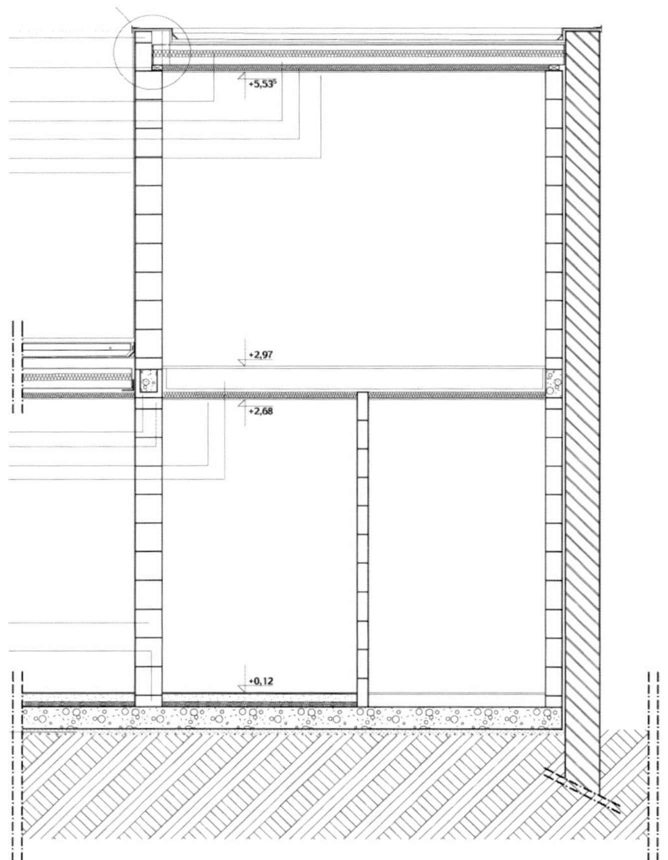

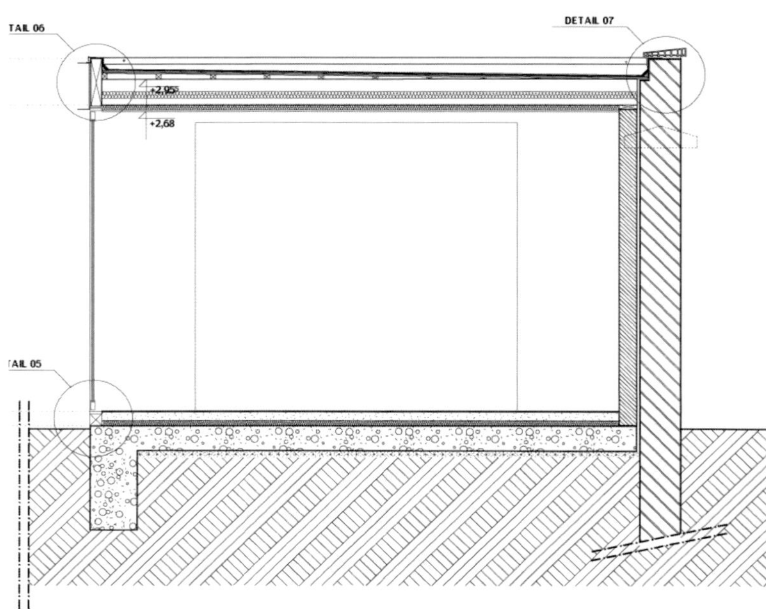

Construction sections

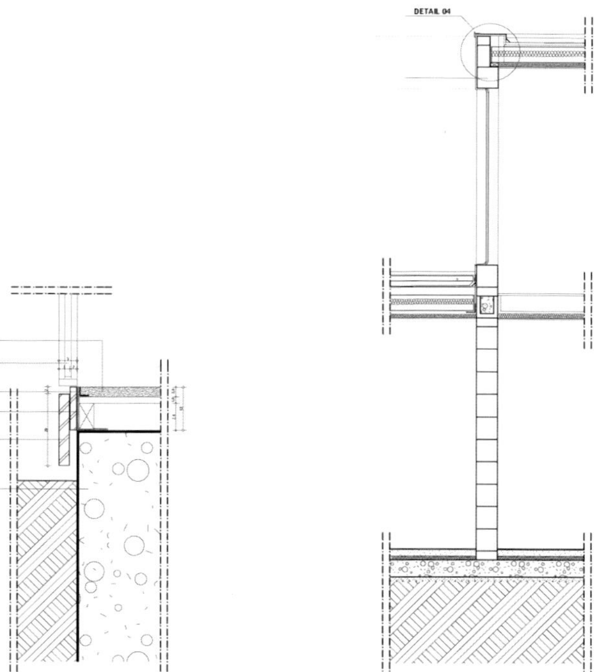

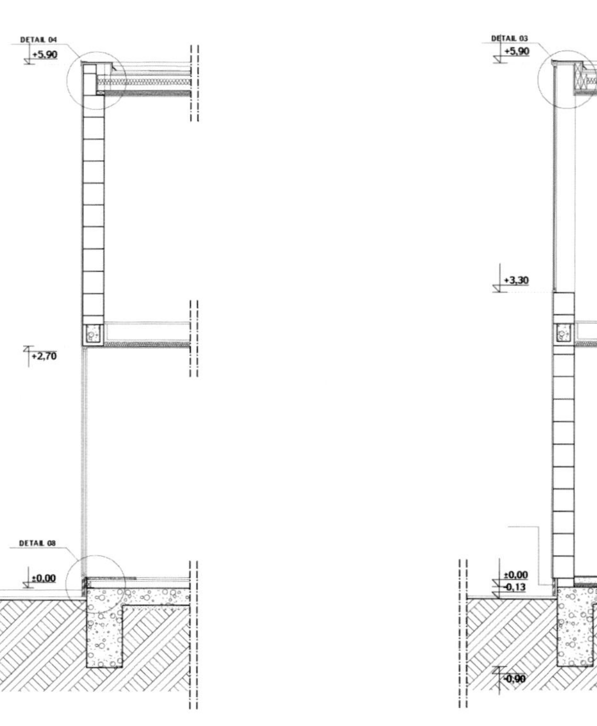

Construction details

Emerald Hill

Architects: WOHA Designs

Photography © Tim Griffin

Location: Singapore, Singapore

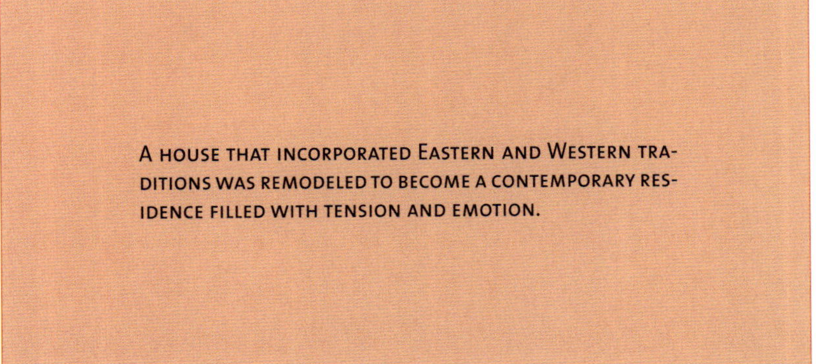

A HOUSE THAT INCORPORATED EASTERN AND WESTERN TRADITIONS WAS REMODELED TO BECOME A CONTEMPORARY RESIDENCE FILLED WITH TENSION AND EMOTION.

Emerald Hill

Many typical houses in Singapore have a family business on their street level floor, whether a store, a restaurant, or a warehouse. These spaces tend to be dark and the residences above them do not have many windows either, because of the hot sun in this region. The plan for the remodeling of this house was to maintain some elements from the old structure while at the same time adapting them to modern lifestyle. Therefore, the original façade was left intact, but beyond the entrance door a magical space is entered since there are a few feet of space between the old façade and the new construction, an emptiness flowing vertically all the way to the top. This solution creates a very somber feeling and a dramatic effect that is caused by the façade, because once inside the house it is perceived almost like a stage set. The rear of the building has a small pool that adds a refreshing element to the environment, and the glass walls allow the sunlight to come in, although it is considerably filtered because of the narrowness of the patio. All the elements of this remodeling project undoubtedly add some tension to the building, and along with the careful design of its architects make this a rare piece full of beauty and comfort.

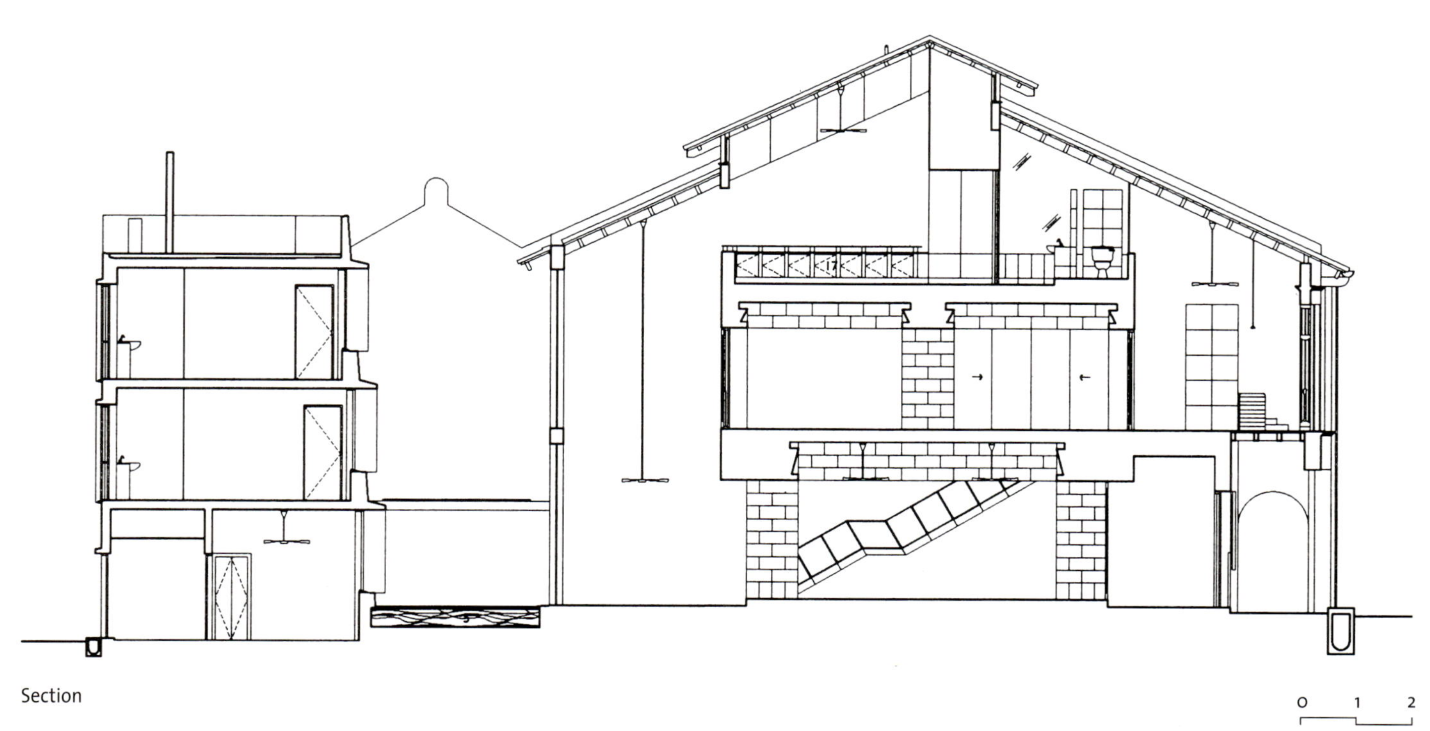

Section

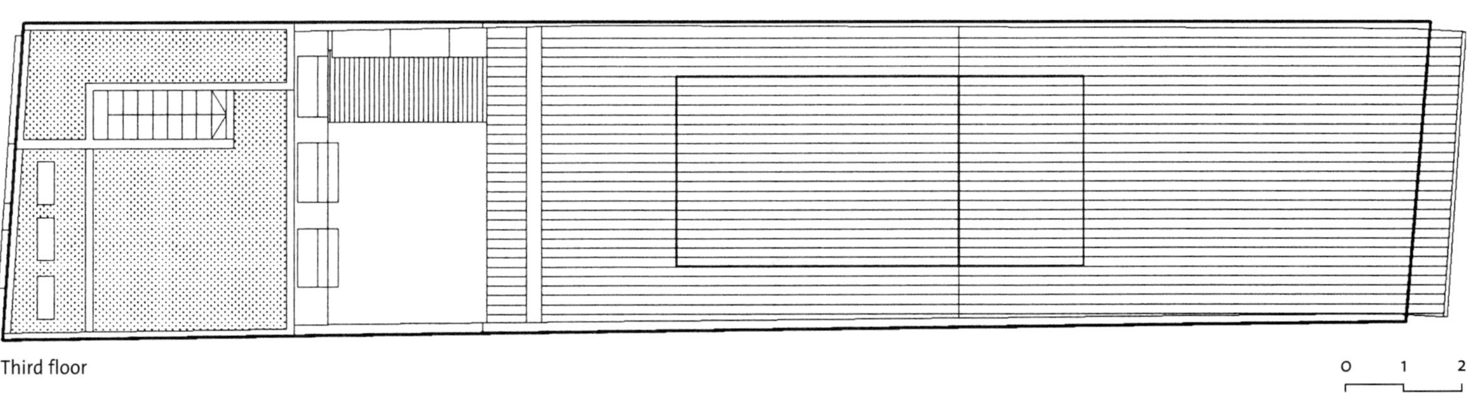

Third floor

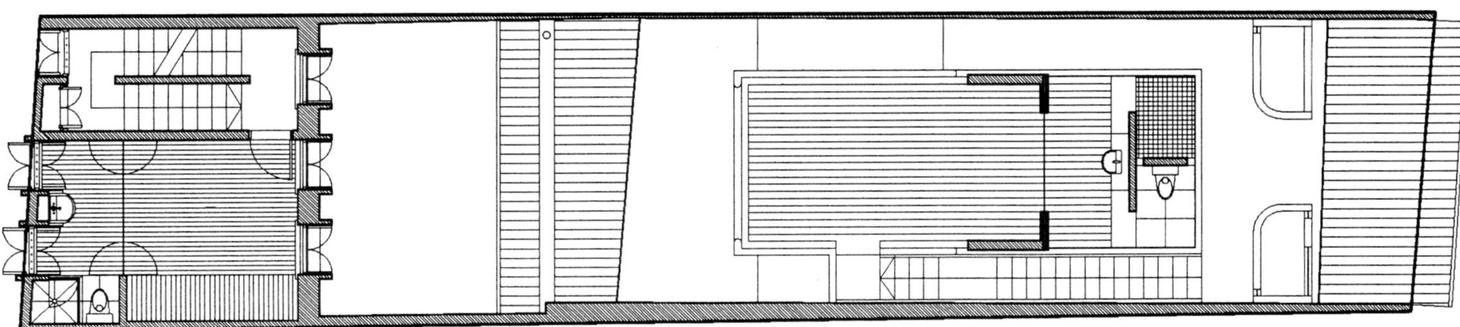

Second floor

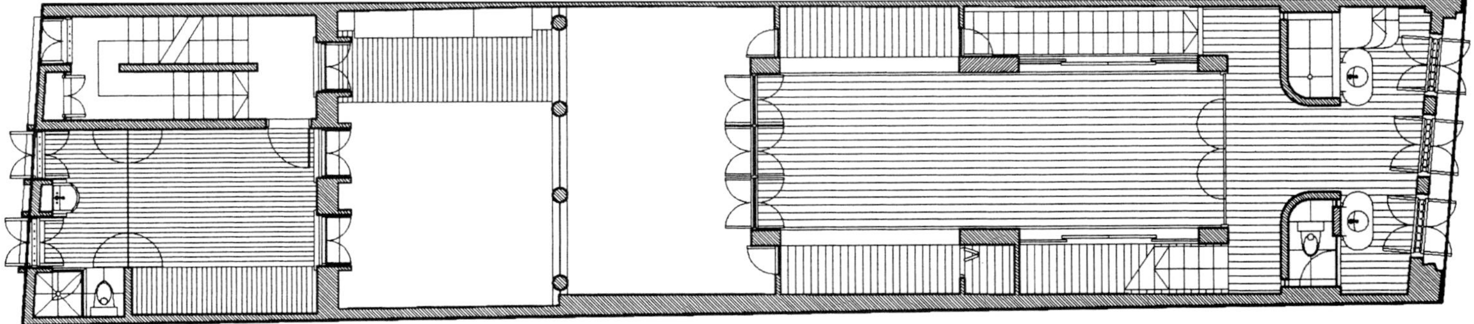

First floor

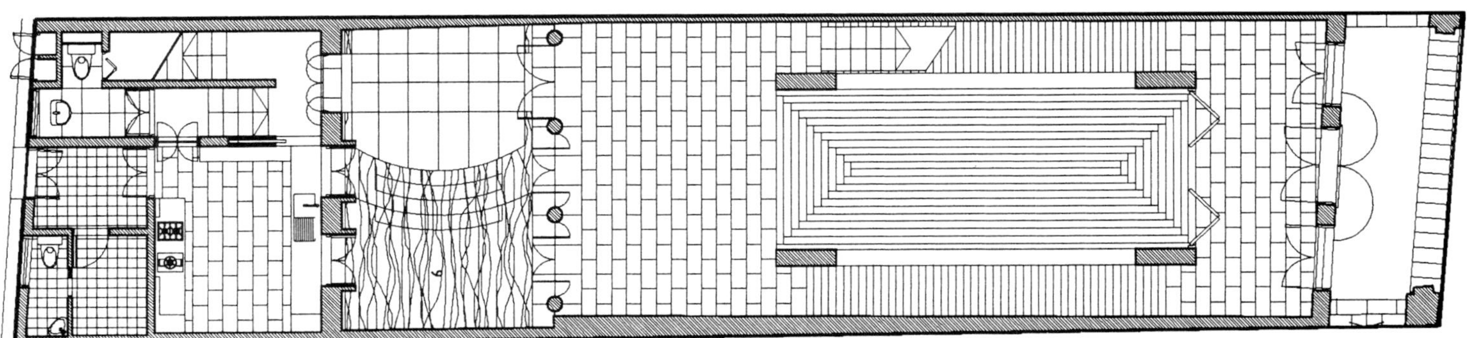

Ground floor

Gold Lane

Architects: Project 35 English and Konu Architects

Photography © Project 35 English and Konu Architects

Location: London, United Kingdom

The rehabilitation of degraded spaces has a social component that also forms part of the responsibility of the architect, who must study and plan the most practical solutions, both physical and human, for his or her works.

Gold Lane

As many as 45 garages were located in Gold Lane: their state of disarray had turned the street into a target for vandalism and presented a safety problem. This was the motivation for a plan to change their use by employing strategies that turned this area into a livable environment. The combination of ecological solutions, affordable prices, and a structure that adapted itself to different lifestyles was key to the project. The most visible solution was covering the roofs with short grass, which is a top notch insulation and is easy to care for because of the English climate. Because of their accessibility, the rooftops became usable terraces, especially on the houses located at the ends of the street, given that they have more surface space. The interiors also incorporate solutions that promote energy conservation: windows that provide the maximum amount of natural light in the rooms, condensing boilers, and good thermal insulation. One solution that demonstrates the strategy of the architects was the planting of climbing plants along the outside walls, with the goal of creating an affordable anti-graffiti wall to help quickly transform the streets with the abandoned garages into a residential area. Other solutions were also applied to make access to the residences easier for low-income families. The Gold Lane Project proves that a pleasant atmosphere can be created with small budgets, while paying attention to details, being respectful to the environment, and that is sufficiently open so that each family can preserve its identity without being encased in a prejudicial architecture.

Rehabilitating several old garages from the turn of the century created a model residential area incorporating a combination of ingredients, like original structural ideas, techniques for energy conservation, and new materials, to generate low maintenance homes.

General plan

0 4 8

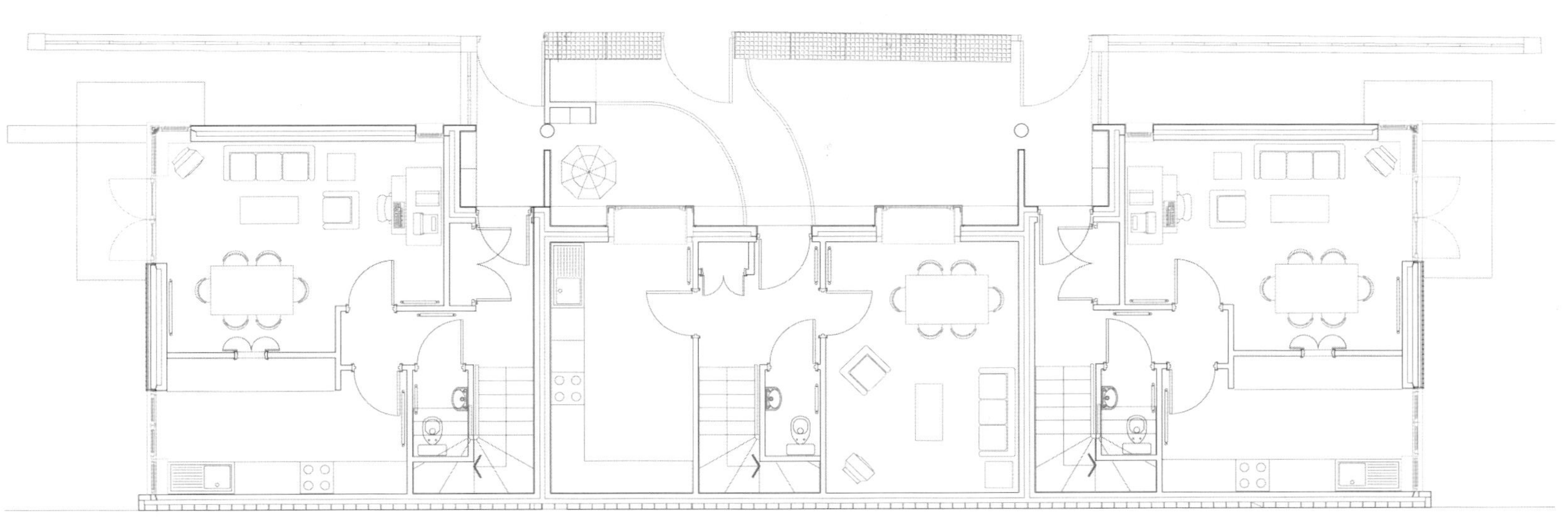

Ground floor

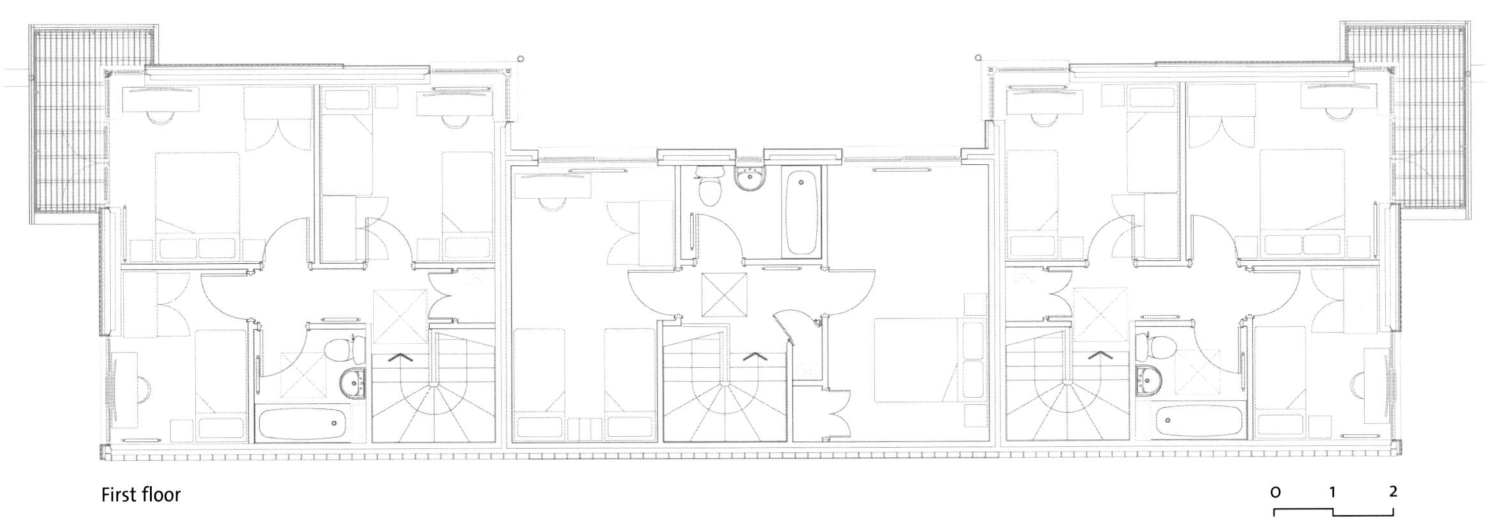

First floor

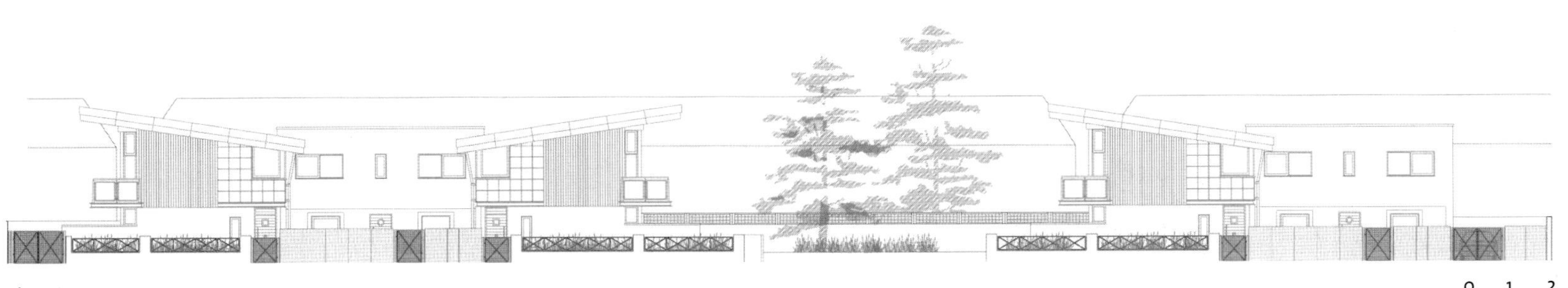

Elevation

Apartment in Sienna

Architect: Giuseppe Chigiotti

Photography © Matteo Piazza

Location: Sienna, Italy

THE IRREGULAR FLOORPLAN RESULTED IN A CREATIVE LAYOUT THAT IS COMPLEMENTED WITH VERSATILE FURNISHINGS: A STEPPED ARMOIRE DOUBLES AS A STAIRWAY TO ACCESS THE MASTER BEDROOM, AND A FURNITURE PIECE FILLS AN EMPTY CORNER ABOVE THE BED.

Apartment in Sienna

This well lit apartment with an irregular floorplan is part of a group of buildings located next to an old medieval wall. Although it was designed as a single space, it can be divided according to the function of each of the rooms, with furnishings that form an integral part of the architecture. One of the outstanding pieces in the residence is a two-level structure in the shape of a tower, which houses the dressing room on the top and the bathroom at the bottom. The dressing room is accessed via a wood stairway-armoire resembling a sculpture that is located in the master bedroom. The remodeling also exposed the paintings concealed by the false ceiling, which were restored and form part of the new decoration. The doors and sliding panels, which take up a minimal amount of room, are examples of functionality, as is the armoire used to separate the bedroom from the kitchen. The space located between the ceiling and the top of the armoire was enclosed with transparent glass, which allows light to flow in.

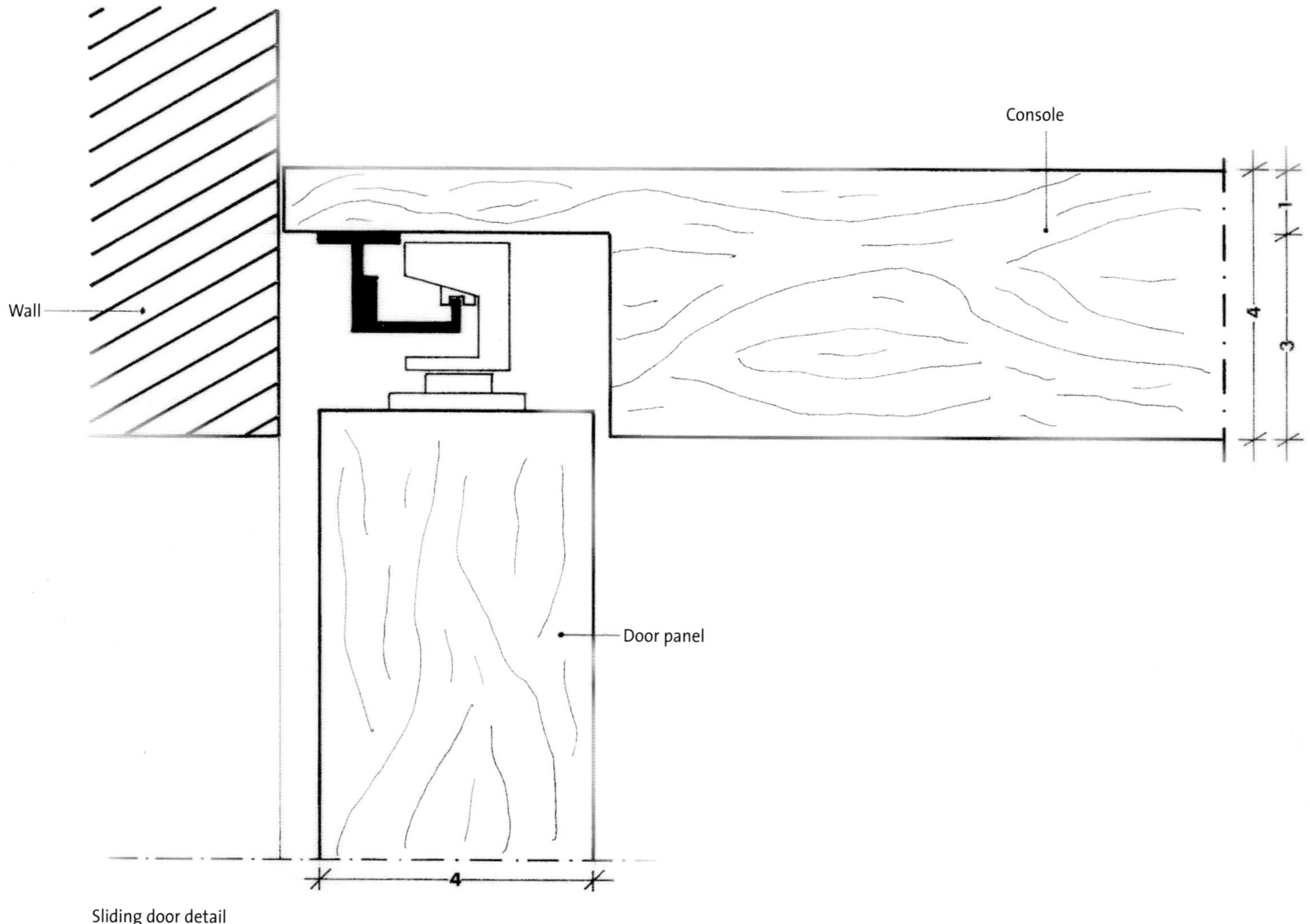

Sliding door detail

Intracranial Vascular Malformations
INTRACEREBRAL HEMATOMAS

THE CONVERSION OF THE INDUSTRIAL ECONOMY INTO A SERVICE BASED ECONOMY HAS RESULTED IN MANY OLD FACTORIES IN LONDON BEING TURNED INTO OFFICES AND RESIDENCES. IN ADDITION TO THE SPACIOUSNESS OF THE ROOMS, THE GOAL HAS ALWAYS BEEN TO TAKE ADVANTAGE OF THE FLAT ROOFS BY TURNING THEM INTO TERRACES.

Loft on Nile Street

This project began with a commission to remodel an old warehouse in a centrally located London neighborhood. The loft occupies the top two floors of the building, which has been able to preserve its factory atmosphere thanks to the good condition of the brick façades that were cleaned and restored in only a few areas. The residence houses a bedroom with a bathroom, the kitchen, dining room, and the living room on the first level, and a multifunctional space that can be used as an additional bedroom on the top floor. This area features a large terrace with views of the city. The brick façades were preserved, however the wood components of the windows, which flood the living spaces with natural light, were changed. The existing structure was also restored and reinforced with exposed concrete. One of the main objectives was to maintain the residence as a container, an empty space that is filled according to the needs of the resident; therefore only two areas were defined, which contain the kitchen and a small office. Both have their own integral electrical installations: spot lights in the studio furniture, and a long fixture over the kitchen counter. The lighting in the dining and living rooms was concealed as well: the recessed fixtures were installed inside a box that runs along part of the ceiling. The surface finishes vary from one element to another: the kitchen was covered with wood slats that give it a rough look; the furniture piece in the office was painted blue, and the floor was covered with resin.

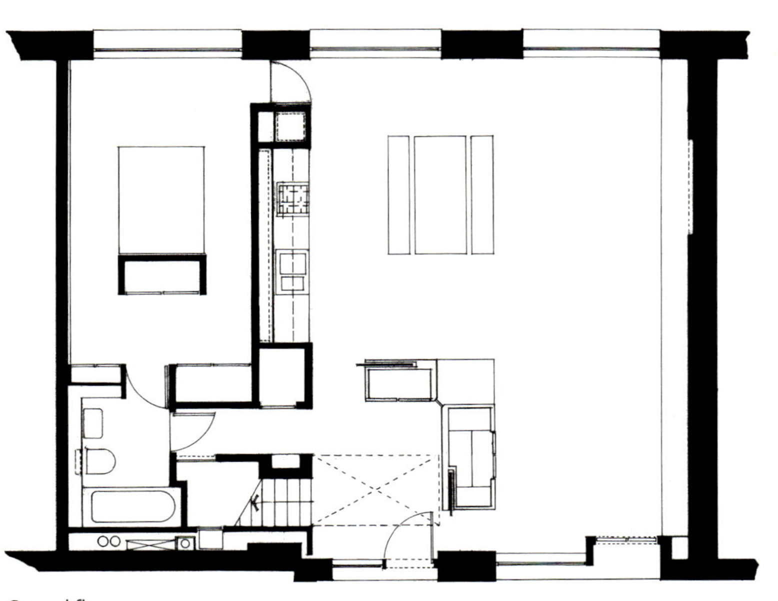

Ground floor

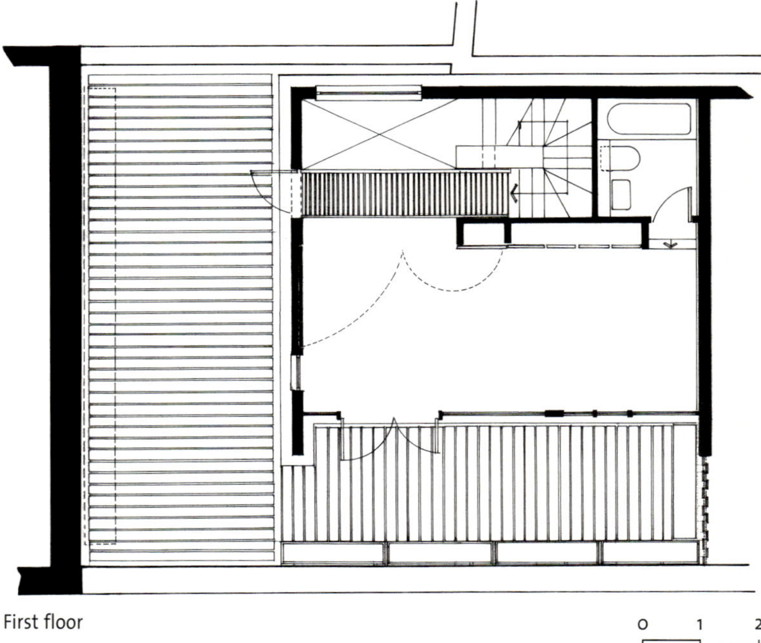

First floor

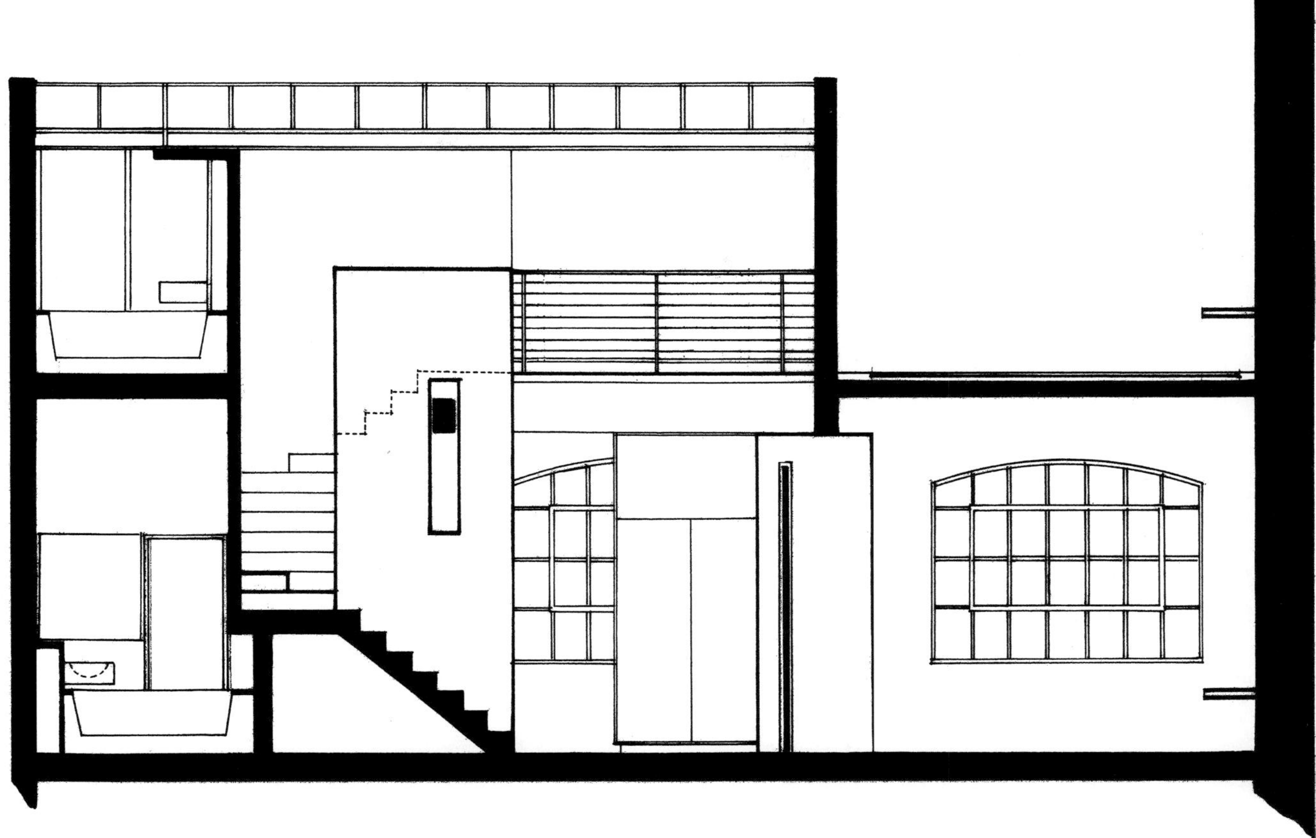

Longitudinal section

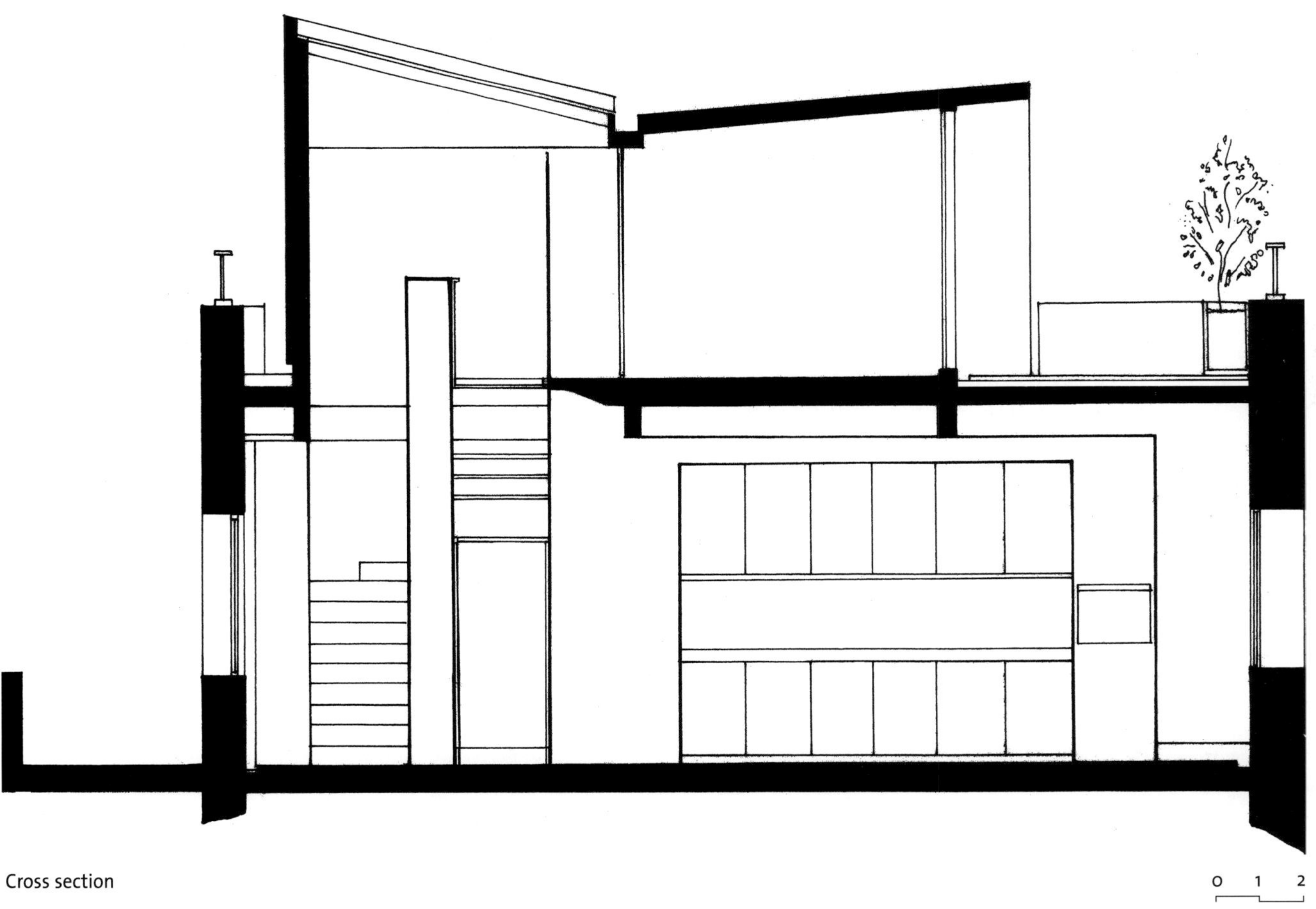

Cross section

Greenberg Loft

Architects: Smith-Miller & Hawkinson Architects

Photography © Matteo Piazza

Location: New York, United States

The mobility of the panels makes it possible to completely change the distribution of the area according to the needs of the moment, whether making several rooms or creating a single space.

Greenberg Loft

The Smith-Miller & Hawkinson team was commissioned to remodel this loft that would include a living area and a space to exhibit works of art. The client, an art collector, wanted these two functions to coexist without strict boundaries between them. With this in mind, the architects developed crossed floorplans in which the gallery blends with the private zones. The plan is divided into two levels: the lower one, which includes the master bedroom, the living area, the dining room, the kitchen and the projection room, a painting studio, a storage area, and a large terrace. The top floor consists of two mezzanines, guest rooms, and a studio. These loft areas did not exist in the original plan but the designers took advantage of the building's height to construct them of reinforced concrete, resting on steel beams painted black with tempered glass banisters. On the lower floor, the concrete is also visible in a few of the pillars and on some of the walls, although they generally opted for concealing it with white plaster on the walls and with maple boards on the floor. One of the most interesting aspects of the project is the way the space is defined with vertical dividers, which transition to the floor with narrow baseboards that create the feeling of floating in space, and with large sliding doors made of sheets of wood, which allows the creation of flexible and interconnected spaces. The remodeling of the northern façade, which is slightly tilted, included incorporating large mechanically operated windows that fill the living/dining room with light and provide splendid views of the city.

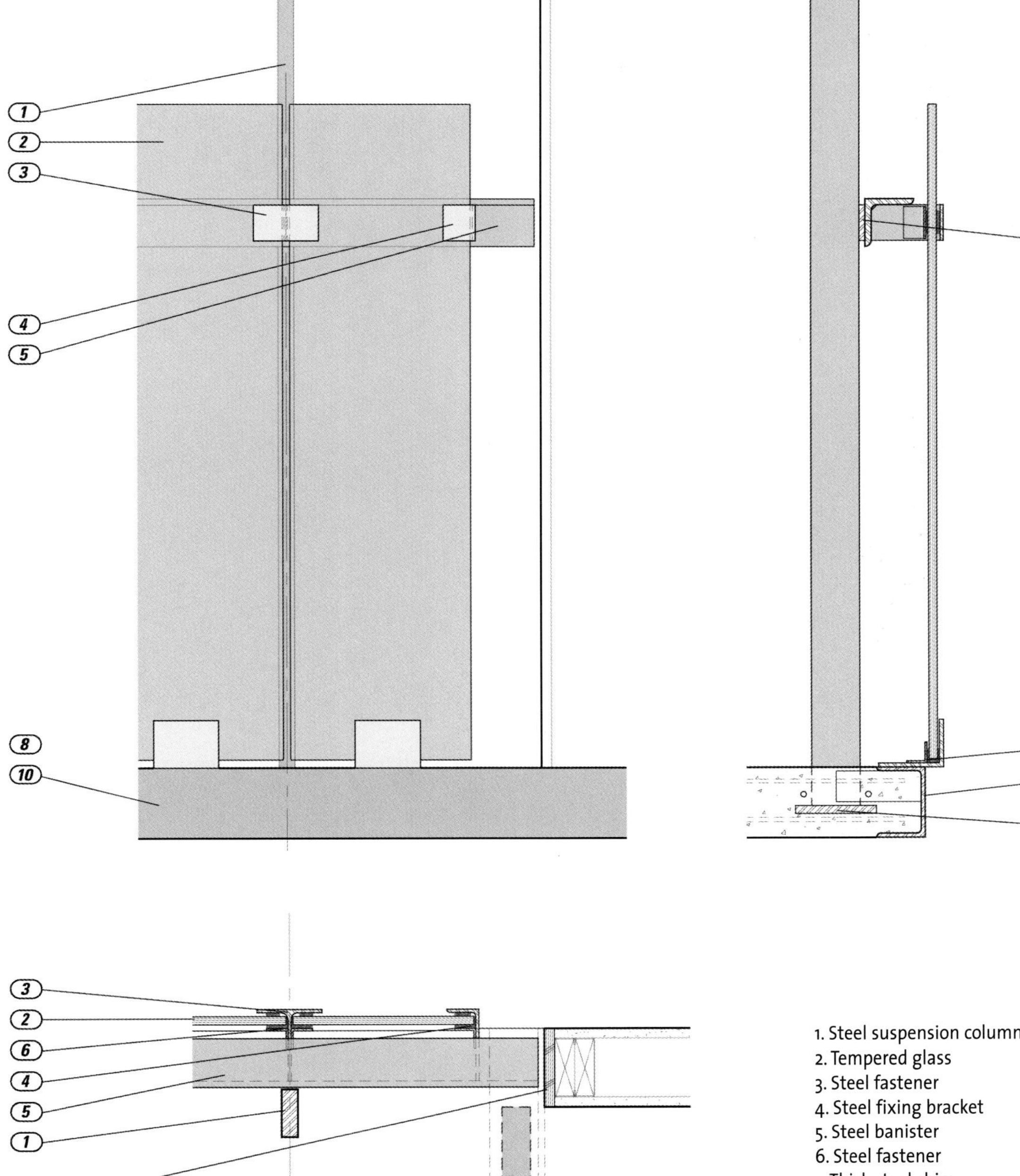

Detail of mezzanine banister construction

1. Steel suspension column
2. Tempered glass
3. Steel fastener
4. Steel fixing bracket
5. Steel banister
6. Steel fastener
7. Thick steel shim
8. Steel bracket
9. Steel fastener
10. Anchored steel channel
11. Steel clamp
12. Steel anchor plate
13. Maple wood end stop
14. Sliding door rail

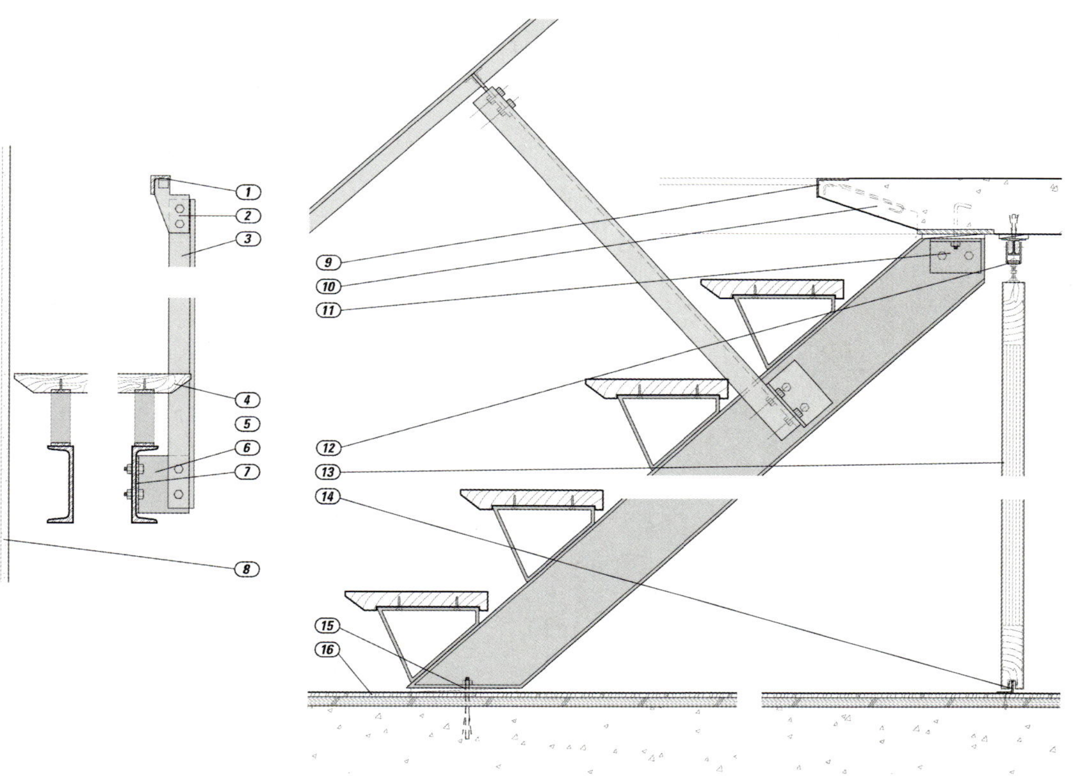

1. Steel banister
2. Steel banister anchor
3. Steel post
4. Maple wood tread
5. Steel clamp
6. Piece bolted to channel
7. Steel channel
8. Plaster wall
9. Embedded steel plate
10. Concrete slab
11. Steel bracket
12. Door hinge
13. Maple wood door
14. Steel guide
15. Expanding shim
16. Maple floor boards

Detail of stairway construction

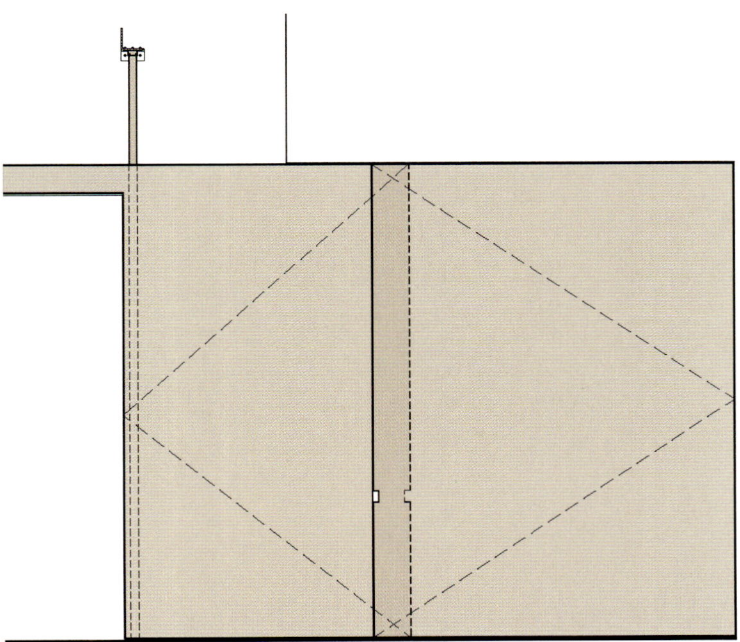

Side view of pivoting door

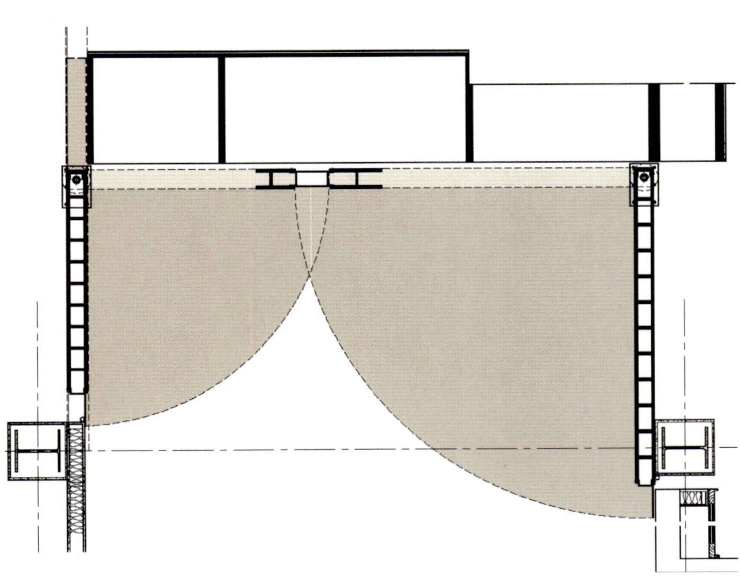

Top view of pivoting door

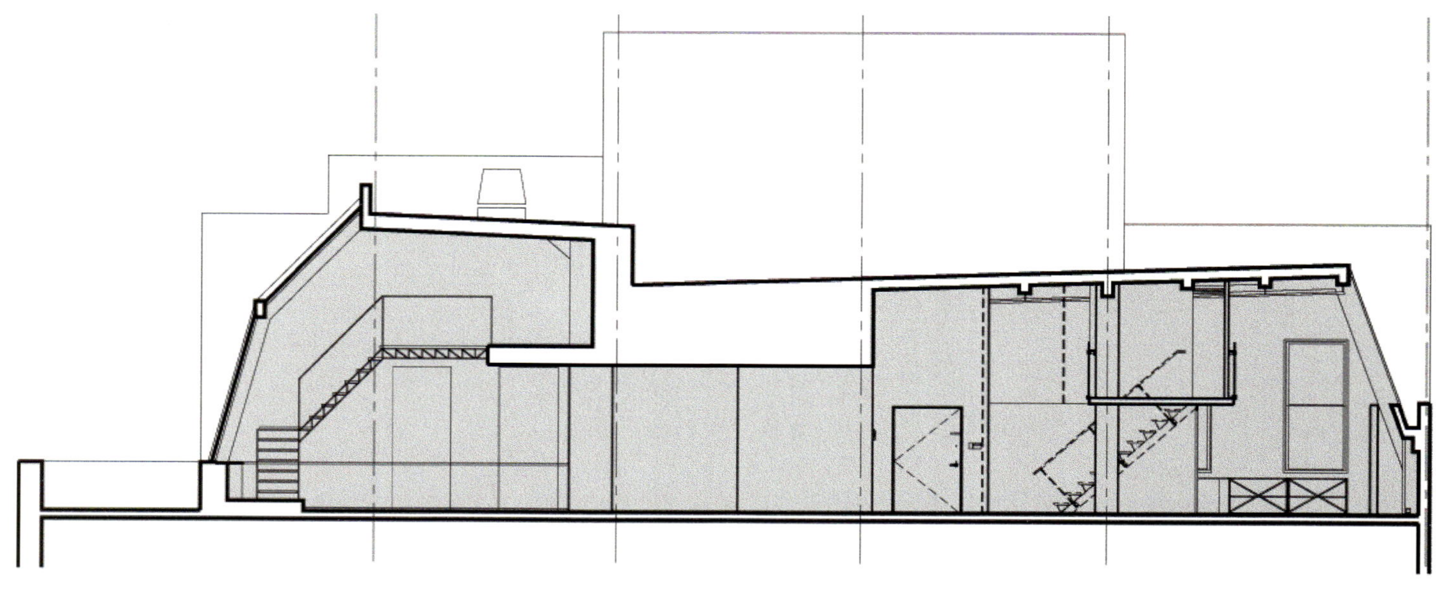

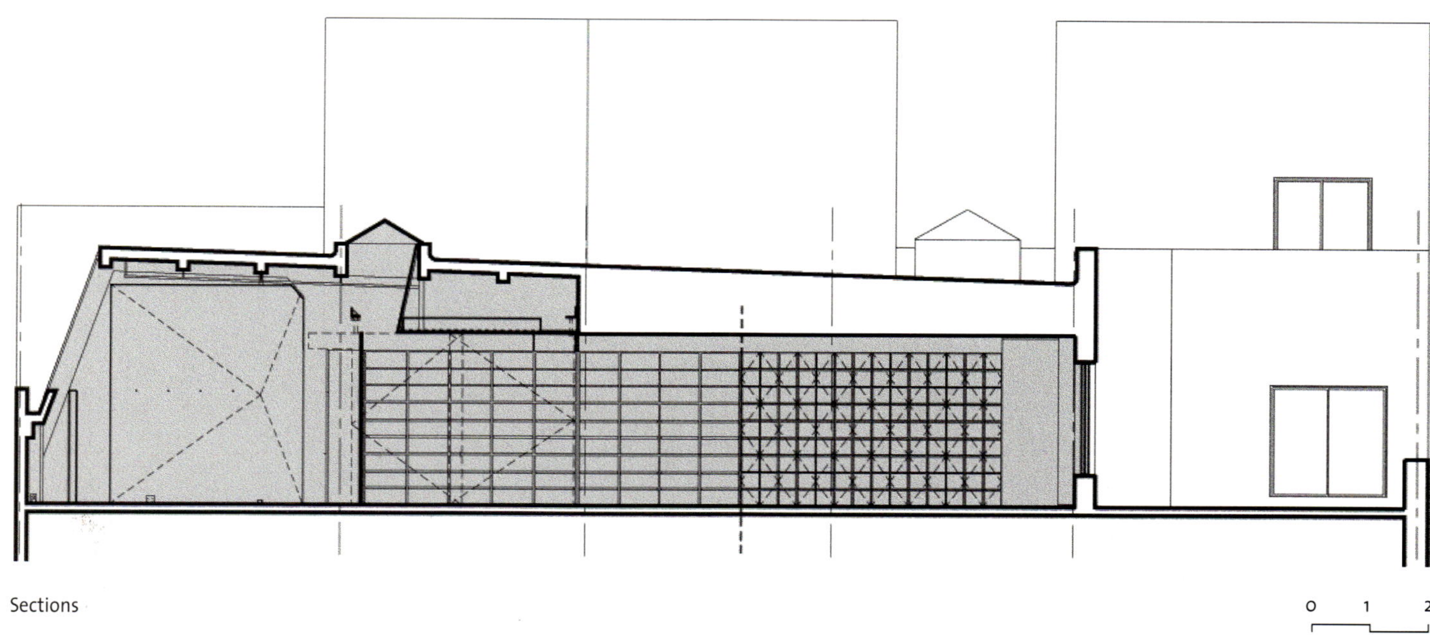

Sections

First floor

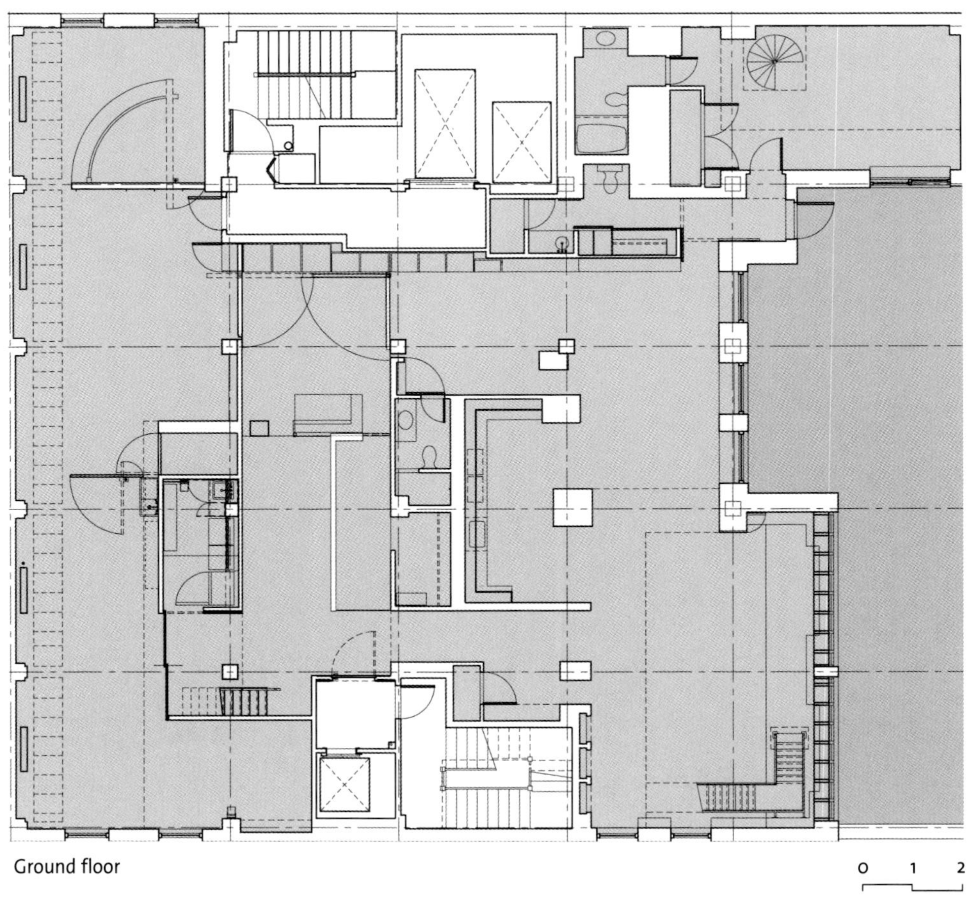

Ground floor

0 1 2

Cristofolini House

Arquitecto: Giuseppe Caruso

Photography © Matteo Piazza

Location: Geneva, Switzerland

The large stairway landing almost works as a transition place between the various rooms. The stairs leading to the upper floor are open, but the continuity with the rest of the staircase is not visible, which creates a very striking effect.

Cristofolini House

The purpose of the restoration of this historical building dating from 1761, later expanded with the construction of a barn in 1878, was to uncover the original structure and at the same time to enhance the monumental aspect of the architectural features characteristic of the farmhouses in the region. Some walls were demolished to recover the original interior space, and the primitive look returned to the area for feeding the animals and for storing the feed, converting it into an impressive 50 foot high (15m) foyer. In addition, the façade was reconstructed preserving the style of the typical agricultural buildings of the Vaud Canton, such as the large door divided into four windows or the small door with an adjacent window. To emphasize the importance and the visual impact of the wood structures (doors, beams, stairs, railings), a system of spotlights was used to bring out their texture while at the same time lighting up the passage areas. Flooring on the first floor made of stone from Burgundy mixed with cement and resin was used to mimic the local stone.

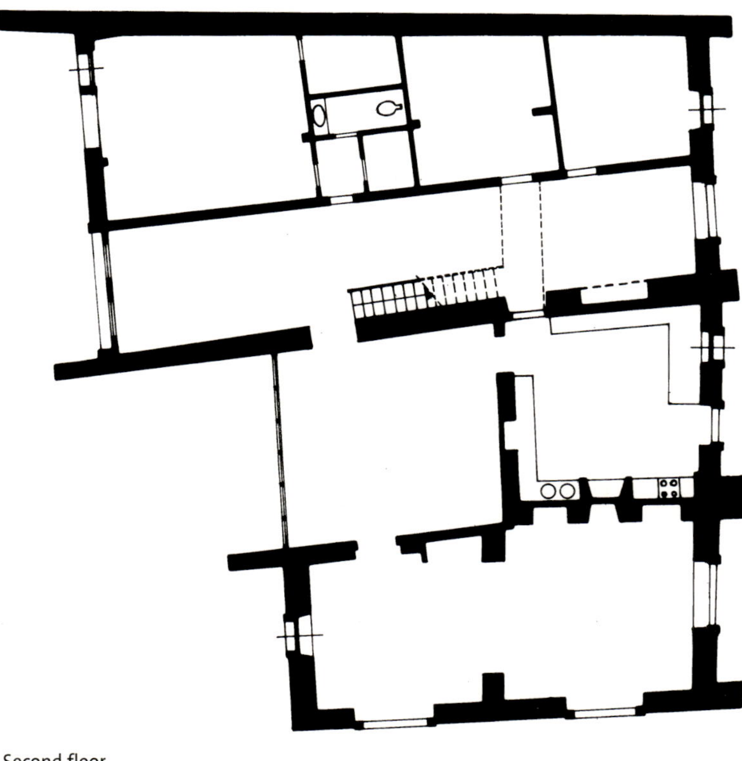

Second floor

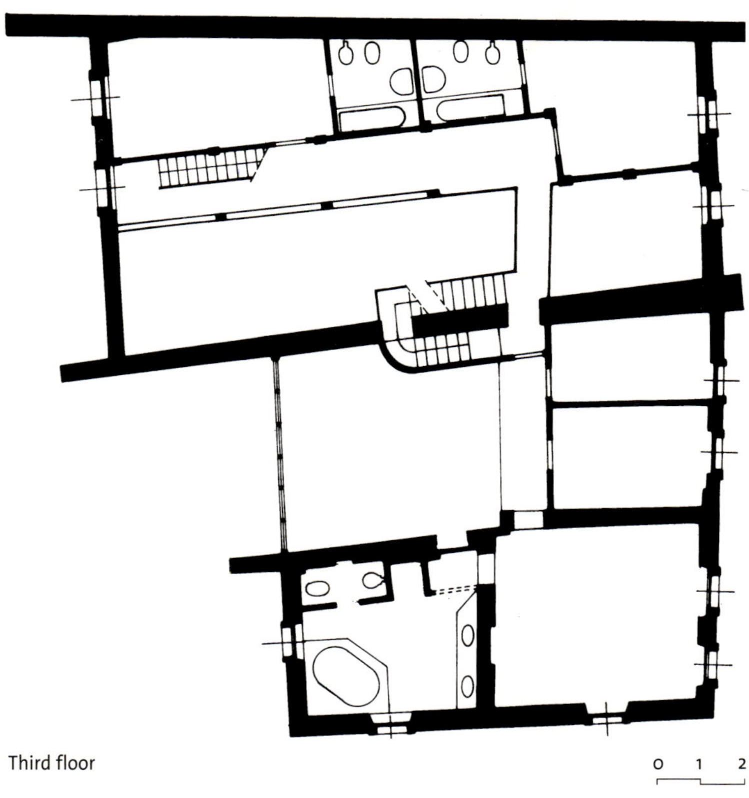

Third floor

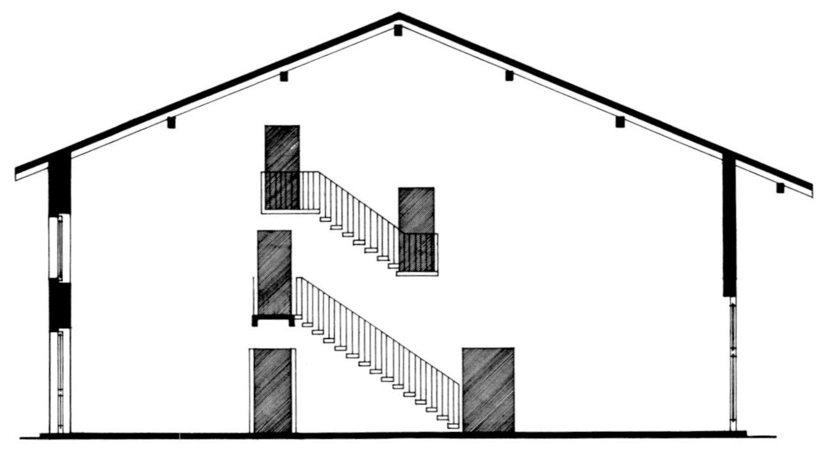

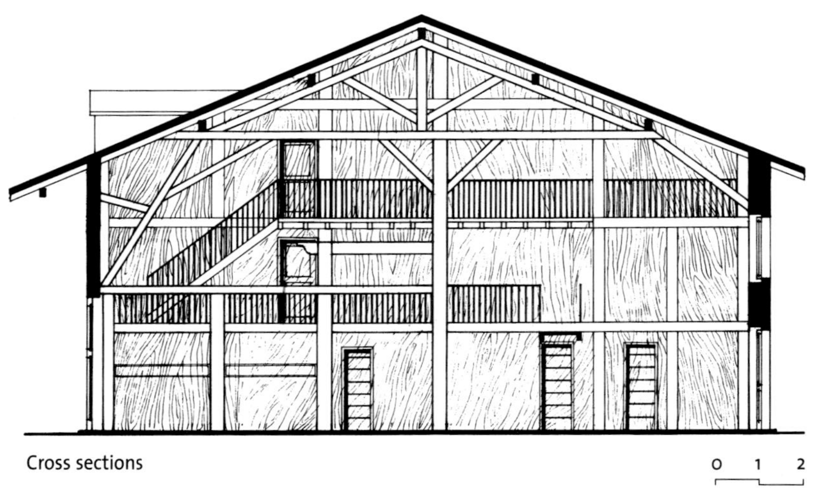

Cross sections

Elevation